THE ENGLISH KING

A STUDY OF THE MONARCHY AND
THE ROYAL FAMILY, HISTORICAL,
CONSTITUTIONAL AND SOCIAL

By Michael MacDonagh

KENNIKAT PRESS
Port Washington, N. Y./London

THE ENGLISH KING

First published in 1929
Reissued in 1971 by Kennikat Press
Library of Congress Catalog Card No: 78-118484
ISBN 0-8046-1233-1

Manufactured by Taylor Publishing Company   Dallas, Texas

CONTENTS

Contents

Book V

THE SOVEREIGN AND PARLIAMENT

Book VI

GOVERNMENT AND ADMINISTRATION

Book VII

IN THE ROYAL CIRCLE

INTRODUCTION

THE British Monarchy is the most ancient in Christendom. Its glory has in no wise worn thin with age. As a pageant it still takes the roughness of this world with splendour and romance. Moreover, Kings and their ways, their personal characters and private lives, as well as their public relations with the State, are, and always have been, of inexhaustible interest. Pope says :

> " Oh, 'tis the sweetest of all earthly things
> To gaze on Princes and to talk of Kings."

And yet, what a strange thing, while there are in text-books on the Constitution chapters galore which deal with the Monarchy, theoretically more or less, and many histories of reigns of Sovereigns, and biographies of Sovereigns, there is no book that purposes to describe with an aim of completeness this venerable human institution, living, active, effective, in all its ramifications, as it exists and works to-day. That is a want which I have tried to supply. The predominant idea of my study, blending its independent books, each dealing with relevant features of the subject, into a coherent whole, is to bring out what may be called the democratisation of the Monarchy (a big mouthful, but not unpleasant to the taste of the age) and also the influence which the personal qualities of Princes and Princesses, Kings and Queens, have had on retarding or advancing the process. I approach the subject through human nature. I am concerned with details of curious interest as well as with constitutional principles. It is surely not out of place to smile when we see the natural man breaking through the purple and gold of Kingship. I tell the story of the Republican Movement—till now an unwritten chapter of national history. After following the movement in the contemporary newspapers of the 'seventies of the nineteenth century, it was a strange experience and unaccountable to search in vain for any reference to it in the standard histories of England, even when these run to several volumes. The movement, it is true, cannot be described as a great, vehement, deliberate attack on the Monarchy, but, all the same, it was a remarkable manifestation of the republican spirit in aristocratic, middle-class, and working-class circles, and, as such, is, I think, well worth the telling, as well as being relevant to my theme. I may add that, for over forty years, I have been associated as a journalist with Parliament and with public life generally. My book, therefore, is based on considerable personal observation of the working of the Monarchy,—supplemented by private information as well as by a long and interested study of the institution from State records, histories, biographies, and memoirs—showing the King in association with Parliament, the Government, and the people.

The conclusion I have come to with respect to the constitutional side of my subject is that the adaptation of the Monarchy to a democratic age reached its completest point in the reign of George V, and that, as a result, it has probably been placed on the securest and most enduring basis. Such attacks as were made on the Monarchy in times past were directed against it chiefly on the ground that its hereditary principle was opposed to logic and equality. It has also been criticised as a political institution in the Party sense—as playing, or endeavouring to play, an effective part in the decision of the political principles upon which the country was to be governed. And, indeed, what could be said for a system in which an individual, solely by the accident of his or her birth, should have, or claim to have, a controlling voice in the affairs of the Nation, even against the Party actually in power, supported by a majority in the House of Commons and millions of the electorate, and be allowed, moreover, several hundreds of thousands sterling a year and many palaces to live in. The Monarchy was a political institution, to some extent, even as late as the reign of Queen Victoria. Liberal Ministers had no little trouble in getting on with her, in her old age, on account of her stubborn opposition to their policies and measures. The Monarchy was a political institution also, though in a far less degree, in the reign of Edward. He exercised considerable influence in foreign affairs, with the knowledge and approval of his Ministers, Conservative and Liberal, be it said, and was largely instrumental in replacing the old policy of "splendid isolation" by a policy of alliance with other Powers.

But the Monarchy has now entirely ceased to be political. It has become wholly a national and social institution, to the greater honour and glory of the country and the contentment of its people. That should prove to be the great constitutional transformation which will make the reign of George V historically outstanding. The King has no personal voice in political affairs, and not only does His Majesty not pretend that he has any, as we will see, but he has taken pains, as we will also see, to repudiate anything coming from an authoritative source which might tend to convey to the public mind an impression that he tries to override the decisions of his constitutional advisers. Aloofness from politics is his policy as King. His only thought in political affairs is to carry out—so far as the executive acts of the Crown that lie in his hands are concerned—the policy of the Party returned to power at the General Election, no matter what their political principles may be. He has adapted Monarchy completely to the needs of a modern democratic State, founding it on the people's will and ruling by that will. He stands above Parties, trusted and revered by them all, as the direct representative of the sovereign people. It is probable that the Monarchy has now become settled in this form in which the democratic theory of popular sovereignty is organic and elemental in its life and in its spirit, as well as in its procedure and functions. In the reign of King George also the Crown reached its highest point of exaltation as the symbol of unity between the United Kingdom, the self-governing Dominions, the Principalities, the Colonies, and the Protectorates, with their diverse races and forms of government, making them all one in name and one in fame as the British Empire, and blending their peoples in a common British citizenship.

The King's moderating and reconciling influence in affairs has thereby been strengthened. The value of the Monarchy in national service has thereby been enhanced. Patriotism more than ever centres round the person of the King, and patriotism is one of the greatest of a country's assets. No Sovereign has surpassed King George in the confidence, esteem, and affection of his people. No Sovereign has come more directly and intimately into contact with his people, and there never has been anything in his conduct, as man or as King, to divert the friendly current, or break the contact. King George is by far the most popular man in the country—excepting, perhaps, the Prince of Wales. Queen Victoria was frequently criticised in the Press. She was once hissed in the streets of London. Even King Edward said or did things which brought him into conflict with sections of public opinion. I have failed to find any reference to King George in any newspaper that was not in his praise. If the Kingship were elective by a direct popular vote His Majesty would easily be far ahead of all other candidates. For, by democratising the Monarchy, King George has also nationalised it in the broadest sense of the term. The King, more than ever before, stands for his country, one and indivisible, and in his presence all class divisions and all the prejudices arising from conflicting political, social and religious opinions disappear. By making the Monarchy safe for Democracy, King George has done a still greater thing—he has made Democracy safe for the Monarchy.

MICHAEL MacDONAGH.

BOOK I

THE OFFICE OF KING

CHAPTER I

SOVEREIGNTY

" THE Pre-eminence, Power and Authority of the King of England." These resounding words are the title of an Act passed in 1534, the twenty-fifth year of Henry VIII, denying any jurisdiction of the Pope in England. In stately language the majesty of the King and the duty of subjects to him are proclaimed—

> By divers sundry old authentic histories and chronicles it is manifestly declared and expressed that this Realm of England is an Empire, and so hath been accepted in the world, governed by one supreme Head and King, having the dignity and royal state of the Imperial Crown of the same. Unto whom a body politic compact of all sorts and degrees of people divided in terms and by names of spirituality and temporality, being bounded and owen to bear next to God a natural and humble obedience.

Then the power and authority of the King are set forth :

> He being also institute and furnished by the goodness and sufferance of Almighty God with plenary, whole and entire power and pre-eminence, authority, prerogative and jurisdiction, to render and yield justice and final determination to all manner of folk, residents or subjects, within this his Realm, in all causes, matters, debates, contentions, happening to occur, insurge or begin within the limits thereof, without restraint, or provocation to any foreign princes or potentates of the world.

The declaration is as true in theory to-day as it was when it was written, but with a tremendous difference in its practical application. The political sovereignty has become vested in the people at large. And while the pre-eminence, power and authority of the King remain, they are exercised by him not as an absolute Monarch, but as constitutional Sovereign on the advice of the Cabinet supported by Parliament—in a word, as the Crowned Head of a democratic system of government, embracing not only the United Kingdom but every Dominion and dependency in the vast and complex political system of which the United Kingdom is the heart.

Whether it was due to the predilection of British genius for constitutionalism, or to haphazard but happy chance, the Monarchy has thus been made at once the symbol of the people's sovereignty and the instrument of the people's will. There are two forms of sovereignty—the legal and the political. Legal sovereignty is the power to make laws; political sovereignty is the power to say what laws shall be made. The first is vested in the Parliament; the second is vested in the people. Legal sovereignty is, consequently, subordinate to political sovereignty. For Parliament, in the long run, is virtually incapable of making laws of which the people disapprove. And the instrument by which the decrees of Parliament—being the will of the people, so far as it can be ascertained at a general election—are given effect to is the King, as chief of the Executive. In this connection " the will of the people," really means the political will, for the time being, of the majority of the electoral body of the Nation. The political will of the entire community never finds, and perhaps never can find, unanimous expression at the polls. " Many men of many minds." It is always broken up into conflicting Party opinions. So unstable is it that frequently it varies from election to election. It is often the sport of transient whims, fancies, fears. What is decided at a general election is the rule of the majority of the electoral body, only for the time. And not always. For it has happened that a Party has been returned to power by a minority of the votes cast at a general election. Such is sovereignty, in the constitutional sense of the term.

But the Sovereignty of the People, rightly interpreted, signifies more than that—far more than that. Embraced in it are all classes of the community, all religions, all shades of political opinion. It means the entire people collectively, and not the Party that may temporarily be in the ascendant. It is the thing that makes a Nation separate and distinct from all other Nations—the national conscience and character, the common principles and ideals, the ruling sentiment or passion of all. This is the high sovereignty which the King personifies.

*   *   *   *   *   *

The most stupendous doctrine that came to be associated with the British Monarchy was that of Right Divine. It held that hereditary kingship was divine and could not be made void. It taught that the King derived his office from God, that he was not answerable to human authority, that to God alone was he responsible for the exercise of his absolute power over his subjects. " The greatest Anglican divines of that age," Macaulay writes of Stuart times, " had maintained that no breach of law or contract, no excess of cruelty, rapacity or licentiousness on the part of a rightful King, could justify his people in withstanding him by force." That belief in such a doctrine could have been entertained at any period may now seem to some minds difficult of comprehension. But to those who look back on the remote past with a sympathetic allowance for its necessarily primitive ideas, the conclusion that so splendid a being as a crowned potentate, occupying, by hereditary right, a station so exalted, must really be God's consecrated representative, appointed to have supreme and uncontrolled dominion over the people of his Kingdom, appears instinctive and natural. It was not something imposed on the kingship ; something foreign to its nature and spirit. It was, in fact, the natural blossoming and fruit of the general conception of the solemnity and power of the office. And surely it must have been a source of satisfaction and contentment to the people to feel that the ruler to whom they owed unquestioned obedience must be wise and right in all things—aye, though his government might appear to be unjust. For did not the light of Heaven inspire his mind and guide his steps !

The most rigid exposition of this supernatural origin, and therefore indefeasible, right of Kings came from James I, the first of the Stuarts. " Kings," he declared in a speech to Parliament in 1609, " are justly called gods, because they exercise a manner of resemblance of Divine power upon earth. For if you will consider the attributes of God you shall see how they agree in the person of a King. God hath power to create or destroy, make or unmake, at His pleasure, to give life or send death, to judge all and to be accountable to none. And this like power have Kings. They make and unmake their subjects, they have power of raising up and casting down, of life and death, they are judges over all their subjects and in all cases, yet unaccountable to none but God. They have power to exalt low things and abase high things and to make of their subjects like men at chess." His subjects responded in like vein. See the dedication of the Bible to " The Most High and Mighty Prince James," where that rather commonplace person is called " Most dread Sovereign . . . the Sun in his strength . . . Your very name is precious . . . most tender and loving nursing Father . . . Your Most Sacred Majesty."

It so happened that the time was equally propitious for a King to exalt his office and for his subjects to think less of it than before. In the profound disturbance in mankind's thought and feeling caused by the Reformation, these conflicting streams of opinion in regard to Kingship had their source. Before the Reformation the King did no more than regard himself as the Vice-Regent of God only in secular affairs. After the Reformation the transference of spiritual and ecclesiastical authority from the Pope to the King made the King also Vice-Regent of God in the domain of religion. The freedom of opinion, the play of reason, the disputing of the claims of authority, engendered by the tremendous clash between the spiritual and the temporal powers at the Reformation, led inevitably to the raising of questions of doubt relating to Kingship. Why should not the liberty obtained in things religious be extended to things political ? If the pretensions of the Pope to bind or unloose in spiritual matters could no longer be tolerated, why should the pretensions of the King to exercise by Divine Right the arbitrary power of life and death over his subjects be not also denounced ?

Men's minds became generally unsettled. That most levelling doctrine, the right of private judgment against Authority, began to be claimed all round. So it came to pass that the theory that Kingship had descended from Heaven and became incarnate in a particular member of a particular family to whom the succession was limited by heredity, was rudely shaken when the head of Charles I fell to the executioner's axe on the scaffold at Whitehall Palace. It entirely disappeared when a boat put off from the ferry at Westminster carrying his son James II, a fugitive from the anger of his oppressed subjects.

For at the Revolution it was declared that James II had abdicated the Throne, and the two jointly appointed Sovereigns, William and Mary, were given a title to reign far better and more enduring than that of Right Divine—the title of Parliamentary sanction.

*   *   *   *   *   *

Great as was the material power of the Kingship, in olden times, its spiritual or occult power bordered on magic. For another attribute of the Monarchy was that of curing scrofula, or the " King's evil," as it was called, by the healing power of the Royal touch. Older than the theory of Right Divine, it sprang from the same belief in the holiness of the Kingship. Edward the Confessor is the first King spoken of in history as having practised the touch. Cromwell played the King, among other ways, by trying his hand at the cure. A ruler even less saintly, Charles II, touched in the space of nineteen years no fewer than 92,798 afflicted persons, according to the official registers. Some of the surgeons of high repute who attended Charles II made profession of their faith in the King's miraculous power.

It says much for the good nature of the gay and irreligious Charles that he never spared himself to give such comfort and ease to his suffering subjects as they might derive from having his hands laid upon them, however unpleasant the ordeal might have been for himself personally. The healing services were held regularly in the Banqueting Hall of Whitehall Palace. The King, robed and crowned, sat in a canopied chair of State, surrounded by nobles, physicians and chaplains. At the end of the hall were assembled the afflicted—men, women and children from all parts of the country. They were led up in small parties, and the King laid both his hands on the cheeks of each, or on the clothes over the part of the person that was affected by the disease. When all had been thus touched they were brought up a second time for the touch-piece—a small medal of gold on which there was a figure of St. Michael spearing the dragon, with the inscription *Soli Deo Gloria*. It was strung on a white silk ribband which the King placed round the patient's neck. At the end of the service nobles

17

brought a basin and ewer and a linen towel for the washing of the King's face and hands. Many cures were effected which medical scientists now ascribe to the powerful shock, mental and physical, given to humble folk by personal contact with a King. So it appears to be true, after all, that Sovereigns, in the days of their deification by their subjects, did have a power of touch which made the sick well.

The first King who refused to touch was William III. He used to say, " Let them go to James II at St. Germains." The custom was kept up by James in exile at St. Germains, outside Paris, where he held a mockery of a Court until his death in 1701, and was continued by his son and grandson, the Pretenders. Prince Charles Edward, during his attempt in the Forty-Five to regain the Crown, held a healing service at Edinburgh. The last Sovereign to touch was Queen Anne, the last of the Stuarts. One of her patients in 1712 was an infant who became Dr. Samuel Johnson. At the age of two years and a half he was brought up to London from Lichfield by his mother, and he used to say in after years that he had a confused recollection of a lady in diamonds and a long B..ck hood. His face, disfigured by scrofula, and his dim vision afforded pathetic evidence that Queen Anne's touch was ineffectual, in his case, at least.

The belief in the Royal touch, after seven hundred years of religious sanction and popular favour, came to an end at the accession of George I. Perhaps it could hardly have survived the uncouth looks, the surly manners, the German tongue, of the first of the Hanoverian Kings. Yet why should that have been so ? George I was not accountable for his unattractive appearance and demeanour. Besides that, he wore the Crown, and it was as much the Kingship, as the particular person who filled it for the time being, that was supposed to possess this divinely endowed grace. Anyway, George scouted the idea that there could possibly be any healing in his touch. Former Kings had thought they had no superior on earth. George recognised that he was subject to the Law which had made him King. The Divine Right of the Kingship had passed away. The Kingship was no longer an earthly manifestation of the Heavenly glory of God. The Revolution established that the authority of the King is derived not from Heaven, but from a contract between him and his people, and that his State actions must be limited and governed by the wishes of his people. Thus the Kingship was established in the world of reality by the levelling tendencies of the modern spirit. Thus it lost its supernatural sanctions and was bereft of its mysterious potency. Thus it became justified to reason and rationality. And withal it remained a wonderful institution, radiant in the glorifying light of romance !

*   *   *   *   *   *

I have opened this chapter with a high-sounding declaration of the Kingship's imperious dignity from the sixteenth century. A fitting close to the chapter is the Proclamation of George V as King, which gives expression to the twentieth-century form of homage and fealty :

> Whereas it has pleased Almighty God to call to His Mercy our late Sovereign Lord King Edward the Seventh, of blessed and Glorious Memory, by whose Decease the Imperial Crown of the United Kingdom of Great Britain and Ireland is solely and rightfully come to the High and Mighty Prince George Frederick Ernest Albert :
>
> We, therefore, the Lords Spiritual and Temporal of this Realm, being here assisted with those of His late Majesty's Privy Council, with numbers of other principal gentlemen of quality, with the Lord Mayor, Aldermen and citizens of London, do now hereby, with one voice and content of tongue and heart, publish and proclaim :
>
> That the High and Mighty Prince George Frederick Ernest Albert is now, by the death of our late Sovereign of happy memory become our only lawful right Liege Lord George the Fifth by the Grace of God King of the United Kingdom of Great Britain and Ireland, and of the British Dominions beyond the Seas, Defender of the Faith, Emperor of India, to whom we do acknowledge all faith and constant obedience, with all hearty and humble affection, beseeching God, by whom Kings and Queens do reign to bless the Royal Prince George the Fifth with long and happy years to reign over us.

The Proclamation was publicly read, with ancient and picturesque ceremonial at St. James's Palace, at 9 o'clock of the morning of May 9, 1910, a few days after the death of King Edward. A Guard of Honour of the First Life Guards rode into Friary Court of the Palace, followed by the band of the Coldstream Guards with draped guns, and by the Army Headquarters' staff in their full and varied uniforms. Then appeared on the balcony overlooking the quadrangle, the Duke of Norfolk, Earl Marshal, and Garter King-of-Arms and Pursuivants of the Heralds' College, all in their robes and attended by State trumpeters. A great crowd assembled for the ceremony.

Four of King George's children looked on from a window of Marlborough House, opposite the quadrangle, and the King and Queen were at another window, though unseen by the people. Garter King-of-Arms read the Proclamation, the young Princes and the troops standing at the salute and the men in the crowd baring their heads. The Earl Marshal led the cry of " God save the King," and it was sung by the people. A Royal Salute of forty-one guns was fired in the neighbouring St. James's Park.

CHAPTER II

THE CORONATION

THERE is no ceremony for the exaltation of man in high office that surpasses in solemnity and splendour of ritual the Crowning of the King of England in Westminster Abbey? Many changes have been effected in the constitutional form of the British Monarchy—some in the tumult of revolutions, some in the silent lapse of events—so as to fit it into the ever-advancing democratic system of government, but the rites of initiation are the same to-day as they were when Edward the Confessor and William the Conqueror were crowned, when the Kingship was regarded as sacrosanct and absolute—denoting the possession, by the Sovereign personally, of supreme dominion, authority, rule.

The Coronation is essentially a religious service. It is conducted by the highest ecclesiastical dignitaries. The great Officers of State who assist at it are but servers or acolytes to the Archbishops and Bishops. It is the finest, perhaps the only, mediæval pageantry in patriotism transfused with religion, that is extant in the twentieth century. The inspiration of Rome is in its solemn ritualism and its gorgeous pomp. And yet throughout the ceremonial there runs a recognition that the King, if but a little lower than the angels, is still a man, with personal feelings, opinions and predilections, and subject to the commonest weaknesses of humanity—its tempers, whims, caprices. Therefore, there are professions of humility on his part as well as anthems of praise to his glorification. Above all, there is an insistence that he must bind himself by oath to his duty and responsibility towards his country, to govern the people according to the laws of the land, to execute justice with mercy; and prayers of intercession are offered up that he may be strengthened for the fulfilment of these obligations. The Coronation, in fact, is of the nature of a solemn covenant between the King and his people —of devotion to their well-being on his part, and, in return, of loyalty on theirs. This assertion of the truth that Kingship must be founded on order and law is brought out and emphasised at all the supreme moments of the elaborate service.

*   *   *   *   *   *

The new King goes to the Abbey for his crowning—as all his predecessors have done since William the Conqueror—the Abbey that is the shrine and temple of English history. Buried in its precincts are thirteen Sovereigns (George II being the last) and fourteen Queens. The King enters by the West door, wearing the crimson Royal Imperial Mantle and the Cap of Maintenance, also of crimson velvet edged with white ermine. Preceding him is the Queen Consort, for she too is to be crowned, attired in purple robes with her hair bound by a circlet of gold. Their Majesties are conducted to the Theatre (as it is called), an elevated square platform between the North and South Transepts (better known respectively as Statesmen's Aisle and Poets' Corner) and before the Sacrarium within which is the Altar. In the South Transept are the Princes of the Blood and the peers in robes of scarlet and ermine, in the North Transept are the Princesses of the Blood and the peeresses, in light Court dresses and jewels. High galleries over the peers contain the Members of Parliament. They have the option of wearing morning dress. So also have the representatives of county councils, municipal corporations, trade unions, friendly societies, who, for the first time, were invited to the Coronation of Edward VII. All other males are expected to come in court dress or uniform. Ladies not of the peerage are restricted to Court dress without trains.

Altogether about 5,000 men and women are privileged to attend the service—an enormous assembly which is made as representative of all classes, and of all callings, as it can well be. For their accommodation galleries are erected on all sides towering to the roof. On the floor is spread a carpet of dark blue. The hangings are of lighter blue and silver grey, behind which the effigies of poets, statesmen, soldiers and scientists, and all the allegories of the dead have disappeared from view. Taking in the scene as a whole it is like a vast living jewelled cross, formed of the Nave, the arms of the Transepts, and the Sacrarium, and glimmering in the grey mist of the Abbey with subdued colour.

The first part of the service represents a survival of the ancient principle of popular election to the Throne. It is called the Recognition. The Archbishop of Canterbury, vested in a cope of white and gold, and accompanied by the Lord Chancellor, the Lord Great Chamberlain, the Earl Marshal and Garter King-of-Arms, all in their respective robes, stands beside the King, and addressing the assembly in a loud voice says, "I here present unto you, George, the un-doubted King of this Realm." In answer there comes a tre-mendous shout, " God save King George," led by the shrill voices of the boys of Westminster School who for many generations have in this service played the part of the crowd at a mediæval Coronation. Four times this is done, to the north, to the south, to the east and to the west—the Arch-bishop presenting the King, the King showing himself to the people, the people greeting him with acclamations, all with one voice crying out repeatedly, " God save King George ! "

The next great moment is when the Archbishop of Canter-bury, addressing the King, says, " Sir, is Your Majesty willing to take the oath ? " the King answers in a loud clear voice, " I am willing." The King is then conducted to the Altar, the Sword of State being carried before him, and there uncovering, taking off the Cap of Maintenance, and kneeling down and laying his right hand upon the Holy Gospel in the open Bible, he swears " to govern the people of this United Kingdom of Great Britain and Ireland, and the Dominions thereto belong-ing, according to the Statutes in Parliament agreed on, and the respective laws and customs of the same," kisses the Bible and signs his name to a transcript of the oath. Its terms were settled at the Revolution of 1688, but in spirit and substance it is the same oath that Saxon and Norman Kings, Plantagenets and Tudors and Stuarts had taken to hold by the ancient laws and to conform to the old liberties. Having thus solemnly sworn to fulfil his bond the King is anointed and crowned as a constitutional Sovereign—consecrated, as Head of the State, to the service of his people. For, as no one recognises more than he, they are his " people," and not his " subjects." This is the most central and solemn part of the service, and for it

23

His Majesty sits in King Edward's Chair, within the Sacrarium and in front of the Altar.

Who that has seen this venerable and time-worn wooden Chair in the place where it is kept, the Chapel of St. Edward the Confessor, behind the Altar, has not wondered, and also indulgently smiled, at the revelation its condition affords of a curious side of the national character. The front of the Chair, made though it is of hard and solid oak, is scratched all over with names and initials. What self-assertion ? What a craving for immortality by associating one's self, if only by one's initials, with an enduring memorial. But the intention has been defeated, for the names and initials are so numerous that it is difficult, if not impossible, to decipher any one of them. And also what a proof it affords of the absence of any proper guardianship and care of this hallowed Chair, during what must have been a long period of time !

Under the seat of the Chair, resting on a bottom board, is a rough lump of stone, over two feet long and a few inches thick, of a sandy granular formation. It is the Coronation Stone of the ancient Scottish Kings which was preserved in the Augustinian Abbey of Scone—a village in Perthshire on the river Tay —until it was carried off by that warrior and statesman Edward I, in 1296, on his return from his attempt to subdue Scotland, and attach it to England, as he had previously done to Wales, in pursuance of his policy of territorial consolidation. He it was who had the Chair made for the stone. But Edward might have left the stone to Scotland without any loss to England. For England possessed a still more ancient Coronation Stone—the stone upon which the Saxon Kings were enthroned and crowned. It may be seen in the Market Place of the old town of Kingston-on-Thames, surrounded by iron railings.

Tradition gives the Stone of Scone a supernatural origin. It was used at Tara in Ireland as the " inauguration stone " of the Irish Kings, before it was stolen in a Scottish raid. In Ireland, where it was known as the " Stone of Destiny," there was a legend that it had been brought thither from Syria, and was, in fact, the very stone on which the patriarch Jacob rested his head when he slept at Bethel and dreamed his dream of the ladder that reached to Heaven. But Geikie, a famous geologist of the nineteenth century, declared that the stone must have been quarried in the sandstone district between Argyll and the Forth. All the Kings since the thirteenth century have been crowned in this Chair. Even Cromwell, when he was installed as Lord Protector in Westminster Hall, had the Chair brought over from the Abbey and was placed in it. The Stone is the " Stone of Destiny " indeed. The Divine right of Kingship and Parliamentary title, inheritance and usurpation, have been alike to it. There could be no finer symbol of Kingship.

*　　*　　*　　*　　*　　*

While the King is being anointed, as he sits in Edward's Chair, a rich silken pall is held over him by four Knights of the Garter, so that he might be concealed from the view of the spectators. The Archbishop of Canterbury dips his fingers in the Holy Oil, which has been poured by the Dean of Westminster into the golden anointing spoon, and makes the form of a cross on the crown of the King's head, on his bared breast, and on the palms of both his hands. Then comes the crowning. The King, having been vested in the Imperial Mantle, or Pall of Cloth of Gold, again, sits down in Edward's Chair. The Ruby Ring, the wedding-ring of the King and his country—ruby signifying faithfulness—is put on the fourth finger of his right hand by the Archbishop of Canterbury. The Sceptre with the Cross, emblematic of regal power and justice, is placed in his right hand, and in his left the Sceptre with the Dove, emblematic of equity and mercy.

The Archbishop is now to be seen at the Altar consecrating the Crown of England. This is, even more than the Coronation Chair, the most interesting item of the Regalia used in the service. Known as St. Edward's Crown, it is the official Crown of England, and therefore the supreme symbol of the British Monarchy. Alfred the Great (A.D. 871) is said to be the first English King who wore a crown. This Crown was inherited by Edward the Confessor and named after him. Each King down to Charles I had it placed on his head at his Coronation. It was lost in the confusion attending the establishment of the Commonwealth, with Cromwell as Lord Protector. At the

Restoration, a new crown was made for the Coronation of Charles II in 1660. This is the Crown that is now about to be used. As it is a replica of the old it is also called St. Edward's Crown.

The Czar of Russia allowed no man to crown him. In all his vast dominions there was no man of the rank and authority and worthiness for so supreme an act—not even the Patriarch and Chief of the Holy Synod. The Crown was placed on the Czar's head by the only being on earth fit for that mighty purpose—his absolute and autocratic self. But the King of England, with a humbler notion of himself, with a higher regard for religion, is crowned by the Archbishop of Canterbury. His Grace, having blessed the Crown, poises it for a few moments above the King as he sits in the Coronation Chair, and then slowly and most reverently places it on His Majesty's head. The moment is marked by a brilliant illumination. The electric lights are turned on. The jewels of the Crown flash into a sudden flame. A wave of gold iridescence passes over the crowd of peers in the North Transept. They are putting on their coronets. At the same moment the great assembly thrill to a profound feeling. With fervour they cry out " God save the King, Long Live the King," to an accompanying fanfare of trumpets and drums. The bells of the Abbey ring out, and the massed guns at the Tower of London thunder the announcement that the King has been crowned. It was the self-same spirit that in ancient times expressed itself in wild barbaric shouts and the gleam of steel as the lieges proclaimed their devotion to the new Sovereign. A great and free people were now doing homage to the King whom they had chosen to reign over them.

*   *   *   *   *   *

But the service is not yet over. A part that is equally lofty and thrilling is still to come. This is called " The Homage." The King, arrayed in all the emblems of sovereignty, robed and crowned, goes back to the Theatre, where a Throne consisting of a Chair of State on raised steps has been provided, and His Majesty is lifted up into this Throne by the Archbishops, Bishops and great Officers of State. Homage is first rendered by the Archbishop of Canterbury, on behalf of the Lords Spiritual. His Grace kneels down at His Majesty's feet— all the other Bishops kneeling in their places—touches the Crown on the King's head and kisses the King's left cheek, testifying that he and his Estate of the Realm do become His Majesty's " liege men of life and limb." The Princes of the Blood Royal, headed by the Prince of Wales, do their homage in like manner. Then the Peers, rank by rank—Dukes, Marquises, Earls, Viscounts, Barons—kneel in their places, and the premier nobles of each rank come to the Throne and, kneeling before the King, do homage on their behalf by touching the Crown and kissing His Majesty on the left cheek.

Here, it must be noted, there is one thing conspicuously wanting. The Commons have no part in the Homage. When the Service was composed " the people " had practically no political existence, and to bring them, or representatives of them, into personal association with anything closely relating to the Monarchy and the Court was unthinkable. The authors of the Service obviously did not indulge in dreaming on things to come, or, if they did, they did not foresee the sweep of the world into a broader day bringing new majesty to Kings of mighty States by political power in widest commonalty spread.

Accordingly, the Coronation of the King is, of the ceremonies of the Constitution, the only one that remains wholly old, fixed and stereotyped, without any of the modern democratic tenets. And thus it is that the House of Commons, in the person of the Prime Minister, or Leader of the House, is not included in the Homage paid to the Head of the State on the day of his crowning. Still, the great constitutional fact remains that the declaration of allegiance by the subjects, represented by bishops, princes and peers, comes after the King has sworn his oath of contract to the country, and he has been duly crowned according to the prescribed rites of the Realm.

The elemental qualities of mankind, which, happily for himself, a King shares with the humblest of his people will out, even as he sits in Cloth of Gold, with jewelled Crown upon his head in Westminster Abbey on the greatest day of all his days, the sole centre and essential figure in a wonderful service. The most moving episode at the Coronation of Edward VII had no place in the official Form and Order of the Service. The Prince of Wales did homage by taking off his coronet, and kneeling before the King, declaring in the prescribed words, a thousand years old—" I, George, Prince of Wales, do become your liegeman of life and limb, and of earthly worship and faith and truth I will bear unto you, to live and die, against all manner of folks. So help me, God." Then, rising to his feet, the Prince touched the Crown on the King's head and kissed His Majesty on his left cheek. As the Prince was about to turn away the King took hold of his robe to detain him. They were no longer King and liegeman, but father and son. The father placed his left hand on his son's shoulder, still holding his robe with his right, and drawing him towards him, kissed him affectionately on each cheek. Then taking his son's hands in his own the father gripped them warmly. This manifestation of paternal emotion illuminated the Service, in the sight of the great assembly, as with a sudden and unexpected accession of glory.

All this time the Queen Consort has been seated within the Sacrarium. It is now her turn to be crowned. A Queen Consort is crowned by Command of the King, and not of necessity by the will of the people as he himself is crowned. The ceremony is in essentials the same as in the case of the King, but the ritual is not so elaborate. Four peeresses hold a pall of cloth of gold over Her Majesty while the Archbishop of Canterbury anoints her on the head, puts the ring on the fourth finger of her right hand, and a crown on her brow. The Queen's Crown is called St. Editha's, in honour of the Consort of Edward the Confessor, though it was originally made for the coronation of Catharine of Braganza, the Consort of Charles II. The Chair in which Her Majesty is crowned was first used by Mary, Consort of, and joint Sovereign with, William III. The Queen then takes her place beside the King on the Theatre, sitting in a smaller or lower Throne. At the moment there is a flash of light, charged with water colour, over the peeresses in the North Transept. They are putting on their tiaras.

* * * * * *

Coronations have not been without the comedy that is in all human things. The official kiss between men, which is so ordinary an occurrence in France, has always been unpopular in England. It is therefore not surprising to learn that when the Order of the Coronation Service was submitted beforehand to William IV that unsophisticated person strongly objected to the Kiss of Homage, and insisted particularly that he must not be kissed by the Archbishop of Canterbury. His Grace just as strongly remonstrated against the omission of the kiss, for it would mean, he contended, a derogation of the position of the Church in the State, and a reflection also on the dignity of its ecclesiastics. It was only when the Archbishop declared that without the Kiss of Homage the service would not be complete, nor the King properly crowned, that William gave way. In the coronation of his successor, Queen Victoria, it was agreed to omit the kissing in the Homage because of her sex and youth. The young Queen had a rosy cheek which the Archbishop, the Princes, and the peers would have been very pleased to kiss no doubt, but they had to be content with kneeling at her feet in testimony of their fealty.

There have also been incongruous incidents and awkward hitches during the service. The stage management, or prompting, at the coronation of Queen Victoria was often defective. The leading performers seemed to be always in doubt as to what was to come next. " Pray tell me what I am to do," said the young Queen to Lord John Thynne, who, by Her Majesty's command, took the place of the Dean of Westminster, " for " —with an angry glance at the Archbishops—" they don't know." Her Ruby Ring was wrongly made for her little finger, which was supposed to be the fourth, omitting the thumb in the counting ; and it was so small that the Archbishop of Canterbury could get it on the proper finger next the little one, only by using such force as to make her gasp and almost scream with pain. She had to steep her hand in iced water after the ceremony, till the flesh shrank sufficiently for the Ring to be removed from the finger for enlargement. The service was also marred by a serious mistake of omission. The Queen, having been told by the Bishop of Bath and Wells, who acted as prompter or Master of the Ceremonies, that the service was concluded, retired to her waiting-room. Lord John Thynne then discovered that a part had been omitted, due to the Bishop having turned over two pages of his copy of the " Form and Order of the Service." What was to be done ? Melbourne, the Prime Minister, was consulted. Indifferent, as usual, he made the characteristic reply : " What does it signify ? " But Thynne thought otherwise, and on his advice the Queen returned to Edward's Chair, and the omitted part was transacted. Again, towards the end of the ceremony, the Lord Great Chamberlain began scattering among the assembly gold memorial medals of the Coronation, and an unseemly disturbance was caused by the maids of honour and the lords in waiting scrambling for them. This old custom of striking a medal and distributing it both in the Abbey and outside was not renewed at subsequent Coronations.

The Chapel of St. Edward, behind the Altar, is used as a retiring room for the Sovereign for rest and refreshment during the long service. Queen Victoria, writing about her Coronation, mentions that Lord Melbourne, the Prime Minister, remarked to her in the chapel that it was less like a chapel than any he had ever seen, for what was called the altar was covered with sandwiches and bottles of wine. It was to this retreat that George IV escaped now and then, from the dazzling and then very protracted scene of his Coronation—the service being meanwhile suspended—to fling off his heavy robes, cast himself upon a lounge, and mop his fevered brow in relief of his physical distress. The Coronation was then four hours long, and William IV and Victoria had to go through the same trying ordeal. As Edward VII had had a serious illness before his crowning the service was reduced to two hours, and the abbreviated form was also observed at the crowning of George V.

*   *   *   *   *   *

The King enters the Abbey for his crowning in a crimson robe. He leaves it in a robe of purple. On his head is a crown— not St. Edward's which is used only in the actual Coronation— but the Imperial Crown. Its chief gem is a ruby, of a value estimated at £100,000, which was given to the Black

Prince in Spain in the year 1367, and was worn by Henry V in his helmet at the battle of Agincourt. In his right hand the King carries the Sceptre with the Cross, and in his left, another ancient symbol of the Kingship, the Orb, a golden sphere enriched with pearls, and surmounted by a Cross—the Cross of both Sceptre and Orb signifying that the worldly power of the King is restrained by religion and morality, that above and beyond the King is the law of God. Thus arrayed the King goes forth with his Consort to show himself to his people, assembled in hundreds of thousands in the streets. As they drive in the old State coach of glass and painted panels, drawn by eight bay horses, to Buckingham Palace, their Majesties look just like a Prince and Princess in a book of fairy-tales.

Does the Sovereign come forth from his anointing and crowning, feeling glorified, puffed up with his own majesty ? Queen Victoria certainly did not. On arriving at Buckingham Palace she heard in the hall her favourite little spaniel barking with joy at the sight of her, and crying out " Oh, there's Dash ! " without waiting to lay aside her crown or purple mantle, she rushed over to take the dog in her arms and caress it. No doubt it was a reaction from the strain of the almost unendurable splendour of the Coronation.

CHAPTER III

THE ROYAL PREROGATIVE

PREROGATIVE means the attributes and privileges of the Sovereign and particularly his power legally to do things affecting the State without the authority of Parliament. The consideration of the Royal Prerogative leads us into the somewhat bewildering implications, if not confusions, of Kingship —vague, elusive, mysterious—so often is the practice in flat contradiction with the theory.

Who can have read for the first time without a start of surprise and incredulity the long list of calamities which, according to Walter Bagehot—acute thinker, banker and man of letters—in his illuminating book on the " British Constitution " (1868), it was in the power of Queen Victoria to inflict upon her unhappy subjects by the exercise of Prerogative, and without the consent of Parliament. Bagehot, in a famous passage, says :

> " She could disband the Army (by law she cannot engage more than a certain number of men, but she is not obliged to engage any men) ; she could dismiss all the officers, from the General Commanding-in-Chief downwards ; she could dismiss all the sailors too ; she could sell off all our ships-of-war and all our naval stores ; she could make a peace by the sacrifice of Cornwall and begin a war for the conquest of Brittany. She could make every citizen in the United Kingdom, male or female, a peer ; she could make every parish in the United Kingdom a ' University ' ; she could dismiss most of the civil servants, and she could pardon all offenders. In a word, the Queen could by Prerogative upset all the action of civil government within the Government ; could disgrace the Nation by a bad war or peace, and could, by disbanding our forces, whether land or sea, leave us defenceless against foreign nations."

We are seriously told that all this Victoria, or any other British Sovereign, before or since, could have done—Heaven save us !—without consulting Parliament, and even without any violation of the Constitution ! And what did Victoria herself think of it ? When the passage was brought to her notice she exclaimed : " Oh, the wicked man to write such a story ! Surely my people do not believe him ? " The good Queen, whose only thought was for the glory of England, and the safety, prosperity and contentment of her people, would not do any of these frightful things, even if she could, and we feel in our inmost convictions—it is a steadying and solacing thought—that no Sovereign could do any of them, even if he would. Wide apart, indeed, are the letter and the spirit of the Constitution.

Yet as we pursue the subject of Prerogative we find, however absurd and fantastic or at variance with common-sense it may seem, that the deeds set out by Bagehot which shocked the Queen and made us lift an eyebrow, are possible—according to the theory of the British Constitution. For Prerogative says the Sovereign is omnipotent. It also says he is never under-age and never over-age. More wonderful still, it declares he never dies. Non-age, that time of life when all subjects according to law and common experience are incompetent to manage their own affairs, does not affect the Sovereign in the discharge of his functions. Lord Eldon, the celebrated judge, explaining this presumption of the Prerogative to the House of Lords in 1830, in the course of a debate on the appointment of a Regency in the event of King William's death before Princess Victoria, Heir to the Throne, had come of age, said : " If an infant Sovereign were to be on the Throne whose head could not be seen over the wig of the Lord Chancellor or the Woolsack, he would be supposed to have as much sense, knowledge and experience as if he had reached the years of three-score and ten."

No risks, however, are taken. It is the custom, at the opening of every reign, to provide for the disabilities of infancy in the case of the Heir to the Throne by making statutory provision for the appointment of a Regency, should he succeed before he had attained his majority, which in his case, is the age of eighteen. Thus Queen Mary was appointed Regent by Act of Parliament passed in 1910, immediately after the accession of King George. It provided that " if on the demise of His present Majesty (whom God long preserve) any child of His Majesty succeeds to the Crown whilst under the age of eighteen years,"

Queen Mary was to be the guardian of such child, and have, " until such child attain the age of eighteen years and no longer, full power and authority in the name of such child, and in the stead of such child, and under the style and title of The Regent, to exercise and administer, according to the laws and constitution thereof, the Royal power and government of this Realm, and all the dominions, countries and territories belonging to the Crown thereof."

*　　*　　*　　*　　*　　*

" Kings should disdain to die and only disappear." So sang Thomas Flatman, a poet—though a very minor one—on the death of Charles II. " The King never dies," is an ancient maxim of the Constitution. Sir William Blackstone, the famous commentator on English laws, says : " Henry, Edward or George may die, but the King survives them all." The term " death," meaning the extinction of life, is never constitutionally or legally applied to the King. What is used is " demise," meaning the transmission of a right or estate. In the words of the Regency Act of 1910—quoted above—" on the demise of his present Majesty (whom God long preserve) " the Kingdom passes instantly to his Heir Apparent. Thus we find that it is not to the Sovereign as human being, but to the Sovereign as ruler, that the law's interpretation of Prerogative gives perpetuity. Thus it remains true that Queen Anne is dead after all. But not for an instant is the Throne vacant. At the moment of the death of the King, or, to use the phrase of Blackstone, " the disunion of the King's natural body from his body politic," that very moment the reign of his successor begins. Fast on the certification of the death of George III by the doctors at Windsor Castle, at 8 o'clock in the evening of January 29th, 1820, a herald appeared at one of the windows overlooking the town, and, after a fanfare by two State trumpeters to arrest the attention of wayfarers, he cried aloud, " The King is dead ! Long live the King ! "

That was the last time this barbaric ceremony took place, but there is an interesting story told of King Edward VII which gives a modern touch to that ancient exclamation— " The King is dead ! Long live the King ! " Queen Victoria died at Osborne. As the body was being borne in the Royal Yacht, *Victoria and Albert*, with King Edward on board, from the Isle of Wight across the Solent through the long lines of battleships displaying their flags at half-mast, King Edward noticed that the Royal Standard on the Royal Yacht was also at half-mast. He summoned the Captain and asked him to explain. " The Queen is dead, Sir," replied the Captain. " The King lives," said Edward, and the Royal Standard was hoisted mast high.

The King is the embodiment of all the power and authority of the State. The Army is the King's Army. It is to him naval and military service is rendered, for the Navy likewise is the King's Navy. When he speaks of them he calls them " My " Army and " My " Navy. The entire revenue of the State is paid to the King. As the guardian of the peace and the source of justice, the King appoints judges and magistrates. The administration of the law throughout his vast Dominions is carried on in his name. The King can pardon prisoners or abate their punishment. The King summons and dissolves Parliament and he may reject Acts passed by both.Houses. He makes and unmakes Governments. The King is the fountain of all State honours, titles, dignities, ranks and offices. As Head of the Established Church, the King appoints archbishops, bishops and deans. In all foreign affairs the King represents the United Kingdom. He sends British ambassadors and ministers as his envoys to foreign States, and receives the ambassadors and ministers of foreign States at his Court of St. James. The King wages war, concludes peace, makes treaties.

These vast powers and privileges are exercised by the King in right of his Prerogative, and yet for their consequences, however evil, he enjoys an absolute immunity. It is a fundamental law of the Constitution that the King can do no wrong. At this point it begins to dawn upon us (if we are not aware of it already) that the King has to be regarded in two separate and distinct roles—as Head of the State, and as a private person. It is as Head of the State that he is omnipotent and infallible in all things. There is a figurative term by which the supreme executive and administrative power of the State is expressed. That is " the Crown." All the powers and rights of Prerogative have been transferred from the King, as an individual, to the Crown. It is in the name of the Crown that the Navy and Army are maintained, and commanded, that appointments to all great positions in the State and in the Church are made; that the Courts of Justice have jurisdiction. Parliament is summoned and dissolved in the name of the Crown. Ministers hold their offices under the Crown. In a word, the Government is carried on in the name of the Crown.

And yet the Crown in this sense is but an abstract entity. The reality, the solid fact, is the Ministry, supported by a majority of the House of Commons. The supreme executive and administrative authority is the Ministry. On the Ministry lies the responsibility for all things done in the name of the Crown, because, though they are done in the name of the Crown, they are done in reality on the advice of the Ministry. Furthermore, as the Ministry is absolutely dependent upon the will of the organised community, we get down to the basic fact that the absolute sovereignty lies not in the Crown but in the people. It is the people, and the people alone, who could do, or rather could command a Ministry returned by them to power to do, all the appalling things which Bagehot declares it was in the capacity of Queen Victoria to do by the Prerogative without saying to Parliament—" By your leave, my Lords and Commons." So it is that the Prerogative, which in the long ago made the British Monarch subject only to his own will and caprice, is now used to execute the will or caprice of the community. It is the Will of the People that has become infallible, omnipotent and perpetual—in constitutional theory.

The most notable instance of the exercise of the Prerogative by the Government in recent times, was Gladstone's use of it in 1871 to abolish the custom of acquiring officer's rank in the Army by buying it. The Liberal Government, in which Gladstone was Prime Minister, first tried to abolish purchase by Bill, which was violently opposed in the House of Commons and held up indefinitely in the House of Lords. It was then found that an Act of George III had abolished the selling of offices in other departments—while retaining to the Crown the discretion of continuing the practice in the Army by the issue of a warrant sanctioning and regulating it—and the

Government circumvented the Lords by issuing under this Act a Royal warrant abolishing purchase. It is said that Queen Victoria made no objection to signing the warrant.

So recently as the reign of Edward VII, one of the last of the prerogatives that had continued vested in the Sovereign was transferred to Parliament—authority for the cession of territory. Under the Anglo-French agreement of 1904 certain territories were to be surrendered and exchanged between England and France. Arthur Balfour, then Prime Minister, stated in the House of Commons that the consent of Parliament to the proposed cession of British territory would be asked in the form of a Bill which the Government would submit. King Edward in a private communication sharply rebuked the Prime Minister for this statement, and insisted that the power to cede territory lay not in Parliament but in the Sovereign. Balfour, however, stuck to his point, being fortified by the opinion of the Law Officers, and the King reluctantly gave way. Thus the residue of arbitrary or discretionary power in the Sovereign passed to Parliament.

*   *   *   *   *   *

A provision in the Act of Settlement expressly declares that the Sovereign should not go out of the Kingdom without the consent of Parliament. It was repealed in the first year of George I to enable His Majesty to visit his beloved Hanover. But the high importance of Kingship in the transaction of affairs of Government daily arising is seen in the arrangements which have to be made for their discharge by proxy during any prolonged absence of the Sovereign from England. One instance, and the most interesting, arose out of the visit of King George V and Queen Mary to India for the Coronation Durbar in 1911. Their Majesties were crowned in Westminster Abbey on June 22nd, 1911. On November 11th, they left Portsmouth for India in the steamship *Medina*, escorted by a squadron of battleships, and were crowned Emperor and Empress of India in Delhi on December 12th. They returned to England, after an absence of three months, in February, 1912. The journey and its object are memorable among events associated with the Monarchy. It was the first time that a Sovereign left the Kingdom to visit a part of the British Empire overseas. Edward VII was proclaimed Emperor of India at a Coronation Durbar in his absence. The presence of King George and Queen Mary at their Coronation Durbar marked the initiation of a new policy of more intimate intercourse being established between the Sovereign and his lands beyond the seas.

The first and second of the Georges often left England for Hanover, of which they were Kings by inheritance, though it was not included in the British Empire. Lords Justices, as they were called, were sworn as a Regency for the administration of the Royal functions during the absence of these Sovereigns. George II was away in July, '45 when the Young Pretender landed in Scotland. He did not get back to London until the end of August, and he then made preparations to go away altogether, in view of the triumphant march of Charles Edward towards London and the apparent indifference of his own English subjects. The King offered a reward of £200,000 for the Pretender's head. The Pretender retorted by offering 200 shillings for the head of the King. George III was never out of his Kingdom of England during his reign of sixty years. He passed his life contentedly between London and Windsor. His longest journey was to Weymouth in summer for sea-bathing. The last Sovereign to make a prolonged visit to Hanover was George IV, in 1821, when, for the last time also, Lords Justices were appointed.

Modern facilities of communication made a delegation of the Royal authority unnecessary during the short visits of subsequent Sovereigns, Queen Victoria and King Edward, to the Continent. In 1845, when Victoria was about to visit France as the guest of King Louis Philippe, Lord John Russell raised the matter in the House of Commons, he being then in Opposition, and urged that provision should be made for the exercise of the Royal authority by the appointment of Lords Justices. But it was decided that as one of the Secretaries of State, in the person of Lord Aberdeen, was to be in attendance on the Queen in France, to advise any exercise of the Prerogative that might be necessary while Her Majesty was abroad, the need for Lords Justices for so short a time did not arise. It was held that any State act done by the Sovereign abroad is as valid as if done within the Kingdom, provided it is done in the presence, and on the advice, of a Minister of the Crown. For legal doubts were raised at the time, as a matter of constitutional law, whether the Queen could do outside the Kingdom what she could do within it.

In the delegation of the Royal authority during the visit of King George and Queen Mary to India the old style of " Lords Justices " was dropped, and " Counsellors of State " —which sounds more democratic—was substituted. Four in number, they are thus sonorously described in the Commission authorised by Warrant under the Great Seal :

> Our Most Dear Cousin and Counsellor His Royal Highness Prince Arthur Frederick Patrick Albert of Connaught, Knight of Our Most Noble Order of the Garter, Knight Grand Cross of Our Royal Victorian Order ; Our Right Trusty and Right Entirely beloved Counsellor the Most Reverend Father in God Randall Thomas, by Divine Providence Lord Archbishop of Canterbury, Primate of All England and Metropolitan, Knight Grand Cross of Our Royal Victorian Order ; Our Right Trusty and Right Well-beloved Cousin and Counsellor Robert Threshie, Earl Loreburn, Knight Grand Cross of Our Most Distinguished Order of St. Michael and Saint George, Lord High Chancellor of Great Britain, and Our Right Trusty and Well-beloved Cousin and Counsellor John, Viscount Morley of Blackburn, Member of Our Order of Merit, Lord President of Our Council.

These Counsellors of State were empowered to do any matter or thing which might appear to them necessary or expedient to do, on King George's behalf, in the interests of the safety and good government of the Realm. But the power of dissolving Parliament and of granting peerages was withheld from them, and they were further bound not to act in any matter or thing on which it was signified by the King—or appeared to them necessary—that His Majesty's special approval should previously be obtained. In fact, as Asquith, the Prime Minister, informed the House of Commons, the King during his absence was in daily telegraphic communication with his Ministers in London, and all matters of gravity and importance were, in the ordinary course, submitted to him. Moreover, Lord Morley humorously confesses in his *Recollections*, " I detected no guilty ambition to expand our privileges."

A similar Commission was appointed in 1925, when King George made a long cruise in the Mediterranean after recovering from an attack of influenza; and again during the serious illness of His Majesty in the winter of 1928-29. The official announcement in the latter case states that a meeting of the Privy Council was held at Buckingham Palace, December 4th, and goes on: " His Majesty in Council was, this day, pleased to declare that having been stricken by illness He was unable for the time being to give due attention to the affairs of the Realm, whereupon the Draft of a Commission making provision for the summoning and holding of the Privy Council and for the transaction of other matters and things on behalf of His Majesty was this day read at the Board and approved." His Majesty was further pleased to nominate the Queen, the Prince of Wales, the Duke of York, the Most Reverend Father in God Cosmo Gordon, Archbishop of Canterbury and Primate of All England, the Right Honourable Douglas McGarel, Baron Hailsham, Lord High Chancellor of Great Britain, and the Right Honourable Stanley Baldwin, Prime Minister and First Lord of the Treasury, "for the purposes therein mentioned and to declare that they should be designated under the style and title of Counsellors of State."

The Council was actually held in the Audience Chamber which was next to the King's bedroom, and the door leading into the bedroom was left open. Sir W. Joynson-Hicks, Home Secretary, standing in the doorway, read out the Order Paper so that the King, who was in bed a few feet away, could be fully cognisant of the proceedings. The King then signed the document with his own hand. This was following a precedent of the first Council held by Queen Victoria after the Prince Consort's death, while Her Majesty was still in the acute stage of her sorrow and felt unequal to presiding in the normal way. The Queen, describing in her Diary the Council which was held at Osborne on January 6th, 1862, says : " Held a Council, which was well and kindly arranged. Lord Granville and others, with Mr. Helps, were in dear Albert's room, and I in mine, with the door open. The business was all summed up in two paragraphs, and Mr. Helps read ' approved ' for me. This was unlike anything which had been done before. The Council after dear Mama died took place in the Red Room, and dearest Albert handed me the papers and was with me. But now ! " Lord Granville was then Lord President, and the two other Privy Councillors present were Sir George Grey, Home Secretary, and the Duke of Newcastle, Colonial Secretary. Mr. Helps, afterwards Sir Arthur, was Clerk of the Council.

*   *   *   *   *   *

All this shows the large share the King personally has in the government of the country. Most of the things done by the Crown, acting as the executive authority, must be authorised by the Royal Sign Manual, as the signature of the Sovereign is called. Apart from papers of high State importance, the documents of a more or less formal nature which the King has to sign are very numerous. This duty cannot be delegated by the King to another person without the consent of Parliament. When George IV lay dying in May, 1830, an Act had hurriedly to be passed to relieve him of the painful task of putting his signature to urgent State documents. Provision was made for the stamping of such documents in the presence of the King, and by his command given by word of mouth, and for the authenticity of this Royal endorsement being testified to by three members of the Privy Council. What elaborate precautions ! The substance of the Prerogative has been transferred to the Ministry ; but all its outward attributes and distinctions, and much of its actual administration, are retained by the Sovereign.

Arthur Balfour, who was Prime Minister when Queen Victoria died in January, 1901, paid a touching tribute in the House of Commons to her laborious life, in the course of which he mentioned that he saw at Osborne, during the last illness of the Queen, a vast mass of papers awaiting the

Sign Manual. " Short as was the interval between the last trembling signature affixed to a public document and the final rest," he said, " it was yet long enough to clog and hamper the wheels of administration." Yet the drudgery of the Kingship had been considerably lightened during the reign of Victoria. At one time all military commissions had to be signed by the Sovereign. In 1862 an Act of Parliament was passed enabling the Queen, by Order in Council, to relieve herself of this task. There were then 15,000 commissions awaiting the Sign Manual. It frequently happened that an officer raised to higher rank received his warrant of promotion only after he had left the Army. The documents which the Queen had to sign, even after this relief, numbered 50,000 a year. When the Queen was out of town six Royal messengers were continually travelling between London and the Palace where she was in residence—Windsor, Osborne, or Balmoral, carrying despatch-boxes filled with State papers which she had to read or sign.

The duties of the office have since been increased, owing to the ever extending activities of the State and the more exacting demands of the people in the way of public functions on the time of the Sovereign. In fact, Kingship is probably the only calling to-day that—despite the growing desire of ease and leisure—is more absorbing and strenuous than it was half a century ago.

Parliaments, Governments, and Cabinets pass, but the Crown remains. They hold power only for a brief time, are dissolved, and return, it may be, composed of different persons with different politics, according to the changing opinions of the electorate from which they spring. The Crown is always in power. The Crown stands for the traditions and ideals, the liberties and loyalties, the possessions and security of the peoples of the Empire, in the Dominions as well as at home. The Crown, of which the King is the titular guardian, is the one continuing and unchanging symbol of that unity of tradition, authority, interests, sentiments, aims, which holds the British Commonwealth of Nations, part to part, as a single system of government animated by a common spirit and alike in all its branches.

CHAPTER IV

PRIVILEGES AND DISABILITIES

THE King has disabilities as well as privileges. The chief disability relates to religion. The King must be in communion with the Church of England. He is absolutely forbidden to marry a Roman Catholic, or indeed a person of any faith or sect but that of the Established Church. It is against the Roman Catholic religion that the ban is strictest. Should the King declare himself a Catholic or take a Catholic to wife he would forfeit the allegiance of his subjects. The Act of Settlement passed in 1701, lays down the law with comprehensive circumlocution :

That all and every person or persons that is, are or shall be reconciled to, or shall hold communion with the See or Church of Rome, or shall profess the Popish Religion, or shall marry a Papist, shall be excluded, and be for ever incapable to inherit, possess or enjoy the Crown and Government of this Realm and Ireland and the Dominions thereunto belonging, or any part of the same, or to have, use or exercise, any regal power, authority or jurisdiction within the same ; and in all and every such case or cases the people of these Realms shall be and are hereby absolved of their allegiance, and the said Crown and Government shall, from time to time, descend to and be enjoyed by such person or persons, being Protestant, as should have inherited and enjoyed the same, in case the said person or persons so reconciled holding communion or professing, or marrying, as aforesaid, were naturally dead.

The Sovereign must make a public profession by oath of his Protestant faith before the assembled Lords and Commons in the House of Lords when he opens Parliament for the first time. This as a rule takes place before the Coronation. For two centuries the oath denounced as blasphemous all the central doctrines of the Roman Catholic Church, such as the Mass and the invocation of the Saints, and this, naturally, gave great offence to adherents of that Church. A milder

43

form was substituted by Act of Parliament in 1910 and was
sworn to for the first time by George V. It is in the following
terms :

I do solemnly and sincerely in the presence of God
profess, testify and declare that I am a faithful Protestant,
and that I will, according to the true intent of the enactments which secure the Protestant succession to the Throne
of my Realm, uphold and maintain the said enactments
to the best of my power according to law.

The Act of Settlement could, of course, be repealed by
Parliament, but while the law stands an occupant of the
Throne who becomes a Roman Catholic or marries a Roman
Catholic would immediately cease to be Sovereign, and thus
no question of the allegiance due to him by a subject could arise
in law.

*   *   *   *   *   *

The King, in the exercise of the prerogative of mercy, can
remit or mitigate sentences on prisoners. This was originally
part of the arbitrary power claimed by Tudor and Stuart
Sovereigns to dispense with the law of the land. The Bill of
Rights made the dispensing power illegal, but retained to the
Crown the prerogative of pardoning offenders or commuting
their sentences. The King is theoretically prosecutor in
criminal cases ; all indictments are drawn up as being " against
the peace of our Sovereign Lord the King, his Crown and
Dignity," and as it is the " King's Peace " that is broken by a
violation of the law, he himself, being the offended party, may
forgive the transgressor.

Formerly, it was the duty of the Sovereign to consider
every death sentence and, in cases where a reprieve was not
granted, to sign the warrant of execution addressed to the
sheriff. In the exercise of the prerogative of mercy the Sovereign always acted on the advice of his Ministers. A curious
case arose in 1830. Peter Comyn, a man of good family
and position in Clare, Ireland, was convicted of arson—
he burned down his own house—and as that was then a crime
visited with the extreme penalty he was duly sentenced to
death. George IV, moved by a petition from the inhabitants

of the county, and without consulting his Ministers, wrote to the Lord Lieutenant directing him to revoke the execution, and substitute for it some other sentence as he might think fit. The Lord Lieutenant had already decided, on the advice of the Irish law officers, that the law should take its course.

Sir Robert Peel was Home Secretary and Wellington was Prime Minister. On hearing what the King had done they decided that it was unconstitutional, inasmuch as His Majesty had not beforehand asked the advice of the Minister who was responsible for the exercise of the prerogative of mercy. Peel wrote to the King to that effect, and also intimated that he must resign if His Majesty did not allow the sentence to be carried out. Moreover, Wellington, in a personal interview with the King, explained that Comyn had committed perjury, as well as arson, in swearing that three innocent men had set fire to the house. In the circumstances the King thought it best to withdraw the order of reprieve, and Comyn was hanged.

The practice of submitting to the Sovereign lists of death sentences with a statement in each case of the circumstances of the crime was naturally found very embarrassing when young Queen Victoria came to the Throne. To relieve her of a most painful duty an Act of Parliament was passed providing that no report in regard to persons sentenced to death should be made to Her Majesty nor to her heirs and successors. The prerogative of mercy lies since then exclusively with the Home Secretary. Attempts were made in Parliament to extend the principle of the joint responsibility of the Cabinet to the decisions of the Home Secretary in such cases, but the Government of the day always stood firm against it. The Home Secretary remains responsible, though the prerogative continues to be exercised, as of old, in the name of the King. " We, in consideration of some circumstances humbly represented to Us "—so runs the order for a free pardon, addressed to the governor of the prison in which the prisoner concerned is confined—" are graciously pleased to extend our Grace and Mercy unto him, and to grant him our Free Pardon for the offence for which he stands convicted."

The King is outside and above the law. His person is

inviolable. He is immune from all suits and actions, either civil or criminal. An Act passed in 1660, after the restoration of Charles II, " for the attainder of several persons guilty of the horrid murder of his late Sacred Majesty, King Charles the First," declares " that by the undoubted and fundamental laws of this Kingdom, neither the Peers of this realm, nor the Commons, nor both together in Parliament, or out of Parliament, nor the people collectively nor representatively, nor any other persons whatsoever, ever had, have, hath or ought to have, any coercive power over the persons of the Kings of this Realm." The law, in fact, endows the Sovereign with the attribute of perfection in thought and deed. " The King," according to Blackstone, " is not only incapable of doing wrong, but even of thinking wrong ; he can never mean to do an improper thing ; in him is no folly or weakness." Blackstone is always interesting on the Prerogative. It is with a smile that one reads the terms of awe and wonder in which he writes of the Sovereign, and then finds that he lived, not in Tudor or Stuart times, but in the last half of the eighteenth century. His *Commentaries on the Laws of England* were published in 1764, after which he was appointed a Judge of Common Pleas. He advises us " out of reverence and decency to forbear any idle inquiries of what would be the consequence if the King were to act thus and thus, since the law deems so highly of his wisdom and virtue as not even to presume it possible for him to do anything inconsistent with his station and dignity, and therefore has made no provision to remedy such a grievance."

We know, nevertheless, that the King, being human, is capable of doing a wrong thing in his private capacity. And what redress has the subject for any injury that may be done in a private or personal action ? None whatever. So that if the Sovereign were, we will say, to forge a cheque he could not be brought to trial, or if he were to defame any of his subjects an action for libel could not be instituted against him. Professor Dicey in his book *The Law of the Constitution* goes so far as to say that if the King were to shoot the Prime Minister with his own hand there is no court of law in which His Majesty could be arraigned. The King, in a word, is personally unamenable. Still, there remains one remedy for supreme acts of wrong committed by the Sovereign. If it be true that the King is above the law, it is also true that necessity knows no law. It is always open to the people, the Government, the Parliament, to break the law, or to ignore it. This was what was done, it will be remembered, in the famous and epoch-making affair of King Charles's head. Most likely the cutting off of a King's head would be thought a very drastic process in these democratic and less bloody days ; but it would be open to Parliament to take the more merciful course of putting the King under restraint, as a lunatic, and appointing a Regent in his place.

The King, though he cannot be sued in his own courts, is entitled to sue in them. He may, for instance, bring an action for trespass in the taking away of his goods. There is, however, one exception to the rule that he cannot be made a defendant. If he submits to the jurisdiction of his courts by instituting a civil action he may be required to comply with an order to put in a defence against a counter-claim in the same proceedings. The King may also forgo his Prerogative by consenting to defend an action for debt or damages or breach of contract, and in such a case the plaintiff—or the " suppliant " as he is more appropriately called—hands in a written statement, known as " Petition of Right," to the Home Office, and the King, as an act of grace, directs that it be endorsed with the fiat, " Let right be done," after which there is a hearing at law in the proper court. As the King cannot appear as a witness in a court of law he is unable to give evidence in any case in which he is a party, whether plaintiff or defendant. Even if judgment be obtained against him under a " Petition of Right," his goods cannot be distrained or taken in execution. Should the Sovereign refuse to pay the debt or the damages the suitor has absolutely no legal remedy whatever.

On the rare occasions that the procedure of " Petition of Right " has been adopted, the matters at issue were claims not against the Sovereign in person, but against the Crown or, in other words, a State department, such as the Board of Trade, the War Office, or the Treasury. It remains true to say that for wrong or injury done by the Sovereign personally there is no remedy at law. The Sovereign of course never allows a person who has suffered injury at his hands to go without redress. When Queen Victoria's yacht *Alberta* in 1875 ran down another yacht, and three of the crew were drowned, Her Majesty, although not legally liable, compensated liberally those who were bereaved by the accident, including the owner of the yacht who was paid £3,000.

The immunity of the King from civil and criminal proceedings does not extend to those who may do wrong on the King's behalf and by the King's command. Those who execute the unlawful orders of the King are amenable to punishment. They cannot plead that they acted on the King's instructions, because, as the King can do no wrong, or even think wrong, it conclusively follows that he cannot give wrongful instructions. The personal servants of the King also enjoy certain immunities. Officers and servants of the Royal Household who are employed in waiting or attendance on the King cannot be taken in execution in civil actions, unless the leave of the Lord Chamberlain of the Household is first obtained. There is a case of a warrant for the arrest of a person in trade, who contracted a debt which he declined to pay, being refused by a court of law on the ground that being also a Royal servant he was privileged from arrest. Officers and servants of the Royal Household are exempted from service on juries. The King's motor-car has no number and is unrestricted by speed limits. It is identified by the miniature Royal Standard—the King's personal flag—that flutters at its bonnet. The King's telegrams have precedence and go free. Indeed His Majesty has little, if any, use for the revenue stamps which bear his image. His letters are franked in the post. There is one legal disability under which he lies because of his pre-eminence. He can hold nothing as tenant, or by service, from a subject. He may buy a house or an estate, but he cannot rent it. Among the minor privileges exclusive to the King is that he may, if he pleases, drive in a horse-carriage down the ride of Rotten Row, Hyde Park. Of course, no King would do a thing so fantastic and absurd. But if he did? One of the early Georges desired to close St. James's Park to the public and make it a Royal Gardens. " What would be the probable cost of the scheme ? " he asked Sir Robert Walpole. " Only three Crowns, your Majesty," said the Prime Minister. This reminds us that what " the King can do no wrong " really means is that " the King must not make a mistake."

The King is free of taxation in respect of income and pro-perty coming to him in right of the Crown. The Civil List, or the fixed annual payments out of the Consolidated Fund, for the maintenance of the state and dignity of the Monarchy, amounting to £470,000, and including the £110,000 to the Privy Purse for His Majesty's personal use, are free of tax and all other charges and deductions, as is also the £60,000 a year which, in addition, the King gets out of the revenues of the Duchy of Lancaster. Income-tax was paid by Queen Victoria and also by King Edward. When the income-tax was first imposed in 1842, Queen Victoria agreed volun-tarily to pay it, as an example to the complaining country, which thought it a monstrous imposition. Payment was continued by King Edward. But in the arrangement of the Civil List at the accession of George V the imposition of the tax was discontinued. Nor does the King pay rates in respect of his Palaces. They belong to the State, and State buildings are exempt from local charges. But the private estates of the King, and any income he may derive from private investments, are subject to all rates, taxes, duties, parliamentary or local, in like manner as the property of any subject. Accounts in respect of these charges are returned, not to the King per-sonally, but to the Keeper of the Privy Purse and are paid out of the Privy Purse. The King does not pay probate duty or death duty on legacies left to him or property he inherits. The will of the Prince Consort, who was supposed to have left considerable property, was not lodged in Somerset House, as all wills must be except those of the Sovereigns. Jurists were divided in opinion as to whether Queen Victoria was within her right in withholding the Prince Consort's will, as the Prince was a subject, but the rule of not lodging the will of the Sovereign cannot be questioned. It is kept strictly private. If it were lodged in Somerset House it would be open to examination and publicity. Nothing was published as to the fortune left by Queen Victoria or as to its disposition, except that it did not go to King Edward. Probably it was distributed among her children and grandchildren whose allowances as provided by Parliament were comparatively limited. The same reticence was observed in regard to the wills of King Edward and Queen Alexandra.

*   *   *   *   *   *

The King must be neutral in political contests. The invigoration of being extreme in anything is denied him. He must keep to the middle of the road—the road that has been trodden out by the continuous and intensive march of the staid and respectable majority of countless generations of mankind, well-balanced in thought and opinion, perhaps, and, also perhaps, conventional. On the polling-day of the General Election of 1922, November 15th, the King was in residence at Sandringham House. His Majesty came out with a shooting party, and on his way to the preserves he saw his servants and the workers on his estate going to the polling-station in the adjoining village of Dersingham to help in giving a majority to one political party or another from which was to be selected the Ministers who were to advise His Majesty in affairs of State. But he himself had no vote. His name was not to be found on the parliamentary register of the parish of Sandringham. The King did not mind. George III would have minded greatly in like circumstances. He probably would have made it his business to direct his servants and labourers how to vote. In the General Election of 1780 he personally canvassed Windsor against the Whig candidate. His method was strange and peculiar. Entering the shop of a silk mercer, he would call out, " The Queen wants a gown— wants a gown ! No Keppel ! No Keppel ! " Entering a grocer's shop he would call out, " The Queen wants a chest of tea—wants a chest of tea ! No Keppel ! No Keppel ! " And the fact that George V did not mind was proof of his emancipation, as King, from political or party considerations. One other incident of the local election, which I also happened to have witnessed as a journalist, must be recorded.

The Labour candidate for the King's Lynn division of Norfolk, in which Sandringham is situated, drove by in a motor-car decorated with red streamers, and was loudly cheered by the beaters in the wake of the Royal sportsmen. The demonstration evidently amused the King, for he was seen to look back and smile very genially. Once when his attention was called to the use of his name on the election card of a Conservative candidate, he caused a reply to be sent saying : "While it is contrary to His Majesty's rule to advise electors how they shall vote, His Majesty is confident they will be showing no disloyalty to him by recording their votes for one candidate or for another."

There remains something of great constitutional importance to be said in reference to the maxim : " The King can do no wrong." It has come down from the far-off days when the Divine Right of Kings was an article of religious belief, and it obtains in the twentieth century, but with a different implication—not in the ancient autocratic sense that the King is humanly incapable of error, but in the modern constitutional sense that as the King can take no action in State affairs without the advice of a Minister of the Crown, it follows that if wrong or injustice should result from anything done in the King's name it is not the King that is to blame, but the Minister on whose advice the King acted. And under the doctrine of Ministerial responsibility there is no executive act of the Sovereign for which some Minister, or the Government collectively, cannot be made to answer either in a court of law if the act be illegal, or in Parliament if the act be contrary to the people's will.

George III, plain and blunt, as well as narrow-minded, was puzzled by the paradoxes of a Constitution which said one thing and meant another, which told him that he was an absolute ruler so morally perfect that he could do nothing wrong, and yet forbade him doing anything but what he was told to do by his Ministers. Speaking to one of his Ministers, Henry Dundas, in 1799, the King said how pleased he was to hear of the contemplated Union between Ireland and Great Britain. " But," he added, " I hope it is not true that the Government is pledged to emancipate the Roman

Catholics at the same time." "No," replied the Minister, "that will be a matter for future consideration." The King protested that as the emancipation of the Roman Catholics would be a violation of his Coronation Oath, which bound him to uphold the Protestant supremacy, he could never consent to it. Dundas endeavoured to explain to the King that he had a dual capacity, executive and legislative, and that the oath bound him as the Crown administering laws but not as the King giving his assent to laws passed by Parliament. "None of your Scotch metaphysics, Mr. Dundas," cried the King. "None of your damned Scotch metaphysics." But it was in fact laid down in the settlement come to after the Revolution of 1688 that the Coronation Oath, or Accession Declaration, was not to bind the King to refuse his assent to laws which Parliament, at a future time, might think necessary to the well-being and security of the country.

*   *   *   *   *   *

One of the most unpleasant disabilities of the King must be the restriction imposed by his station on his movements—his isolation and aloofness from the common round and daily experiences of ordinary people. He cannot take a walk down Piccadilly. At least, were he to do so the congestion of traffic, vehicular and pedestrian, would be enormous. But that he is above the law he might, in such circumstances, be "run in" by a policeman. An example of this aloofness of Royalty and its results is afforded by a remark made by Queen Victoria in the year before she died. It came out in casual conversation that she supposed a railway ticket to be a thin sheet of paper. "I do not think I ever saw a railway ticket," said she.

In spite of the popular belief to the contrary, the King always pays for the use of the box in each theatre which has come to be known as the Royal Box. He goes to the play as a private gentleman. No announcement of his proposed visit must appear in the newspapers beforehand—except on occasions of gala performances or performances for a charity —and his entrance must not be disclosed to the audience by the playing of the National Anthem. The King has only one gift or perquisite, so far as I can discover. On each anniversary of Blenheim, the Duke of Marlborough, and on each anniversary of Waterloo, the Duke of Wellington, presents the King with small replicas of the Royal Standard of England and the French flag of the time these battles were fought and won. On the occasion of a visit of representatives of French municipalities to Windsor Castle, King Edward, with characteristic thoughtfulness and tact, had the flags removed out of sight. At each presentation the standards and flags of the past year are given to the Officer of the Guard on duty that day. To the Guards are entrusted the safety of the King's person. They are on active duty always on that account. Hence the officer whose duty it is to see that watch is duly kept is the officer-in-charge of outposts—not the orderly officer, as in the line, but the picket officer.

CHAPTER V

" THE KING ! GENTLEMEN ! "

EDWARD VII was the first Sovereign to be styled " of the British Dominions beyond the Seas, King." Joseph Chamberlain, who was Secretary of State for the Colonies in 1901, at the accession of King Edward, had an Act of Parliament passed thus recognising in the Royal title the importance of the Dominions to the Empire. The full style and title of the Crown accordingly became : " By the Grace of God, of the United Kingdom of Great Britain and Ireland, and of the British Dominions beyond the Seas, King, Defender of the Faith, Emperor of India."

It was a happy thought, as events have proved. There was a time when the " Colonies," as they were first, somewhat disparagingly, called, were regarded as more of a burden than an advantage. Statesmen differing so widely in political opinion as Cobden and Disraeli, were united in thinking that if the Colonies would but cut the painter attaching them to England, they would be a happy riddance. The argument that a strong Navy and Army were needed for the protection of the Colonies drew from Cobden the exclamation, " Where is the enemy that would be so kind as to steal such property ? We might as well say that it is necessary to arm in defence of our National Debt." Disraeli, Chancellor of the Exchequer, writing to Lord Malmesbury, Foreign Secretary, in 1852, said, " Those wretched Colonies will all be independent in a few years, and meanwhile are a millstone round our necks."

The Colonies at that time did appear to be drifting apart from each other and away from England. Then they began to draw closer together and to turn lovingly to the mother-country, recognising the prestige and protection they derived from their common descent from England, and their relationship, each with the others, in blood and kinship. And at home statesmen began slowly to recognise that in times of difficulty the mother-country might draw much help and comfort from her scattered children beyond the seas, united in a partnership or family of sister nations with common ideals, and common interests, which they were prepared to defend by concerted action. This change in feeling on both sides was manifested in a wonderful way at the Diamond Jubilee of Queen Victoria in 1897. All the Dominions, Dependencies, Principalities, Crown Colonies, Protectorates, took part in the celebrations. It was then most vividly realised that the Empire was composed of many distinct and separate races, differing in origin, language, religion, law, and custom ; differing also in their systems of government, ranging from self-governing Commonwealths of the most democratic types to Dependencies and Protectorates to whose inhabitants the methods of democratic government would be incomprehensible. Then arose the conception of the interdependence of the Empire, of unity in diversity, with the Crown as the keystone binding together the whole of this vast fabric, in which people so opposite dwell—black men, yellow men, red men, white men—and tending at least to soothe the prejudices of colour, and the conflict of different civilisations by participation in a common British citizenship.

But for the golden link of the Crown all the independent Commonwealths would probably have cut themselves adrift, and each gone off on its own account. To the peoples of the Indian Empire the only thing understandable in our Constitution is their Emperor. There are millions of native races in the subject Colonies and Protectorates who have never heard of Cabinet, or Prime Minister, or Parliament, or, if they have, find it hard to grasp intelligently what it implies. But the King they can understand. They know that he is a real, living, all-powerful being, standing high and apart, in whose name all the acts of government in their own lands are done. They acknowledge him as their Overlord. He is the centre of their life. They know that their protection and security lies with him. So they look up to him with homage and devotion. For no symbol of Imperial authority but the Kingship could they have the feeling which we call allegiance. And, in the last resort a subject in any of the Colonies or Dominions asks for justice of the King in person through his Privy Council. All appeals from the courts of the Dominions are heard by the

Judicial Committee of the Privy Council. Kingship, in a word, makes the British Empire one and indivisible.

At the Imperial Conference held in London in November, 1926, it was declared by the Prime Ministers of the Dominions that the group of self-governing communities composed of Great Britain, the Irish Free State, and the Overseas Dominions were " equal in status, in no way subordinate one to another in any aspect of their domestic or external affairs, though united by a common allegiance to the Crown, and freely associated as members of the British Commonwealth of Nations." The more the constitutional ties between the Dominions and the Mother Country have been relaxed by the action of the Dominions in enlarging each its own independence, the more uniting the Crown has become. In the address which the Dominion Prime Ministers presented to the King on the conclusion of their labours—" knowing your Majesty's deep interest in all that touches your people's happiness "—they well expressed the height and depth of the affectionate esteem in which he is held by our kith and kin across the seas. " We have been conscious," they said, " throughout our deliberations, of a unanimous conviction that the most essential of the links that bind our widely-spread peoples is the Crown, and it is our determination that no changes in our status as peoples or as Governments shall weaken our common allegiance to the Empire and its Sovereign." To this emphatic declaration of loyalty the King made a fine reply. Where, he asked, could one find such ample testimony to their common allegiance to the Empire and its Sovereign as in their noble self-sacrifice during four-and-a-half years of the World War ? The Monarchy keeps to the front the common blood relationship. It encourages also closer intercourse between the separate self-governing communities for mutual benefit. The dissolution of the British Monarchy would probably mean that the British Empire would fall to pieces. General Smuts, the South African statesman, speaking in London in 1917, of the influence of the hereditary Kingship in keeping together the British Empire, said " You cannot make a Republic of the British Commonwealth of Nations," for the process of electing a President for such a vast and complicated organisation would "pass the wit of man to devise."

At home in Great Britain the reconciling and uniting influence of the Monarchy is also seen. The Monarchy is the symbol of the home life of the Nation. It is the symbol of the people's greatest common measure of agreement. It enshrines all the ideals and causes upon which the people are united. Of the three great national institutions concerned with the destiny of the country and its welfare, the Monarchy, the Parliament, and the Church, the Monarchy alone stands fixed and stable, unaffected by the conflicts of parties and sects which divide and distract the people. The Church—using the term in its widest sense—is riven into sects almost numberless. Parliament is a tumult of political and social theories. The House of Commons is always in a state of flux. Members sent there by the people are constantly coming in through its swing doors and going out never to return. A Prime Minister, or an Archbishop of Canterbury, could never become an object of deep and continuous regard, not to say of worship as a national hero.

There is only one man who stands for the whole Nation—above all its sectional interests of party and class, above all its strifes, political, religious, social, above all its diversity of opinion, feeling, and sentiment—and he is the King. For, despite the divisions of politics and religion and social state, there exists in all circles of society an abiding sense of a common national history, of a corporate life and needs in the immemorial structure of their political society, which inspires and gives an ardent zest to patriotism. Is not England a land of ancient renown ? Is she not great and powerful ? Is she not the traditional home of freedom ? Is not the King the head of the oldest Royalty in Europe ? Is not the British Throne the most glorious in the world ? This collective sense of the greatness of the country, this national fellowship of spirit, finds its completest expression in loyalty to the Throne. All the national traditions are monarchical. The unity of British history and its continuity are realised in the Monarchy. Attachment to the Throne is in the air, is in the soil. It is bred in the people's bones ; it runs in their blood. Kingship has launched a thousand historical and constitutional panegyrics. Poets in their attempts to interpret its mysteries and defend its sanctity have hung about it the filmy stuff of which visions are made. What gives it its brightest glory is that element of romance that is in the soul of man. Its great strength lies not in logic and reason, but in instinct, intuition, sentiment, emotion—all the innate subconscious forces of the natural man. It is really the most wonderful thing among human institutions. All the glories of the past, and all the vital things of the present, are associated with the Monarchy. There have been tremendous changes in national life since its establishment—changes in ideas, in moral issues, in religion, as well as changes in society and in the Constitution. And through it all one sees at the head of affairs a man or woman, in purple and ermine robes, with a crown of gold and pearls, a sceptre and a sword—commanding to the Crown, reverence ; to the Sceptre, obedience ; to the Sword, fear.

* * * * * *

Too often in the remote past the King as a man was hated, and his office was regarded with an awe that was inspired more by fear and terror than by reverence and devotion. Henry VIII, for instance, received flatteries and genuflections of an Eastern subserviency. It was the custom in the House of Lords for the peers to rise from their seats and bow their heads at every mention of the King's name. And when Henry was present in Parliament, Lords and Commons together knelt down, and gazing in seemingly wrapt devotion at the round-bellied and puffy-faced man with the stubbly reddish beard seated on the Throne—knowing well, too, that he was a selfish and cruel egotist, steeped to the lips in sensuality—they hailed him as " His Most Sacred Majesty," and thanked God for His goodness in having given them so great a Prince to rule over them so long. Perhaps it was the office they saw and not the man. Perhaps they could not see the man so overshadowed was he by the office. The Kingship, perhaps, evoked in them the twin emotions of terror and enchantment—terror at the ruthlessness of its power, enchantment at its Divine origin and splendour.

But what a contrast that spectacle presents to the scene often witnessed at a race meeting on Epsom Downs in the first decade of the twentieth century! In the crowded Royal enclosure of the grand stand, King Edward VII—an elderly bearded gentleman, stout and jovial, wearing a silk hat and light dust coat, and smoking a cigar—could be seen moving freely among the throng. However well-known one may be to a Royal personage one must not presume to address him, but must wait for him to give the recognising nod, or smile, or word. This rule of etiquette affords to Royalty some protection from social snobs and tuft-hunters, eager for notice and pushful. Nevertheless, intercourse between the King and the company at Epsom was of the freest kind. His Majesty had something pleasant to say to acquaintances whom he encountered as he moved about the enclosure, each raising his hat in acknowledgment of the recognition. He was addressed, not as " Your Most Sacred Majesty," but as " Sir." They treated him as they knew he desired to be treated. They admitted him to easy gossiping companionship. There was no undue familiarity on their part ; nor was there, on his part, undue reminder of his exalted position. He was perfectly natural. They were quite at their ease. Then from the immense multitude outside on the course came loud cheers for the " King of Sportsmen." His Majesty smiled and raised his hat in appreciation of the popular greeting. More than that, there were scenes of unparalleled excitement at the Derby of 1909 when his horse, Minoru, carried his colours to victory —purple, gold band, scarlet sleeves, and black velvet cap. It was the first occasion that the Derby was won by a King. Edward left the enclosure to lead in the horse and mounted jockey. The crowd pressed closely round him, rejoicing in his triumph, and, in their endearing familiarity patted him on the back and hailed the greatest of Kings, the occupant of the most ancient of Thrones, as " Good old Teddy."

It was not that kingly degree and rank were forgotten. This was vividly present in the mind of the crowd. They afterwards sang in mighty chorus, " God Save the King." It was that the grovelling adulation, or the slave spirit of the past, had given way long since to esteem and affection. Edward

VII was the first Citizen King. The British Monarchy had lost nothing of its ancient allurement—nothing of its romance, and nothing of its wonder. But it had gained enormously in popularity. What other King but the British would have dared thus to trust himself in a densely-packed and excited crowd? " The King, Gentlemen ! "

 END OF BOOK I

BOOK II

THE ROYAL FAMILY

CHAPTER I

ANCESTRY

" Wha the deil hae we gotten for a King,
But a wee, wee German Lairdie."

So the first of the Hanoverian Monarchs, George I, is contemptuously spoken of in a contemporary Jacobite ballad ; and a ludicrous picture is drawn of him " delvin' in his kailyardie " for leeks, with nothing on but the " breeks," when the deputation of the Whig Government of the day " gaed ower to bring him hame." But George I, despite his German birth, his ignorance of English, and his boorish ways, was really as much a Stuart in blood as his immediate predecessor on the Throne, Queen Anne. Anne, by the way, is called in history the last of the Stuart Sovereigns, though she desired her dynasty, or family, to be known as " D'Este," which was the name of the second wife of her father James II—Mary d'Este, daughter of the Duke of Modena, and the mother of the first of the Stuart Pretenders, Chevalier St. George, whom Anne desired to succeed to the Throne when she herself was gone. Anne was the granddaughter, and George I was the great grandson, of the first of the Stuart Kings, James I. George I and Chevalier St. George were cousins of the Blood Royal, the only difference between them in their common descent from a common ancestor being that the Pretender was in the direct male line from James I, and King George I was in a collateral female line through James's daughter Elizabeth, who married the Elector Palatine of the Rhine. This difference was, by the law of heredity, in favour of the Pretender. Accordingly, though the succession to the Throne was changed at the Revolution of 1688, the association of the Stuart blood with it was preserved, and also, of course, the Tudor, Plantagenet, Norman, and Saxon blood. The story of the ancestry of the Royal Family provides wonderfully impressive evidence of the enduring fabric of this Realm, of the continuity of its national life, under its truly national Throne, from far-off ages to the present day.

The flight of James II from the Kingdom was meant by him to be temporary only. He never resigned the Crown, and never intended to resign it. Even if he had abdicated he would not, thereby, have prejudiced his son's title to succeed. The Convention Parliament, composed of Lords and Commons sitting together, which met to consider the situation, declared that James, " having withdrawn himself out of the Kingdom," had, in fact, abdicated. Glad of the chance to get rid of a Monarch who was a Roman Catholic, and aimed at being absolute, they declared the Throne to be vacant, setting aside James's son, as well as James himself. This was a decision of momentous constitutional importance. It ran counter to the old theory that the King never dies—that the very instant a King passes away another King succeeds him, that the Throne never is and never can be vacant. Here was the Throne declared vacant by Parliament, and here was Parliament looking around for someone whom it could elect or select to fill it. Fortunately, the Lords and Commons were in the position of being able to keep the succession still in the Blood Royal by availing of a collateral, if foreign, stream. For this recognition of heredity made the change over easy by affording a salve to the tender consciences of most of the Royalists who remained stout adherents of legitimacy.

The Protestant Dutchman, William Prince of Orange and Stadtholder of Holland, to whom the Crown was first donated by Parliament jointly with his wife Mary, daughter of James II, was a grandson of Charles I—his mother being a daughter of that unfortunate monarch—and he was therefore a nephew of James II as well as his son-in-law. Another daughter of James, Princess Anne of Denmark (who had been brought up a Protestant) was declared to be Heir Presumptive—William and Mary having no children—in the line of direct hereditary descent from the deposed Monarch, and subsequently, by the Act of Settlement, 1701, the succession was limited to the Hanoverians, descended from that Elector Palatine of the Rhine who had married Elizabeth, daughter of James I, and aunt of James II.

Thus, while the title of the Hanoverians to the Throne was strictly parliamentary—and there could be no better one in a democratic age—the first of the Georges had in his veins a mingling of the blood of all the preceding Royal Houses of England—Stuart, Tudor, Plantagenet, Norman, Saxon. His son, afterwards George II, did make that proud boast on coming to England from Hanover with his parents. " There is not a drop of blood in me that is not English," said he. The declaration was made in broken English, with a pronounced German guttural accent. In a way, the blood in his body resembled his mode of speaking. There was a strong German element in it. In fact, the original Stuart blood had already had an infusion of German blood. The wife of James I and mother of Charles I was Anne, daughter of Frederick II of Denmark by his wife, Sophia of the House of Mecklenburg.

$$*\qquad*\qquad*\qquad*\qquad*\qquad*$$

The present Royal House is the most ancient of the Sovereign Houses now reigning in Europe, much diminished in number by the World War. There were breaks in the direct line of succession. Kings and Queens died leaving no offspring. The Crown, therefore, reverted to collateral branches. There were usurpations. Kings possessed themselves of the sceptre by strong and bloody hands. Then there was the Revolution. A King was brought from Holland. But the Royal Blood of England was in the veins of all that long line of Sovereigns extending through many centuries of chequered history. That being so, King George V can trace his ancestry back in an unbroken line—though not in the direct male line—not only to William the Conqueror but to Saxon Kings who are dim and shadowy figures in the misty dawn of British history.

The ancestry of each and all of us extends, of course, as far back as the ancestry of King George, though most of us can trace our pedigree only to our great-grandfathers, paternal or maternal. But however we may be prone, therefore, to smile at the claims of long descent, we must have wondered, now and then, who was our living progenitor, on any great day in history—any day when a great historical thing was done. The King can tell more than that. At the most solemn moment of his Coronation in Westminster Abbey, when the Archbishop of Canterbury placed the Crown on his anointed head—

a moment for the mood of vision and inspiration—George V, attended also by the august and moving memories of the Abbey, might well have felt exalted by the grandeur of his destiny as the heir of all the ages, had he reflected on the number of Sovereigns who before him held the British sceptre, on their extraordinarily varied character, and on the different influences they have had upon the fate and fortunes of the country. There have been thirty-seven Kings and Queens since William the Conqueror. Before that there had been twenty Kings. Egbert, the Saxon King of Wessex, who by bringing the scattered and independent petty kingdoms of the Heptarchy under his central domination, making England one, was the founder of the English Monarchy which exists to-day. That was about the year 828. King George's ancestry goes even further back into the legendary ages, relying, in the absence of written records, on the heroic lays and legends of chroniclers and romancers. But confining himself to the period of authentic British history His Majesty could follow the careers of his forefathers through fourteen times a hundred years. For Cerdic of Wessex, from whom the Saxon Kings were descended, comes well within historic times, and back to him King George could trace his pedigree, step by step, without gap or flaw.

Egbert was succeeded by fourteen Saxon Kings. The greatest of them all was Alfred—Egbert's grandson—soldier and law-giver. His blood runs in the veins of George V. Then came the intervention of three Danish Kings. The Saxon dynasty was restored by Edward the Confessor (1042-1066) the son of King Ethelred and Queen Emma, daughter of Richard, Duke of Normandy. Edward died unmarried. Then followed the Normans. The first of them, William, Duke of Normandy, seized the Throne by force. He was illegitimate, his mother being the daughter of a tanner, but he was able to advance a claim by descent, though it was a weak one, in that Queen Emma was the sister of his father's father. However, his youngest son, Henry I, united the Saxon and Norman claims to the Throne by marrying Matilda, daughter of King Malcolm of Scotland, and of Margaret, granddaughter of Ethelred, and sister of Edgar Atheling, the last of the Saxon Princes. In the person of Henry II the Crown was restored to a descendant of Cerdic in the female line. Then came the Plantagenets and the Tudors. The mingled blood of all these streams flows in the veins of George V.

Yet this is by no means all. Not many of his people realise how extraordinarily varied are the lines of descent, foreign as well as British, combined in the person of George V. It is no heraldic fancy, but a genealogical fact, that His Majesty is descended from the High Kings who ruled over Ireland long before King Egbert founded the English Monarchy. One of the most ambitious of the Anglo-Norman lords who obtained vast tracts of land after the Conquest of Ireland in 1171 was Hugo de Lacy. In 1178 he married the daughter of Roderick O'Connor, the last High King of Ireland. The main line of de Lacy ended in a sole daughter who married another notable Anglo-Irish noble, Walter de Burgh, and, in time, the main line of de Burgh ended also in a sole daughter, Elizabeth de Burgh, Countess of Ulster in her own right. As she was the King's ward, as well as a great heiress, she was wooed and won by no less a personage than Lionel Plantagenet, Duke of Clarence, son of Edward III and brother of the famous Black Prince. It was from Lionel and his other brother, John of Gaunt, that the rival branches of the Plantagenet family, York and Lancaster, were descended. The bloody struggles of the two factions for the Throne ended with the death on the field of Bosworth of Richard III, whose despairing cry in Shakespeare's tragedy " A horse, a horse, my Kingdom for a horse," has rung through the centuries. The Crown of England, which was carried by Richard into battle, was found when the fight was over, and was placed on the head of the Earl of Richmond, who, on the field of his victory, was hailed as " King Henry VII," the first of the Tudors. Henry's marriage with Elizabeth of York, daughter of Edward IV—the first of the Yorkist Kings—united the claims of the Lancastrians and Yorkists, and the succession of the son of the marriage, Henry VIII, to the Throne was the first undisputed title for more than a hundred years. It was through Elizabeth de Burgh that the blood of the last High King of Ireland descended to the Stuarts.

With the death of Queen Elizabeth the direct line of the

House of Tudor came to an end and the dynasty of the Stuarts began. The title of the Stuarts to the English Crown was derived from Margaret Tudor, the eldest daughter of Henry VII and Elizabeth of York, and the sister of Henry VIII who married James IV of Scotland. Their granddaughter was Mary Queen of Scots, whose story is immortal, for in it are those two inextinguishable elements of human interest, romance and tragedy. Mary's son, James VI of Scotland, succeeded Queen Elizabeth as James I of Great Britain by reason of his descent from Margaret Tudor. Thus it was through James, the first of the Stuarts, that the blood of the ancient Kings of England, Scotland and Ireland were inherited by the present Royal House. The union of the Stuarts with the House of Hanover came about—as we know—through the marriage of Elizabeth, daughter of James I, with Frederick V, Elector Palatine of the Rhine and King of Bohemia, and the marriage of their daughter, Sophia, with Ernest Augustus, Elector of Hanover. The Electress Sophia died on June 8th, 1714, losing by not quite two months the succession to the Crown of England. Her son, George, Elector of Hanover, ascended the British Throne as George I, on August 1st, 1714. It is curious to think that the hot, passionate, reckless blood of Mary Queen of Scots flowed in the veins of this uncouth " wee, wee German lairdie." Perhaps there was only a little of it.

Through the Hanoverians the Royal House reaches back to Princes who reigned upon the Italian side of the Alps long before the time of the Crusades. For the Electors of Hanover were descended from the Este family, one of the ancient Princely houses of Italy, which survived until the consummation of Italian Unity in 1860, when the territory of Este in Northern Italy was absorbed into the new Kingdom of Italy. In the eleventh century Azp d'Este, Marquis of Este, Milan, went to Germany and espousing a rich heiress, Cunigunda, daughter of Guelph III of Bavaria—Guelph as a name had also resounded through Europe in the Middle Ages—had a son called Guelph d'Este, who was the ancestor of the House of Brunswick. It is an interesting circumstance, by the way, that Azo d'Este married a second time Ermengarde, daughter of the Count of Maine, and that from Falk, the son of this marriage, descended the other line of Este, Dukes of Modena, to which the wife of James II and mother of the first Pretender belonged.

Thus, in one way or another, George V is descended from almost all the greater dynasties and races that have held sway in Europe since the fall of Imperial Rome. Queen Victoria carried her line still farther back. She favoured the theory that the English were descended from the Lost Tribes of Israel, and was convinced of her own descent from the Royal House of David. In 1869 when an Anglican clergyman, the Rev. F. R. Glover, addressed to Her Majesty the results of his researches into her pedigree, which convinced him of her descent from the Psalmist, she was exceedingly pleased and commanded his attendance at Windsor, when, he said, she informed him that the descent was part of the secret history of her house, and showed him a Royal pedigree with David as its root. But confining oneself to authentic and undisputed records, think of all that long history in England, Italy, Germany, with its great personages, its mighty episodes, being to-day concentrated in one man. The Imperial Crown of England is hallowed by the thought. The King himself, as he sat crowned on his Throne in the Abbey and thought of his pedigree, the most magnificent in Europe, might well have said to himself, " Saxon, Scottish, Irish, Dane, Norman, am I, with a rich infusion of Italian, German, and French blood, but above all, I am English." King George is the most truly English of all the Sovereigns since Queen Elizabeth. He wears the oldest Crowns in the World. Japan claims that her Crown stands first in antiquity. But as *Burke's Peerage* well says the antiquity of the Crown of Japan " cannot be tested by the rigid tests of accuracy that we apply in this country."

*　　*　　*　　*　　*　　*

Queen Victoria had a greater pride in her remote than in her more immediate ancestry. She often declared she was a devoted adherent of the House of Stuart. The story of the misfortunes of the Stuarts appealed to her, as it appeals to most people, for the soft romantic feelings it engenders. She regarded the execution of Charles I as the greatest crime in

English history. The King was venerated by her as the Blessed Martyr. In the decoration of the Palace of Westminster, the meeting-place of Parliament, memorials have been provided in statuary, fresco, painted window and stone-carving, of all the rulers of England from Alfred the Great to Victoria the Good—with one exception, Oliver Cromwell, perhaps the ablest and most powerful ruler the country has ever had. Cromwell was excluded by command of Queen Victoria. The command was conveyed by Prince Albert to the Commission, of which the Prince was Chairman, appointed to superintend the adornment of the building. Considering these glowing associations of Kingship, what was Cromwell but a coarse upstart who made a sort of King of himself and had the wickedness to cut off the head of a real King—a King by virtue of the sacred principle of hereditary succession! So Victoria argued.

In 1895, during the administration of Lord Rosebery, the House of Commons was asked to honour the memory of the Protector by erecting a monument to him within the precincts of the Palace at the public expense. The vote was passionately opposed. Members of Royalist sentiment and the Irish Nationalists united in condemning the executioner of Charles I and the author of the massacres of Drogheda and Wexford, with the result that the project was defeated. Four years later Lord Rosebery had erected at his own expense the bronze statue of Cromwell on the sunk grass-plot by the side of Westminster Hall. He presents a stern figure in his leather service dress, broad hat and great wide boots, with sword in one hand and Bible in the other, his swarthy and swollen countenance turned to Westminster Abbey where his body was laid only to be dug up at the Restoration by order of Parliament, his head placed to rot over the gateway of Westminster Hall, his other remains scattered to the winds. " Happy," said Lord Rosebery, in a speech after the inauguration of the statue in 1899, " happy is the dynasty which can permit without offence or without fear the memory of a regicide to be honoured in its capital. Happy the Sovereign and happy the dynasty that, secure in their constitutional guarantees and in the world-wide love of their subjects, can allow such a ceremonial as this to take place without a shadow of annoyance or distrust." As it happened, the Sovereign was not at all happy.

A proposal was made in both Houses of Parliament to have this statue removed. It failed in the Commons. Lord Hardwicke, who moved and carried his motion by a few votes in a small House in the Lords, had the satisfaction of receiving from Queen Victoria the gracious expression of her thanks for his effort to avert this gratuitous insult to her person, her Crown and her people. But the statue remains.

Macaulay states in his Diary, under the date March 9th, 1850, that the Queen, when he was with her as Minister in attendance, talked about his History and owned that she had nothing to say for her poor ancestor James II. The historian in Macaulay moved him to put her Majesty right. " ' Not your Majesty's ancestor,' said I. ' Your Majesty's predecessor.' " " I hope," he adds, " this was not an uncourtly correction. I meant it as a compliment, and she seemed to take it so."

Mary Queen of Scots was Victoria's ancestor, and she was to Victoria what Mary's grandson Charles I was also to her—a sacred canonised memory, while Queen Elizabeth was by her as much detested as Cromwell. She dropped a tear on the grave of the unfortunate James II in the parish church of St. Germains, outside Paris, when she stood beside it with Napoleon III in 1855, and told the Emperor with pride and gratitude how her uncle, George IV, had High Mass for the dead chanted over the grave when it was discovered during structural alterations in 1824. Victoria also had the tomb restored. She even objected to Prince Charles Edward being called " the Young Pretender," regarding it as a term of disparagement. In the Diary of her life at Balmoral in the Scottish Highlands she writes of a visit she made to the Pass of Glencoe where the Jacobite followers of Prince Charles Edward were massacred by the Duke of Cumberland. After describing the stern and rugged valley, the precipitous rocky sides, she says—" The place is one which adds to the horror of the thought that such a thing could have been conceived and committed on innocent sleeping people." " How and whither could they fly ? " she asks. " Let me hope that William III knew nothing about it." There is, however, nothing to show that Victoria disagreed with the general opinion that the expulsion of the Stuarts was a good riddance for the country. How could she? If the Stuarts had been allowed to remain who would ever have heard of Victoria? Would she have been born at all?

It is said indeed that the succession of the Electress Sophia of Hanover and her descendants to the Throne was carried by one vote only in committee of the House of Commons in 1701. If that vote had been otherwise cast the long and great reign of Queen Victoria would have found no place in history. For this romance of history there is no authentic and undisputed authority. It is certain that the Act of Settlement passed in the House of Commons, *nemine contradicente*, on May 14th, 1701. Yet the Bill was but languidly supported. Many of the members in attendance, never more than fifty or sixty, appear to have felt that the calling of a stranger to the Throne was detestable, but it was decided that, on the whole, it was the least of the evils before the country. The earlier proceedings of the Committee appointed to draw up the resolutions upon which the Bill was afterwards founded, were, however, private. There is, therefore, nothing extant to show that the Hanoverian succession was determined on by a single vote. At that time no record of members voting in a division in Committee was officially kept. All that the Committee reported to the House, according to the entry in the Commons' Journals, was the resolutions they had come to.

Two stories are told of the alleged close division in Committee. One is that the single vote which secured the reversion of the Crown to the Hanoverians was that of a member named Sir Arthur Owen who travelled post-haste with relays of horses from Wales to London to be in time for the division. The other is that Sir Arthur Owen and another Welsh member, Mr. Griffiths Rice, also a supporter of the Hanoverians, met in the lobby and stopped to talk just as the Government had decided to take a snap or sudden division. One of the opponents of the Bill immediately rushed out of the House to rally any friends he might find, and thinking that Owen and Rice were against the Bill called them in. This member of the Opposition thus defeated his own object. Had he remained in his place Owen and Rice would have been locked out when the doors of the

Chamber were closed for the division, and the Bill would have been defeated. According to another story, Sir John Bowles, the mover of the resolution that the Electress Sophia and her offspring be nominated heirs to the Throne on the death of Queen Anne, was a member of very little weight and authority, who was even then thought to be disordered in his mind and who eventually died mad.

CHAPTER II

NAMES, STYLES, AND TITLES

MEMBERS of the Royal Family are given no surnames in their birth certificates. They are identified by Christian names only. King George V was baptised, " George Frederick Ernest Albert." But if he were to abdicate, lose all his titles and assume the position of a commoner, or ordinary citizen—which Heaven forfend ! (as our pious ancestors used to pray)—he would be known as " Mr. George Windsor." In similar circumstances King Edward would have been called " Mr. Albert Edward Wettin," and Queen Victoria, before her marriage, " Miss Guelph."

The family name of the House of Hanover to which Queen Victoria and her predecessors belonged was " Guelph," or as some say " Guelph d'Este." Did she change her surname on her marriage with Prince Albert of Saxony (or Saxe-Coburg and Gotha) whose family name was " Wettin " ? Every girl who marries is required by law to assume the name of her husband. Was Queen Victoria ? That is a question which never arose, for the reason that her husband's status was inferior to hers. She being Queen regnant and he only her Consort, it may be assumed that she retained her own family name borne by her before her marriage. But the name of a dynasty, or succession of Sovereigns, is derived from and through the male line, changing in the case of a Monarch who succeeds his mother, and accordingly King Edward's House took its name from that of his father, " Saxe-Coburg and Gotha " (the family name being " Wettin ") of which, in turn, King George was also a member.

On July 18th, 1917, during the World War, there appeared in the newspapers an announcement by King George, affecting the Royal Family, of peculiar and exceptional interest. Signed at a meeting of the Privy Council, held the day before at Buckingham Palace, it set forth :

We, out of Our Royal Will and Authority, do hereby declare and announce that as from the date of this Our Royal

Proclamation Our House and Family shall be styled and known as the House and Family of Windsor, and that all the descendants in the male line of Our said Grandmother Queen Victoria who are subjects of these Realms, other than female descendants who may marry or may have married, shall bear the said Name of Windsor :

And do hereby further declare and announce that We for Ourselves and for and on behalf of Our descendants and all other the descendants of Our said Grandmother Queen Victoria who are subjects of these Realms, relinquish and enjoin the discontinuance of the use of the degrees, styles, dignities, titles and honours of Dukes and Duchesses of Saxony and Princes and Princesses of Saxe-Coburg and Gotha, and all other German degrees, styles, dignitaries, titles, honours and appellations to Us or to them heretofore belonging or appertaining.

Thus was affected the complete and irrevocable severance of the Royal Family from all association with Germany, greatly to the national gratification. Edward VII was the last Sovereign of the Brunswick-Hanoverian Line. George V became the first of the British Line.

Still earlier in the War, in 1915, the German Emperor, the Emperor of Austria, and six German princes and dukes who were Knights of the Garter were expelled from the Order. This took place privately in St. George's Chapel, Windsor. The names of the eight enemy Knights were struck off the Roll. Their banners were taken down ; their surcoats, helmets and swords were removed; their stalls were dismantled. The ceremony, for the number and exalted positions of those degraded, has no parallel in the history of Orders of Chivalry. Two members of the House of Lords, the Duke of Cumberland and the Duke of Albany (both cousins of the King) who had joined the King's enemies were, by Act of Parliament, deprived of their peerages. In accordance with the King's decree that those members of the Royal Family residing in England who bore German titles, should relinquish such titles and adopt British surnames, peerage patents were issued incorporating into the British Peerage, the two brothers of Queen

75

Mary, the Duke of Teck, as Marquis of Cambridge, and Prince Alexander of Teck as Earl of Athlone, both assuming the surname of " Cambridge " ; and the King's two cousins, Prince Louis of Battenburg as Marquis of Milford Haven, and Prince Alexander of Battenburg as Marquis of Carisbrooke, both assuming the surname of " Mountbatten."

*   *   *   *   *   *

King George also resolved to restrict the use of the titles " Royal Highness," and " Prince " and " Princess," in future to the children of the Sovereign, and, in the case of grandchildren, to those of the male line only. Letters Patent gazetted under date, December 11th, 1917, declared that :

> The children of any Sovereign of the United Kingdom, and the children of the sons of any such Sovereign, and the eldest living son of the eldest son of the Prince of Wales, shall have and at all times hold and enjoy the style, title, or attribute of Royal Highness, with their titular dignity of Prince or Princess prefixed to their respective Christian names, or with their other titles of honour : that save as aforesaid the titles of Royal Highness, Highness, or Serene Highness and the titular dignity of Prince or Princess shall cease, except those titles already granted and remaining unrevoked.

Edward Freeman, the historian, who was a sturdy Radical, asserts in his *Growth of the British Constitution* (1872) that the custom of calling all the children of the Sovereign " Princes " and " Princesses " is a " modern vulgarism." " As late as the time of George II," he says, " uncourtly Englishmen were still found who eschewed the foreign innovation and who spoke of Lady Caroline and Lady Emily as their fathers had done before them." "Prince" and "Princess" are but titles of courtesy which confer no privilege, no legal status above other commoners, save in the cases of the Sovereign's eldest son and eldest daughter.

The Select Committee of the House of Lords, appointed in 1915 to consider the Bill for depriving enemies of the King of their British titles and dignities, reported that they had also inquired into the title of " Prince " and had come to the conclusion that it conferred a legal status only on the eldest son of the Sovereign who, they say, is by birth " Prince of Scotland " and is created, by Letters Patent, " Prince of Wales." They add that by long custom the children and grandchildren of the Sovereign have been known as " Princes " and " Princesses," and, further, that these titles have been recognised in various Royal Warrants and Letters Patent dealing with questions of precedence. The committee does not refer to the title of " Princess Royal." Since the time of George II this title had by custom been conceded to and borne by the eldest daughter of the reigning Sovereign without the issue of any special Warrant. Victoria, eldest daughter of Queen Victoria, was Princess Royal from her birth in 1840, and she bore the title until her death as Empress Frederick of Germany in 1901. Four years afterwards, in 1905, the then King, Edward VII, issued a Royal Warrant conferring the title of " Princess Royal " on his eldest daughter, Louise, who was married to the Duke of Fife in 1889.

All the other children of the Sovereign are commoners, even though they be called " Princes " and " Princesses." In fact it is only because the eldest son is born Duke of Cornwall, that he also is not a commoner but a peer of the realm before he is created Prince of Wales. The King may raise his other sons, as he may raise any other of his subjects, to the Peerage. And he always does so by making his sons Dukes when they come of age. While they are commoners there is nothing to hinder any of them being elected to the House of Commons. George III was so displeased with his third son, Prince William (afterwards William IV) that for a time he refused to make him a peer. " Well," said the Prince, " if the House of Lords is to be closed against me I'll get into Parliament through the House of Commons." He went so far as to select Totnes, Devon, as his constituency. To stop him going further the King made him Duke of Clarence. William was twenty-four years of age at the time. Prince Leopold, who was supposed to be the cleverest of Queen Victoria's sons, was nearing thirty before he was raised to the peerage as Duke of Albany. While he was still awaiting his title, Lord Houghton happened to ask him why it was he did not use the House of Lords as a field for the display of his abilities. " I don't know the cause of the delay in making me a peer," said Leopold. " I tell them that if they put it off much longer I'll stand for the House of Commons as a Liberal." And the Prince laughed at the thought of the look of displeasure such a suggestion would bring to his mother's face, and her sharp reproval of his levity. There is, of course, a recognised convention that the Royal Family takes no part in politics ; but constitutionally any Prince who is not in the House of Lords is eligible for election to the House of Commons.

*   *   *   *   *   *

But of all the steps taken by King George in those historic days of the World War, the boldest and most democratic was that of adopting the name of "Windsor" for his House and Family. Never before in British history did a Sovereign proclaim his choice of a surname for himself and his descendants. The early Kings of England appear to have had no surnames. They are called in history Norman, Plantagenet, York, Lancaster, but these are titles to distinguish different dynasties rather than family names. Tudor is a family name, and so are Stuart, D'Este, Guelph and Witten. King George could have made no happier choice of a name for his House and Family than that of his most ancient palace and chief seat. " Windsor " appeals to the pride of patriotism. It is expressive of the island's long history and traditions. The Castle, with its ancient towers rising on the banks of the greatest of the country's rivers makes a picture that conjures up the pageant of Kingship—grandly imposing, calmly majestic, with a touch of feudalism. It has been associated with the fate and fortunes of English sovereignty from Saxon times. Certainly " Windsor " is characteristically English and national. The titles of " Prince " and " Princess," being now limited to the children of the Sovereign and his grandchildren of the male line, any great-grandson of the male line will be a commoner with the courtesy title of the son of a Duke—a title given as an act of courtesy, not of absolute right—such as " Lord John Windsor " (assuming that the custom of making the Sovereign's sons dukes will be maintained) and any great-great-grandson of the male line will be plain " Mr. Windsor."

The Royal Family, by gradually merging first in the nobility and subsequently in the commonalty of the Kingdom, will become, in time, part and parcel of the people, bone of the people's bone, flesh of their flesh, ceasing to be a small exclusive caste—kindly British of the British, neither Hanoverian nor Saxe-Coburg-Gotha. That was King George's intention. He established a truly national dynasty. He made the British Monarchy more British than ever.

The intermarrying of Royalty with the aristocracy and commonalty had already begun. The Duke of York, second son of George V, was the first Prince of the Hanoverian Line to take a commoner for wife—Lady Elizabeth Bowes-Lyon, daughter of the Earl of Strathmore. They were married in Westminster Abbey in April, 1923. Daughters only of the present Royal House had previously married into the nobility. Princess Louise, fourth daughter of Queen Victoria, was the first English Princess for centuries who took a husband who was not of Royal birth. The Marquis of Lorne was son and heir of the Duke of Argyll, and afterwards succeeded to the dukedom, but he was a commoner when the Princess married him in 1871. The country approved of the match on the ground, generally, that the Princess was not marrying " another German." Disraeli, writing to Queen Victoria on the announcement of the engagement, said " What is about to happen seems to me wise as it is romantic. Your Majesty has decided, with deep discrimination, to terminate an etiquette which had become sterile." What the Queen herself thought of the engagement is expressed in the following extract from her " Diary "—" Louise told me that Lorne had spoken of his devotion to her, and that she had accepted him, knowing that I would approve. Though I was not unprepared for this result, I felt painfully the thought of losing her. But naturally I gave my consent."

In 1889 another Princess Louise, the eldest daughter of the then Prince of Wales, married the Earl of Fife. A story went the rounds that Queen Victoria was not, at first, disposed to regard the match with favour. She went to Sandringham to

79

discuss the matter with the Prince and Princess of Wales.
Princess Louise met her at the door and with tears in her eyes
protested that if she was not allowed to marry MacDuff—the
family name of Lord Fife—sl.e would die an old maid. " But,
my dear," said the Queen soothingly, " I hardly know him.
I must see something more of him, and judge what he is like."
Lord Fife was made a duke. His position was not enhanced
in the order of precedence at Court, but when his father-in-
law became King it was decided that the duke should be
regarded as of the Royal Family in family affairs. The Duchess
subsequently became Princess Royal, and her two daughters
were granted the title of " Princess " with the style and attribute of " Highness " without " Royal," and given precedence
immediately after all members of the Royal Family having the
style of " Royal Highness." Another marriage which raised
the question of Royal titles was that of Princess Patricia of
Connaught, niece of King Edward, to Captain Ramsay, a
younger son of Earl of Dalhousie. She gave up the titles of
" Royal Highness " and " Princess " and as the daughter
of a duke, the Duke of Connaught, became Lady Patricia
Ramsay.

The next marriage of a lady of the Royal House into the
aristocracy was that of Princess Mary, only daughter of King
George V, to Viscount Lascelles, son and heir of the Earl of
Harewood, in 1922. She is styled, " Princess Mary Viscountess
Lascelles." At the presentation to Lord Lascelles of a portrait
in oils of the Princess as the wedding gift of the Harewood
tenantry, the Earl of Harewood made an interesting little
speech to the tenants, which, perhaps, affords some indications
of the views of the aristocracy regarding the choice by a
Princess of a husband from their class. " To-day," he said,
" you are welcoming Princess Mary who, despite her exalted
rank, has condescended to devote her life to the happiness
of her husband, my son." Possibly wives who regard devotion
to husbands as the first principle of their duty will indulgently
smile at the earl's idea of condescension in a wife, even though
she be a Princess ; and as for those married men who like to
think of wives, irrespective of rank, on their hands and knees
to their husbands, the heresy of the remark is calculated almost

to take their breath away. The democratic view of the marriage was humorously expressed by one of the tenants of the estate. " I hope," said he, " that when Princess Mary dipped into the matrimonial lottery she got as good a husband as my wife got."

The son and heir that was born to Princess Mary and Viscount Lascelles in February, 1923, was called simply "Master Lascelles." The child's father, being heir to an earldom, bore the title of Viscount, but such titles are called courtesy titles, as they are unsupported by legal right, and the son of such a Viscount has no title until his father succeeds to the earldom when he in turn assumes the courtesy title of Viscount. Here, then, was a grandson of the reigning Sovereign who was not only not a Prince, but had no title. That is all the more remarkable because " Master Lascelles " at his birth was sixth in the order of the succession to the Throne as King and Emperor. That he would succeed was, of course, a very remote contingency at the time, but it was a possible one. If the Prince of Wales and his three brothers—the Duke of York, the Duke of Gloucester, and Prince George—had died, leaving no issue, male or female, and Princess Mary survived them, Princess Mary would have succeeded to the Throne, and at her demise she would have been followed by her son—no longer " Master Lascelles," of course, but Prince of Wales. As Princess Mary, however, she conferred no style or title on her son.

There is an old maxim that while a wife cannot confer upon her husband any honours she may possess in her own right she shares in all his honours. In a word, she takes the rank of her husband. Accordingly, Lady Elizabeth Bowes-Lyon, who before her marriage with the Duke of York was a commoner, became " Her Royal Highness the Duchess of York," with the status of Princess, as valid as though she had been of the Blood Royal. She also became the fourth lady in the land, the first three being the Queen, Queen Alexandra, and Princess Mary— a position from which she could be displaced only by a Princess of Wales, and stood in direct and close succession to the Throne as the wife of the second in the line. The birth of a daughter to the Duke and Duchess of York in 1926, put Master Lascelles' nose completely out of joint. Princess Elizabeth of

York, as the daughter is styled, became third in succession to the throne.

It is improbable, if not impossible, that any doubt can ever arise as to the member of the Royal Family who is entitled to succeed at a demise of the Crown. For there is a settled and indisputable law of succession which marks out the next successor to the Throne, and after him, or her, the order in which all the other members of the Royal Family stand as heirs. The Crown descends lineally to the children, male or female, of the reigning Sovereign, or to the grandchildren, male or female, if none of the children survive. But there is this important qualification—in the direct line preference is given to the male. The Sovereign may be a female as well as a male. The Salic Law excluding females does not prevail in this country, and never did. The first Queen regnant was Mary I, daughter of Henry VIII, by his first wife Catherine of Aragon. In the first year of Mary's reign, Parliament passed an Act which declares that " the regal power of the Realm is in the Queen's Majesty as fully and absolutely as ever it was in any King." Mary succeeded on the death, without issue, of her half-brother, Edward VI. His mother was Jane Seymour, the third wife of Henry VIII, and he was Mary's junior by thirty years. This case shows the position which Princess Mary, Viscountess Lascelles, held in the order of succession, at the time of her marriage. A female succeeds only when there is no male heir in the direct line. The youngest son would inherit to the exclusion of a sister who was born before him. After the sons the daughter would come in as heir before an uncle, or nephew or male cousin. But should the reigning Sovereign have no children or grandchildren, male or female, alive at his demise his next brother and the children of his next brother would successively come to the Throne. For example, William IV, having no children, and his next brother, the Duke of Kent, having died before him, the Duke's only child, who happened to be a daughter, Princess Victoria, succeeded King William on the Throne instead of the Duke of Cumberland who was next surviving brother to the late King. Thus Princess Elizabeth of York, ranking after the Prince of Wales and her own father, is third in the succession to the Throne.

Prince Henry and Prince George come fourth and fifth, brothers taking precedence of sisters in the line of succession, and Princess Mary, Viscountess Lascelles, although she is senior to both brothers, fills the sixth place, and her two sons the seventh and the eighth place.

There is still another distinction between males and females in the order of the succession. If the heir to the Throne is a son or grandson of the reigning Sovereign he is styled " Heir Apparent." Any other member of the Royal Family who may be heir is called " Heir Presumptive." Even if the heir be a daughter of the reigning Sovereign it is " presumed " that there may be born a son to displace her.

*　　*　　*　　*　　*　　*

The original style and title was, as we have seen, simply " King of the English." Not the least interesting part of the story of the British Monarchy is that which tells how and in what order, in the course of many centuries, it came to possess its present style and title.

Wales was the first of the three Celtic countries to be incorporated with England under one Crown. In 1283 it was subdued by Edward I—its last Prince, Llewelyn, having been earlier killed in battle—and transferred to the King's dominions. It brought no addition to the then Royal title, " King of England." But Edward's consort gave birth, at Carnarvon Castle in 1284, to a son who was styled " Prince of Wales," the title since then of the Heir Apparent to the British Crown. Next came Ireland. The country was invaded by the English in 1169. Two years later the King, Henry II, crossed over to exact from the Irish chieftains recognition of England's domination. He appointed his son, Prince John, Lord of Ireland. It was intended to make John King of Ireland, and a crown of gold was sent to him by the Pope, but the Coronation never took place, and the idea was not revived until more than three centuries later. Henry VIII, who had previously been styled " Lord of Ireland " assumed the title of King of Ireland in 1542.

" King of France " had already been added to the style of

the English Sovereigns. Edward III assumed it in 1340, the thirteenth year of his reign, by right of his mother, Isabella, daughter of Philip IV, King of France, despite the fact that the Salic Law, excluding females from the succession, applied to the French Crown. The title was strengthened in a sense by Henry V who, after the overwhelming defeat of the French at Agincourt, entered Paris in triumph, and had himself acknowledged King, and by Henry VI who had himself crowned at Rheims. But supposing the English title to the French Crown was acknowledged by France, and supposing also that in the chances and changes of time France become the predominant partner, and made England the dependency that England sought to make of France ? That contingency was foreseen and was guarded against by an Act passed in the reign of Edward III. " The realm of England and the people thereof," it proudly declared, " shall not at any time to come be put in subjection to nor in obedience of the King, his heirs or successors, as King of France."

Accordingly, from Edward III to Henry VIII, the Sovereigns were styled, " By the Grace of God, King of England and France, and Lord of Ireland." The eighth Henry had the style of the Crown considerably augmented. Not only did he call himself King of Ireland, but in return for a book he wrote—or got written in his name—refuting the heresies of Luther, and a copy of which, bound in gold, he presented to Pope Leo X, His Holiness conferred on him the title of " Defender of the Faith," which he added to the style of the Crown. After Henry's break with Rome, and the repudiation of the Pope's spiritual authority in England, Pope Paul III cancelled the title. Henry retained it nevertheless, obtaining for it parliamentary sanction. In 1543, an Act was passed " for the ratification of the King's Majesty's style " which set forth :

Whereas our most dread natural and gracious sovereign liege Lord the King hath heretofore been, and is justly, lawfully and notoriously known, named, published and declared to be, " King of England, France and Ireland, Defender of the Faith, and of the Church of England and also of Ireland on earth supreme Head," be it enacted that the same style be united and annexed for ever to the Imperial Crown of England.

The longest and most resounding style was that of Philip and Mary. Mary was styled the same as her father, Henry VIII, until her marriage with Philip of Spain, when both were styled, " Philip and Mary by the grace of God, King and Queen of England and France, Naples, Jerusalem and Ireland, Defenders of the Faith, Princes of Spain and Sicily, Archdukes of Austria, Dukes of Milan, Burgundy and Brabant." The next addition was that of " King of Scotland." England and Scotland were brought under one Sovereign by the accession of James VI of Scotland to the English Throne as James I. He was styled " King of England, Scotland, France and Ireland, Defender of the Faith." It was not, however, until the Parliaments of England and Scotland were united in 1707 by the passage of the Act of Union, England and Scotland being declared by the same statute to be one Kingdom called " Great Britain," that " England " as well as " Scotland " disappeared from the titles of the Crown. Anne, who was then reigning, became " Queen of Great Britain, France, and Ireland, Defender of the Faith."

The claim to the Throne of France survived the Revolution of 1688. The Bill of Rights, 1688, and the Act of Settlement, 1701, conferred " the Imperial Crown and dignity of the realm of England, France and Ireland," first jointly to William and Mary, next to Anne, and subsequently to the Hanoverians. Having been adhered to for more than four centuries and a half, the claim was dropped on January 1st, 1801, when the Parliaments of Great Britain and Ireland were united, and George III, the reigning Monarch, was styled by Royal Proclamation— " By the Grace of God, of the United Kingdom of Great Britain and Ireland, King, Defender of the Faith."

" Empress of India," as an addition to the Royal title, was assumed by Queen Victoria on New Year's Day, 1877, under an Act which Disraeli, then Prime Minister, carried through Parliament in the session of 1876. That was nineteen years after the control of affairs in India was taken over from the East India Company, and the Crown became ruler in fact as well as in theory. Joseph Chamberlain (another great Imperialist, like Disraeli), who was Secretary of State for the Colonies in 1901 at the accession of Edward VII, had an Act passed recognising in the Royal title the important position held by the Dominions in the Empire. Edward VII was accordingly styled on his accession, " By the Grace of God, of the United Kingdom of Great Britain and Ireland, and of the British Dominions beyond the Seas, King, Defender of the Faith, Emperor of India." And so was George V. But during the reign of George V in 1927 another change was made in the style and title of the King. This was due to the establishment of the Irish Free State as a Dominion. The term " the United Kingdom of Great Britain and Ireland," was altered to " the United Kingdom of Great Britain and Northern Ireland." Southern Ireland, or the Free State, comes into the term " the British Dominions beyond the Seas."

CHAPTER III

A KING IN THE MAKING

THE education of the eldest son and heir is a matter of concern in the domestic circles of the upper classes. Naturally, it is more so in the Royal Family.

Princes have always been educated in their earlier years at home by private tutors. The Public School provides the surest foundation upon which the English character at its best is built—that is according to tradition, which is questioned by some persons in the light of experience. But the Public School is not open to a Prince. For a Prince would be unable to sink his individuality in the general mass of the boys, however much he might desire to do so. He would be placed on a pedestal, as it were, and in that conspicuous position would be the mark for attentions not always friendly. The average schoolboy is a leveller in feeling and in action.

Besides that, it is supposed that if a Prince were to mix indiscriminately with the boys at a Public School he would run the risk of forming undesirable acquaintances. A Prince is presumed to be more liable than a youth of any other class to be beset by the designs of the wicked, as well as by the wiles of the flatterer and toady, who, particularly, if the Prince is the Heir to the Throne, might use the influence they obtained over him for unworthy purposes when he became King. Accordingly, it is contended that if the Heir to the Throne is deprived of the stimulus to thought and conduct afforded by the free companionship and competition in lessons and sports with youths of his own age, he has the countervailing advantage of being guarded against temptations to which in the circumstances he would be peculiarly exposed, and which, if yielded to, might cast a shadow over all his later life.

What, then, is the best form of education and training for a King that is to be, in his own personal interest and in the interest of the countries and peoples whose welfare he will one day hold in trust? The answer to such a question must surely depend entirely upon the mind and disposition and understanding of the Prince—upon his character, its strength and its weakness. The youth of King Edward VII was made unhappy by the anxious and watchful care which his parents, Queen Victoria and the Prince Consort, bestowed upon his education, intellectual, moral and physical, without any regard to his own natural bent. It vexed and wearied him for years and ultimately drove him into revolt.

The Prince Consort's conception of his duty as head of the Royal House is seen in a story told of him at the birth of his first-born. He was disappointed on hearing that the child was a girl. Then, brightening up, he said, "I must set about compiling a dissertation on the duties and responsibilities of a Princess Royal." When a boy came the Prince Consort thanked God for having put into his hands the moulding of the character of a future King of England. That happy event took place at Buckingham Palace. In accordance with ancient custom the Government were represented at the birth of an heir to the Throne. This is traditionally intended to prevent the danger, which appears to have been very real in mediæval times, of a supposititious child. The Prime Minister, Sir Robert Peel, and Lyndhurst, the Lord Chancellor, were waiting in a room adjoining the Queen's bed-chamber, and when the nurse, very soon, brought in the infant, they signed the declaration that a male heir to the Throne was born.

Queen Victoria participated in her husband's ambition of making the child the paragon of his age in scholarship and virtue. As Prince, he was to be a shining pattern to the young of the country in the avoidance of youth's follies and indiscretions. As King, he was to be the noblest of his long line—notable for industry, prudence and wisdom. Their first concern was to find the infant a fitting Christian name. They found that only in the Saxon age had there been Kings who were given special appellations expressive at once of their own personal qualities and their people's love and esteem, such as " Alfred the Great " and " Edward the Confessor." They also discovered that all the Edwards, six in number, had been good Kings. Therefore, though the first name given to the child was " Albert " after his father—it was the constant prayer of the mother that the son should resemble the father in mind and body—his second name was " Edward " which, it was decreed, he should be known by when, in the course of nature, he ascended the Throne.

The Prince Consort's idea of Kingship was that it should be a moral agency like the Church, but more concentrated, and, for that reason, more powerful in its influence for good. The King should be seen as the personification of honour, virtue, justice, in the fierce light that plays about the Throne—at once an example and a blessing to the worshipping Nation. To fit " Bertie "—as the boy was called in the family circle—for this high destiny he was to pass his early years at home in the charge of tutors, under the jealously watchful eyes of his parents, and in an atmosphere of religious and virtuous domesticity. As a boy Bertie was never left unattended. There was always a tutor to hold his hand.

*   *   *   *   *   *

" Bertie " was made Prince of Wales and Earl of Chester— the two titles go together—when he was four months old. This title is not one of succession by hereditary right. It is conferred by the Sovereign on the Heir Apparent at his pleasure and by personal investiture. The eldest son of the Sovereign is born Duke of Cornwall to which large properties are attached. He is also born Duke of Rothesay, Earl of Carrick, Baron of Renfrew, Lord of the Isles, and Prince and Great Steward, or Seneschal, of Scotland. This imposing series of Scottish titles were borne by the eldest son of the King of Scotland, and when James VI of Scotland became James I of Great Britain and Ireland they passed to the eldest son of the British Monarch. At the union of the two Crowns, Scottish and English, a still loftier title was added, that of "Prince of Great Britain and of Ireland," but it never came into favour, though it still survives, and the more ancient honour, " Prince of Wales,"—first conferred by Edward I on his second son, Edward of Carnarvon (afterwards Edward II) in 1301—remains the most popularly recognised title of the male Heir to the Throne.

The investiture of " Bertie " took place at Windsor Castle, in February, 1842, and was carried out by his mother, Queen Victoria, assisted by the Prince Consort, the Lord Great

Chamberlain and the Home Secretary. According to the Letters Patent issued on the occasion the child was ennobled and invested with the style and title of Prince of Wales by the Queen girding him with the Sword (it was hung round his neck), placing a Coronet on his head, a gold ring on the third finger of his left hand, and the Golden Verge (a rod or staff) in his right hand. The infant was then placed on his knees before the Queen to do homage for the Principality of Wales, after which the Queen raised him in her arms and kissed him on each cheek—more as his mother, we may be sure, than as his Sovereign.

All this did not make Bertie " a good boy," as the term is understood in the family circle. Often, when he committed some slight act of disobedience, the Queen, there and then, in the presence of the ladies and gentlemen of the Court, would put him across her knee and whack him with her slipper. The slipper was not to be spared if it would spoil the Prince. His father allowed him but few toys in his nursery, and these tended to the end that was always kept in view—efficiency, by their pointing a moral and adorning a tale. As he grew to boyhood he was subjected to a strict discipline of manners and morals. He was to be hardened against the allurements of the World, the Flesh, and the Devil, which, in the opinion of his parents and their advisers, are more insidious in their attacks on young Princes than on other mortals. The simplest tastes were inculcated. Self-indulgence of any kind was repressed. The Prince was not allowed as a boy to read Scott's novels even. The one recreation given him was the writing of summaries of Gibbon's *Decline and Fall of the Roman Empire*. As a young man he was set to learn all modern languages, all philosophies, all science, all history, and, to infuse some sweetness and light into this mass of erudition, the course of studies was widened to include literature, art, music, of the more bracing or less enervating kind.

This system of training was recommended by Baron Stockmar, a German physician and confidential adviser of Queen Victoria and the Prince Consort. He pointed out that the " iniquities " of George IV—as he called them—which so weakened the influence of Royalty, were due to the failure to graft the principles of truth and morality on his mind in early youth. This opinion was endorsed by Melbourne, the Prime Minister. The training of the Prince must be such as would enable him " to withstand the temptations and se-ductions with which he will find himself beset." The Prince was to be a perfect gentleman as well as a great ruler. A long and confidential memorandum was drawn up " for the guidance "—as it said—" of the gentlemen appointed to attend on the Prince of Wales." It insists that the Prince must be not only a gentleman but the first gentleman of the country, and it sets forth, as follows, the qualities which distinguish a gentleman in society :

1st. His appearance, his deportment, and dress.
2nd. The character of his relations with and treatment of others.
3rd. His desire and power to acquit himself creditably in conversation, or whatever is the occupation of the society with which he mixes.

As regards religion, the boy was brought up an Anglican of the Low and Broad Church, to which both the Queen and the Prince Consort were attached. " I am quite clear," the Queen wrote in a memorandum on the subject, " that he should be taught to have great reverence for God and for religion, but that he should have the feeling of devotion and love which our Heavenly Father encourages His earthly children to have for Him, and not one of fear and trembling ; and that the thoughts of death and after-life should not be represented in an alarming and forbidding view, and that he should be made to know, *as yet*, no difference of creed, and not think that he can only pray on his knees, or that those who do not kneel are less fervent or devout in their prayers." Religion with Queen Victoria was a matter of simple undogmatic piety. She looked with extreme suspicion on the High Church party and had little or nothing in common with the Evan-gelical section.

The Prince Consort seems to have been a severely con-scientious man. Gladstone in his *Gleanings of Past Years* (1879) says his chief characteristic was " a manifest endeavour

91

to turn every man's conversation, every man's particular gift and knowledge to account for his own mental improvement." This was a most laudable desire, Gladstone thought, but it deprived the Prince Consort of " the charm of absolute ease in his intercourse with the world." The Prince Consort must, indeed, have been a bit of a bore in his search for information and instruction when he proved tiresome to Gladstone who, by all accounts, loved to pour out his knowledge of, and reflections on, things, persons, affairs, on every occasion.

Another curious trait of the Prince Consort, in relation to the upbringing of his son, was that he did not like women to have much to do with the education of boys. At an early age the Prince was transferred from his governess, Lady Lyttelton—wife of the third Lord Lyttelton—to a tutor, the Rev. Henry Birch, an assistant master at Eton. The Prince Consort had a still worse defect, one which is common with men of his type, and a cause of much suffering to those over whom they have direction. To him all children were alike ; all were cast in the same mould. If some failed to grow up to be good men and good women, it was due to errors in their education and training. He does not seem to have had any true comprehension of the diversity of innate intelligence and disposition in the young. He certainly thought that if the Prince of Wales did not avail to the utmost of the learning and culture spread so liberally at his feet, it would be solely because the desire to do so was wilfully lacking. But nature had made the boy temperamentally different from his father. He was not intellectual and he was not studious. Books and lessons made no appeal to him. He could not see things with his parents' eyes ; he could see only with his own, and, looking through his own eyes, what he saw spread at his feet was not the world of learning, but the world of companionship and games ; and he saw himself, not as the future King of England, not even as the Prince of Wales, but as a boy with the normal boy's natural desires for sport and play with his fellows. Even his tutor, the Rev. Henry Birch, complained of the rigour of the Prince's education. The tutor himself was allowed only a fortnight's holiday in the year. He used to say that he felt in that fortnight like a discharged prisoner.

* * * * * *

The Prince of Wales was sent to three Universities, first to Edinburgh, next to Oxford, and then to Cambridge, so that he might have the advantages of all that is good in their separate systems as a grand ending to his scholastic education. It was felt also that this arrangement would prevent jealousy among the Universities with respect to Royal recognition and patronage. In Edinburgh the Prince had apartments at Holyrood Palace, with his personal suite and tutors. When he had been there his three months, in September, 1859, the Prince Consort visited him to see how he was getting on. An " educational conference," attended by the persons assisting in the education of the Prince, was held. " They all speak highly of him," writes the Prince Consort, " and he seems to have shown zeal and good will." The Prince was given lectures on chemistry in relation to manufactures, and on Roman history. The language course consisted of Italian, German, and French. He also had instruction in English law and history. And all in the one term.

At this time the Prince had reached manhood. Twenty-one is the age in all other ranks of society. The Prince of Wales attains at eighteen to what is called his legal majority. Had he succeeded to the Throne before that age he would have been regarded as a minor, and a Regency would have been appointed to discharge the duties of Kingship until he was eighteen. Having been born on November 9th, 1841, he was not eighteen, by the usually accepted notation, until Nov. 9th, 1859. But his parents held that the first anniversary of his birth was his second birthday, and so, according to this reckoning, November 9th, 1858, was his eighteenth birthday. On that day Queen Victoria wrote him a long letter of " warning and admonition." He was now to consider himself his own master. His parents would never intrude any advice on him, though they were ready to give it whenever he thought fit to seek it. " You may have thought," his mother said, " that the rule we adopted for your education a severe one, but your welfare was our only object, and well knowing to what seductions of flattery you would eventually be exposed we wished to prepare and strengthen your mind against them."

The Prince went to Oxford, as an undergraduate of Christ Church at the opening of the Michaelmas term, 1859. He did not live at the College. He was still in a state of tutelage. Frewen Hall, a large private house with grounds attached, was taken for him, and there he resided with his " Governor," Colonel Bruce (brother of Lord Elgin), who had commanded a battalion of the Grenadier Guards, and also with three others —his tutor, his director of studies, and his chaplain. It was the tutor's duty to send to the Queen and the Prince Consort daily reports of the Prince's studies and relaxations, mentioning particularly where he had been to and whom he had met. It was only on the sports side of University life that the Prince was allowed the companionship of young men, and these were carefully selected, being limited in numbers and being socially of a superior kind.

The relations between students were not then so free as they became in later and more democratic times. At Christ Church, undergraduates of noble birth were distinguished from common scholars by the wearing of gold tassels in their college caps, and they dined at a table on the dais while the undergraduates of a lower social degree appropriately sat below in the hall. The Prince was permitted to join a select social and sports club called the Bullingdon. Cricket was the game they played. They were identified by a ribbon of blue and white on their straw hats, and by stripes of the same colours down their flannel trousers. They were still more gorgeous at their dinners, which were given in a barge on the river, mingling the festive with the grave. Their evening dress was blue with a velvet collar to the coat, a display of gilt buttons, and a bright blue tie. The Prince also attended the debates at the Union, but only as a listener. Failure attended the attempts by jocose undergraduates to draw him into the political discussions, for the fun of it. He never could be got to declare whether he was a Whig or a Tory. He never voted in the divisions. When revolutionary and republican doctrines were preached in language of frightful violence, his flesh refused to creep. Only his sense of humour was tickled. He laughed at it all in his easy affable way. Undergraduates might poke fun at him, but they could not " pull his leg," as they would themselves term it. In photographs of him taken at this time we see a handsome young man with soft chubby cheeks and plenty of hair showing a tendency to curl. But the expression of the face is unexpectedly shy and phlegmatic— unexpectedly to anyone who can recall the genial, good-humoured, laughing King Edward VII.

A. Cambridge, which he entered as an undergraduate of Trinity College, in January, 1861, he was confined within even a narrower circle of friends and movements than at Oxford. He lived at Madingley Hall, an old Elizabethan manor three miles away from the town, with his tutors and his Governor, Colonel Bruce. He took no part in the corporate life of the University. He was negligent in attending lectures. He declared he was utterly tired of being educated. He felt a revulsion against science, philosophy, history, mathematics, languages, and against Cambridge, because the University was obsessed by these repellent things and by these alone. And, oh, for the freedom of being able to go about by himself, and unknown! One day he was missing. It was found that he had gone to London by an express train to have a day off doing things he was not authorised to do. What was it but the bubbling of healthy effervescent youth! But, alas, at Paddington he was confronted by the station-master and two Royal servants with a carriage in waiting.

A telegram had been sent to Buckingham Palace. The Prince, seeing that he was foiled, entered the carriage and said sarcastically to the footman, " Drive me to Exeter Hall " —then the well-known home of evangelistic services in the Strand. He was driven instead to Buckingham Palace, where he admitted, without sorrow or contrition, to his angry parents, that what he had done was a deliberate act of rebellion against his long tutelage. It was decided to terminate his University studies at Christmas. One good story of his Cambridge career survives. Professor Goldwin Smith had been lecturing on Elizabethan statesmen, and especially on Sir Walter Raleigh, and at the end the Prince said to him, " I think, sir, that you have forgotten Raleigh's most important gift to his country-men." " What was that, sir ? " asked the Professor. " The introduction of tobacco," was the reply. All through his life Edward was a devoted smoker.

*　　　*　　　*　　　*　　　*　　　*

The Prince was even more anxiously shepherded on his visits abroad. At the balls he attended during his tour of the United States in 1860 he danced only with ladies selected for him, and these, as a rule, were the wives or sisters of members of the Government. An American paper calculated that the combined ages of his partners aggregated nine hundred years. He stayed at the White House, Washington, the guest of President Buchanan, who would not allow dancing for fear it might be a cause of scandal to religious people. No wonder the Prince was detected letting himself down by a rope from his bedroom window. It is related that his grandson, Edward, Prince of Wales, when he visited America, was told this story and shown the bedroom by President Wilson. Evidently the Prince could, from his own experiences, appre-ciate his grandfather's feelings, for turning to the President with an assumed air of sadness he asked : " Would a twisted sheet do as well as a rope ? "

CHAPTER IV

THE KING AS HE'S MADE

THE ambition which King Edward's parents desired to see realised in him was that he should be known as a Monarch who had made all knowledge his province. But it happened that a very essential thing was missing from the curriculum they provided for him, and that was—real life. He was to learn as little as possible of living, toiling, scheming humanity in the world of bustling affairs. To mingle this in his upbringing would be corrupting, in the opinion of his parents. And yet, without it he could never really understand himself as King and his relations as King with his kind. By a strange and happy chance, as things turned out, it was for this very knowledge that King Edward was most noted as Sovereign.

His scholastic attainments, as they are called, may have been meagre compared with those of the average man who has had to the full the advantages of Public School and University. But being very human himself, and of quick human sympathy, he came to possess an uncommon understanding of human nature in all its phases. He had acquaintances larger in number and more varied in kind than any man of his time. None of his predecessors had ever come into contact so intimate with his people of all classes, or conversed with so many different individuals from every rank of society. He was thus made a shrewd man of the world—as good a judge of character, and as tactful in the management of men, as one could possibly be.

For the higher duties and responsibilities of Kingship, he was trained in the best of all possible schools—personal intercourse with monarchs, presidents, statesmen, diplomatists, administrators, soldiers, sailors, members of both Houses of Parliament, ecclesiastics, lawyers, physicians, officials of trade unions, and leaders of all sorts and kinds of social and philanthropic movements. As Prince of Wales, as well as King, his love of a life of pleasure did not prevent him from availing of the extraordinary facilities at his service of meeting the finest minds of his age. He could consult the authority on any subject at first hand, and listen to his living voice expounding his views. Like most persons who lead lives full of many concerns King Edward read few books. His knowledge was assimilated from those with whom he conversed, and from things he saw in his wide travels. In this way he became one of the best-informed persons in the Kingdom, and had the knack of making what he learnt readily available, particularly in regard to questions relating to the government and welfare of the community.

Yet Queen Victoria rarely, if ever, consulted Edward, Prince of Wales, on home affairs. She was disappointed in him, he fell so far short of the Prince Consort, the most perfect of men, and that despite all she had done and all the prayers she had said that he might resemble his father. She held him in tutelage even in the advanced years of his manhood. The only great horse race which he never saw was the Grand Prix of Paris. As that in his day was always run on a Sunday, one year when he was in France he telegraphed—according to a story current in Paris—to the Queen for permission to go to see the race. What, on the Sabbath! The answer he got was in the negative. He was forty-two years old at the time. It seems never to have entered the mind of Queen Victoria that she might have been wrong in the treatment of her son and heir. She had the habit of having little statues made in silver of those she was attached to, among members of her family and domestics, when they passed away. Her gift to her grandson, Prince Albert Victor, at his baptism, was a statuette of the Prince Consort, over three feet in height, clad in gilt armour, copied from the effigy of Warwick, the King-Maker, in St. Mary's church, Warwick, but representing Christian in *Pilgrim's Progress*. On the plinth was the inscription from Timothy : " I have fought a good fight, I have finished my course ; I have kept the faith." On a panel was the verse :

" Walk, as he walked, in faith and righteousness,
    Strive, as he strove, the weak and poor to aid,
  Seek not thyself but other men to bless,
    So win like him a wreath that will not fade."

There was a further inscription which she herself wrote and had placed under figures of Faith, Hope, and Charity :

> " Walk, as he walked—in Faith
> Strive as he strove—in Hope
> Think as he thought—in Charity."

These pious aspirations were probably intended for Prince Albert Victor's father more than for Prince Victor himself. For the tutelage of the Prince of Wales was not yet at an end. His functions were largely ceremonial—the laying of foundation stones and the opening of institutions. Queen Victoria retained almost to the last full control and responsibility for public affairs. To the very end she had little trust in the Prince's judgment, and still less in his discretion. She always feared that at dinner-tables and in smoking-rooms he would babble of things that should be kept secret. For he was prone, or was supposed to be prone, to unguarded utterances in the intimacies of social intercourse.

* * * * * *

The faults of the system of which he had been the sore victim were not lost upon King Edward when being still Prince of Wales, he had to decide how his own sons, Prince Albert Victor and Prince George, should be educated. Their natural tastes and dispositions were borne in mind in the programme of their early studies. They were not too much troubled with tasks from books. When they grew up they joined the Navy, which has always been regarded as a great school of character and as affording a far more democratic discipline than a Public School. Their training ship was the *Britannia*, anchored in the estuary at Dartmouth, then used as a college for naval cadets. Prince George was twelve years of age at the time. There were two hundred cadets on board. The hammocks of the two Princes were slung in quarters of their own. This was the only concession to their royalty. In matters of discipline and study they were treated no differently from the other boys during their two years of training.

The uniform of the college was navy blue with brass buttons, and a cap with a gold band. The cadets rose at half-past six, winter and summer alike, and after a bath drilled from 7.15 to 8, when they assembled for prayers and breakfast. The rest of the forenoon was devoted to study. Dinner was served at a quarter to 12, after which the cadets had an hour on shore. Returning to the ship, they resumed their studies until 4 o'clock, when they again went on shore and played cricket or football, according to the season, for two hours and a half. Tea was served at 7 o'clock. Then followed another hour's tuition. At a quarter-past 9 the cadets assembled for prayer, and by half-past 10 all were in bed. The two Princes took their seats at the mess table with the other cadets. They attended the drills. They had to darn their own socks and mend their own clothes. They saluted their seniors as " Sir." Prince George, who was intended for the Navy, passed out very creditably in seamanship.

In 1879 the two Princes were sent on a voyage round the world as midshipmen in the cruiser *Bacchante*. The cruise lasted three years, and covered over 54,000 miles. The other midshipmen, eleven in number, were selected for their fitness as companions to the Princes. There were officers, men, marines, and boys to the number of 450 on board. A clergyman, the Rev. J. N. Dalton (afterwards Canon of Windsor) went as chaplain to the ship and guardian and tutor of the Princes. Their studies were modern languages, history, and mathematics, in addition to their regular instruction in the duties of midshipmen. Every night they had to write in their diaries a description of what they saw and did during the day, with comments. From these diaries two volumes entitled *The Cruise of the Bacchante*, were compiled by Mr. Dalton and dedicated to Queen Victoria " by Her Majesty's affectionate and dutiful Grandsons."

During the voyage the country was startled by a statement widely published in the newspapers that the Princes, landing at Bermuda, had each had his nose tattooed with an anchor. It was feared in the Royal Household that the story might be true, because of Prince George's addiction to pranks and practical jokes, for which he was known in the home circle as the " Royal Pickle." Once at a family luncheon at Windsor Castle, in his childhood, he incurred the displeasure of the severe, as well as august, Queen Victoria, and as a punishment was sent under the table until he was in a fit mind to behave himself. After a while he was heard to say, " Grandmamma, I'm quite good now." " Very well, then," said Grandmamma, " you may come out." Out he came, wholly naked and un-ashamed, having in his banishment divested himself of every bit of clothing. There was no knowing what a boy like that might be up to. Anxious telegrams were sent to the ship, and greatly to the relief of the country, as well as of the Royal Family, it was announced that the story was unfounded. What had happened was that the boys ornamented each others noses with pollen from the brilliant orange stamens of the Bermuda lilies. From that day to this yellow noses are regarded as the height of fashion in the island, especially by the native ladies.

It was as a midshipman on the *Bacchante* that Prince George took up stamp-collecting, to satisfy the possessive instinct of the boy. It was a good hobby to have selected, for postage-stamps do give a breadth of vision, what with the vivid colouring, the heads of potentates, the pictures, and names of far-off places, so suggestive of romance. As the King told the Junior Philatelic Society in 1920, he has pursued it with " unabated interest " ever since. His collection of stamps is said to be the completest in existence.

Before he left home for this voyage he promised his mother to read the Bible daily. The Pocket Testament League in 1912 wrote to Buckingham Palace asking if it was true that King George followed the practice of daily Bible reading. " It is quite true," Lord Knollys, the King's Private Secretary, replied, " that he promised Queen Alexandra as long ago as 1881 that he would read a chapter of the Bible daily, and that he has ever since adhered to this promise."

At the end of the cruise in August, 1882, the two brothers parted company. Prince Albert Victor was destined for the Army, and the succession to the Throne ; Prince George adopted the sea as his avocation. After serving for more than two years as senior midshipman on the *Canada* in North American and West Indian stations, he returned to complete his naval education at the Royal Naval College, Greenwich. In 1886 he was appointed lieutenant on the *Thunderer*, and after service on other ships of the Mediterranean Fleet spent three years on the *Alexandra*, the flagship of his uncle, the Duke of Edinburgh.

Prince George was an efficient officer. He was devotedly attached to his calling, although like Nelson and other distinguished sailors, he suffered from seasickness. The Navy is at once an autocracy and a democracy. No rank except service rank is recognised. Obedience must be rendered implicitly, without question, to superiors. Thus originates the bluff heartiness of manner and freedom from airs and pretensions which distinguish the Naval officer. No distinction was made between Prince George and his shipmates. He was all that " sailor " and " naval officer " imply. There was not a trace of affectation in his manner. He was a good singer of comic songs, and the humour of a situation appealed to him. Once when his ship was in Turkish waters a Pascha came on board to pay his respects to the grandson of the Queen of England and son of the Prince of Wales. It happened that the Prince that day was having his turn in the duty of coaling, and when he appeared on deck from the stoke-hole his overalls black and his face and hands grimy with coaldust, even the Eastern calm of the Pascha was ruffled at the sight.

The Prince endured the responsibility and discomfort of commanding in small and precarious craft. At the age of twenty-four, in 1889, he had his first independent command in the torpedo-boat 79 of the Channel Squadron. His skill and daring in rescuing a disabled torpedo-boat off the coast of Ireland during Naval manœuvres of that year—towing it safely into harbour in rough weather—earned him his appointment as Commander of the first-class gunboat *Thrush*. In 1891 he was appointed commander of the new second-class cruiser *Melampus*. His ambition was that one day he would have the pride and joy of hoisting his Flag as an Admiral on the active list. He used to say how glad he was that he would not have to be King, as he wanted to remain a sailor.

* * * * * *

In January, 1892, the whole outlook of Prince George was unexpectedly changed. By the premature death of his brother,

Prince Albert Victor, Duke of Clarence, he came into the direct line of succession to the Throne. After sixteen years' continuous service afloat, his career at sea was abruptly terminated. He was raised to the peerage as Duke of York, and was introduced in the House of Lords by his father. The education and training he had had in the Navy was of a solid, practical kind. There was nothing abstract about it ; it was in touch, all the time, with human nature, and realities. Thus equipped he turned to the study of matters more closely related to the high office to which he was ultimately to be called—the working of the English Constitution and the various departments of public life, and he did it, as is his way, with quiet, unostentatious and thorough diligence. During the ten years of the reign of King Edward, he was, as Prince of Wales, the companion and coadjutor of his father in the business of Government. This was an experience which few Kings of England have had. The aim of Prince George as Heir Apparent was to make himself a personal link between the United Kingdom and the Commonwealth of British Nations overseas. In March, 1901, shortly after his father's accession to the Throne, being then Duke of Cornwall—in which he succeeded his father—as well as Duke of York, he set out, with the Duchess of York, on a tour which embraced India, Australia, New Zealand, South Africa, Canada. They travelled over 50,000 miles, of which 38,000 were at sea. The ceremonial side of the journey is brought out by a few figures. The guns fired in their honour numbered 11,390. The Duke received 544 addresses and made eighty-six speeches. He met all the leading men of the Dominions. He laid twenty-one foundation stones and shook hands with 35,000 persons. It was on his return home in March, 1902, that the Duke was made Prince of Wales. Speaking at a luncheon given at the Guildhall by the Lord Mayor and Corporation, he said : " If I were asked to specify any particular impressions derived from our tour I should unhesitatingly place before all others those of loyalty to the Crown and attachment to the old country." It was on this occasion that he delivered a memorable exhortation : " Wake up, England ! " It was a call for settlers for the " boundless tracts of country yet unexplored, hidden mineral wealth calling for development; vast expanses of virgin soil ready to yield profitable crops."

The Navy was King George's Public School and the British Empire his University. He has given the same training, almost exactly, to his son, Edward, Prince of Wales. Unlike his father, King George is a great reader of books—history, biography, travel, and explorations being his favourite subjects. He differs from his father in mind and temperament and individuality. He has more reserve and unobtrusiveness of manner, the result partly of an unassuming nature, and partly of a high seriousness and sincerity. His deep-set eyes are expressive of thoughtfulness. The whole bearded countenance bespeaks a union of gravity and friendliness. He has not his father's enjoyment of the light side of life—in social relaxations. He is most happy as a private gentleman in the quiet of family life. But he is not self-centred. As King he is a serious and laborious worker, incessantly engrossed in State affairs and business, and it affords him the greatest pleasure to appear informally at great gatherings of his people, seeing them at their sports and amusements.

He is not so jovial as his father was, but he has more urbanity. He is approachable, friendly, and sympathetic in bearing. King Edward would sternly dismiss anyone whom he thought was presuming too far. King George would not hurt the feelings of even the most pushful by a look of displeasure or annoyance. He graciously receives everyone who approaches him, however ordinary, and bends himself to listen with an air of earnest expectation as if there was an important message about to be delivered, and when he has heard it he responds with a kindly comment and an understanding smile. He has certain simple and fundamental qualities of character which are very endearing. He is as popular as his father was. The devotion in which he is held is less familiar, but more profound. Seeing King Edward, one felt that one saw him through and through—light-heartedly satisfied with himself, and, in the main, with everything else in this best of all possible worlds. King George possesses a deeper and more sensitive nature—a region of reserve in which to meditate over the inequalities and sorrows of life, for to him the sufferings of others is a personal grief. Like all persons of this disposition, he has the widest social sympathies. Yet no one would think of patting him on the back, saying " Good old Georgie " in the way his father was hailed as " Good old Teddie." In the applause that greets him there is not the boisterous laughter that edged the cheers which his father aroused. There is in it the unqualified note of warm affection and absolute confidence.

King George can well be pictured, standing, by reason of his training and office, on a great tower that commands the widest possible prospect of the scattered Commonwealth of Nations over which he reigns.

END OF BOOK II

BOOK III

MARRIAGES IN THE ROYAL FAMILY

CHAPTER I

CONSORTS OF THE FIRST HANOVERIAN KINGS

THE Royal marriage which, for many a year, gave the completest satisfaction to national sentiment was undoubtedly that of George V and Queen Mary—or the Duke of York and Princess Mary of Teck, as they were styled at their wedding in 1893. For the first time for more than two centuries a future King of England had chosen a bride who was born and reared in England. The last English Prince in the line of succession to the Throne to marry an English girl was the Duke of York (afterwards James II), the girl being Anne, daughter of Edward Hyde, Earl of Clarendon and Lord Chancellor of England. She became the mother of two Queens regnant—Mary, wife of William III, and Anne, the last of the Stuarts. Princess Mary was not of English blood like Anne Hyde—her parents, the Duke and Duchess of Teck, having been of German origin—but she was born, brought up, and educated in England, and was known to be distinctively English in habits, tastes, and opinions. Anne Hyde died before her husband ascended the Throne as James II. Queen Mary, therefore, was the first Queen Consort for several centuries who spoke English as her mother tongue. For a Queen Consort who, before Queen Mary, was English by birth and speech—excluding the English women whom Henry VIII is supposed to have married—we have to go back to Elizabeth of York, daughter of Edward IV, who married the first of the Tudors, Henry VII, and was the mother of Henry VIII. The native stream of the Blood Royal has had since then regular alien infusions through the Consorts of the Kings.

The wives of the four Georges and William IV were German by birth and nationality. Only in Germany could the Kings and Heirs Apparent of the Hanoverian line find Princesses of Royal Blood—for Royalty then married only Royalty—and also of the Protestant faith, to which the Queens Consort as well as the Kings were legally bound to belong. Nevertheless, to the British people, with their traditional dislike of foreigners, this settled practice had become repugnant. It was first happily broken by the marriage of Albert Edward, Prince of Wales (afterwards Edward VII) to Princess Alexandra of Denmark. For though both the parents of Alexandra were originally German—Prince Christian of Glucksburg and Princess Louise of Hesse, to whom, under an agreement come to by the Powers of Europe it was arranged that the Crown of Denmark was to pass at the death of the reigning childless King, Christian VIII—the Princess herself was born and reared in Denmark, and on her mother's side was not only descended from the Danish Kings of Denmark, but could trace her ancestry back to Cánute, who was monarch both of England and Denmark in the first half of the eleventh century. Tennyson, therefore, was not indulging merely in a poetic fancy when, as Poet Laureate, he hailed her as " Sea-Kings' daughter from over the sea, Alexandra ! " Her youth and loveliness captivated the hundreds of thousands who thronged the streets of London to welcome her as a worthy bride for their young Prince, and they rejoiced in her all the more that she did not come from Germany.

*   *   *   *   *   *

There could not have been a less inspiring succession of Kings than the Four Georges and William IV. Romance took flight from the history of the British Monarchy when George I became King, and did not return again until a June morning in 1837, when at Kensington Palace a young girl, Princess Victoria, was aroused from her sleep, and told she was Queen of England. The wives of the Hanoverian Kings emphasised, rather than relieved, the commonplaceness of their husbands. It is true that in the domestic annals of the Royal Family those German wives have that kind of fame which all good and sensible women would desire. They were excellent wives, and as such retained the respect and confidence at least of their husbands. We see them in the drawing-room after dinner knitting woollen comforters and stockings, and though one might not be able to follow their guttural talk in the German tongue, we feel sure it was quite blameless. But they were not queenly dames. They were without grace and style and distinction. They were plain-featured, and had that full habit of body so characteristic of German Fraus, and furthermore they were unendowed with any endearing feminine quality which, carrying its glamour and allurement beyond the family circle, would have touched a cord in the heart of England. Poor things, it is our pity and sympathy they deserve. They were temperamentally alien to their surroundings. England was to them a foreign land, having habits and customs that were strange to them, and speaking a language they did not understand.

The first of the Hanoverian Kings, George I, was a married man when he came over from Germany in 1714 to succeed Queen Anne. He did not bring his wife with him. She never saw England. She was his cousin, Sophia Dorothea, daughter and heiress of the Duke of Brunswick and Zelle, whom he married in 1682, when he was twenty-two years of age and she only sixteen; but her heart was elsewhere, and he repudiated her and had her locked up in a lonely castle twenty years before he became King of England. Her lover was Count Konigsmark, and the Jacobites of the time used to protest that they saw in George II, her son, a striking likeness to that gallant cavalier. Instead of a wife, George I brought with him (according to Walpole) a seraglio of German women, fat, gross, ugly. They were laughed and hooted at as they drove through London. One of them, putting her head out of the carriage window, said, " Ye Englishes people, why you abuse us ? We come for all your goods." " And for our chattels, too," retorted a voice from the crowd. George Augustus—afterwards George II, had married Caroline, daughter of the Margrave of Brandenburg-Anspach, nine years before his father became King. They accompanied George I to England and were made Prince and Princess of Wales. George II was not a romantic figure any more than his father. He was coarse in tastes, and, as he used to protest in his German guttural, " didn't like boetry and didn't like bainting." But he was a good soldier. At the Battle of Dettingen his horse was shot under him. " Now," he cried out to his men, " I know I shall not run away." He was the last English Sovereign to have been under fire.

Frederick, Prince of Wales, son of George II, was twenty-eight years old in 1735—he was born in Hanover in 1707 before his grandfather was yet King—and greatly to the concern of the English Government he appeared to have, as yet, no thought of taking a wife and becoming the father of legitimate children. He had just discarded his mistress, a young lady of the Court named Miss Vane, generously allowing her a pension of £1,600 a year at the expense of the taxpayers, and the hope of the Ministers that this was a preliminary step to marriage was grievously disappointed. For the Prince put in her place another lady of the Court, Lady Archibald Hamilton, a wife thirty-five years old and the mother of ten children. Accordingly, there was talk in Parliament of the two Houses adopting a joint address to the King praying His Majesty to see to the marriage and settlement of the Heir to the Throne. It was not the scandal of the free living of the young Prince which troubled Lords and Commons. That was regarded at the time as but an amiable failing in Kings and Princes, abroad as well as at home. What they were anxious about was the succession to the Throne, for Frederick was the only child, and there was no prospect of the ageing King and Queen having any other children.

It happened that the King was then on one of his frequent visits to his beloved Hanover, and looking round him for a wife for the Prince of Wales he selected Princess Augusta, a daughter of the Duke of Saxe-Gotha. Frederick and Augusta had never met, and neither had even seen a picture of the other, and yet they both accepted with perfect content the match arranged by their parents. Ah, those poor Princes and Princesses of the past ! They were seldom allowed to choose their mates. The ancient primitive custom of marriages being arranged by the elders of the tribe, collectively, for the good of the tribe, and not by the pair individually according to their personal tastes and pleasure, survived in Royal Families. Seldom for them was there a pleasant wooing-time. They rarely had the rapture of hearing the happy " Yes " faltering lovingly on the lips of the beloved. They rarely looked into each other's eyes until the day they met to be married. Their marriages were of convenience simply, undertaken as a matter of duty for the sake of the children who were needed to make secure the regular succession to the Throne.

Augusta was seventeen when in 1736 she landed at Greenwich. She was escorted from Germany by two members of the English peerage, but was unaccompanied by a single female attendant of her own race. She had a cold reception. No member of the Royal Family met her. At Queen's House, a Royal dwelling place then in Greenwich Park, only the servants were there to wait upon her. A few days later she was conducted by land to Lambeth, crossed the Thames by boat to Whitehall, and thence was carried in a sedan-chair to St. James's Palace, where she was to be presented to the King and Queen and Prince of Wales. As she stepped out of the chair at the door of the Palace, Frederick took her by the hand and kissed her twice on the lips. By the second kiss the Prince meant to convey that he liked her. She was very young— a great attraction in a bride of those days—if not beautiful, and it was for her youth, no doubt, that the Prince was thankful.

That evening they were married in the Chapel Royal by the Bishop of London. After the service a heavy German supper was served. It lasted till midnight. Then followed what was called the bridal-chamber reception. The Prince was accompanied to the chamber by the King and Queen with a retinue of noblemen in attendance. He wore a nightgown of silk brocade in gold and silver. On his head was a cap of the finest lace. The bride was found sitting up in bed arrayed in a lace nightdress, with her bridesmaids standing around. The Prince took his place beside her. And sitting up together in bed the Prince and Princess spent half an hour receiving company! The Princess was much abashed. She was but a simple girl, almost a child. For many months subsequently her only pastime was playing with a doll— dressing and undressing it, fondling it, and nursing it. And Lady Archibald Hamilton, her husband's mistress, was her Mistress of the Robes, at a salary of £900 a year!

*   *   *   *   *   *

Frederick, Prince of Wales, died ten years before his father,

George II, and when that King passed away in 1760 he was succeeded by his grandson—Frederick's firstborn son—George, Prince of Wales, as George III. The new King was only twenty-two, and unmarried. The Royal House of England has, like all Royal Houses, its secret annals—of doubtful authority, fictitious, concocted. A romantic chapter in those annals is concerned with the story of Hannah Lightfoot, the pretty and demure young Quakeress, daughter of a shoemaker of Wapping, who was said to be the lawful wife of George III, and as such, England's Queen, and the mother of children who were rightful heirs to the Throne. In truth, the episode differs in no degree from intrigues of the kind in which, as history relates, Princes in the past were prone to become involved. There was a love affair between George, when Prince of Wales, and the Quakeress.

George had his first glimpse of Hannah at the door of her uncle's shop as he rode through St. James's Market one day. He became enamoured of her, and, she on her part, found the advances of a Prince irresistible. But George did not make Hannah his wife. The marriage-certificate given in a pamphlet called *The Appeal for Royalty*, published in 1858—a hundred years afterwards—were pronounced " gross and rank forgeries " by the High Courts. And Hannah Lightfoot having become the mother of children by Prince George, disappeared as the wife of one of her old sweethearts, Isaac Axford, a grocer's assistant on Ludgate Hill.

There is another love-story in the life of the King George III which is better authenticated and possesses more human and romantic interest. George III has the distinction of being the first of the Hanoverian Kings of England to be born and brought up in the country over which they ruled. In the very first Speech from the Throne which he read to the Houses of Parliament he said : " Born and educated in this country, I glory in the name of Briton." The speech, as originally prepared by Lord Chancellor Hardwicke, did not contain this famous passage. It was inserted by the King in his own handwriting and on his sole initiative. " It was not suggested to me by anyone," he said afterwards. But his English education was so imperfect that he spelt " Briton "

" Britain." Moved also, perhaps, by this racial pride, the King was at first disposed to choose as his Queen Consort an English girl—English by blood as well as English by birth and upbringing. The object of his early and spontaneous affection was Lady Sarah Lennox, the youngest sister of the then Duke of Richmond, not quite sixteen, and a pretty girl of uncommon attraction.

A happy issue to this love affair was frustrated by the contrary natures of the parties themselves. The King was sluggish in temperament, and shy in manner; the lady was high-spirited, wilful, and coquettish. He was prodigal of infatuated looks whenever he encountered the lady about the Court, though they took the most unromantic and disconcerting form of staring. But he found it impossible to bring himself to use even the simplest and most direct proposal : " I love you ; will you marry me ? " He had to declare his affection through a third party. He said to another lady of the Court, Lady Susan Strangeways, there would be no coronation until there was a Queen, and he thought Lady Sarah Lennox was the fittest person to be his Consort. " Tell her so from me," he added. Lady Susan did convey the King's message to Lady Sarah. Shortly afterwards His Majesty made bold to ask Lady Sarah what she thought of it. " Nothing, sir," was her reply. " Nothing comes to nothing," said the King in a huff as he walked away. What girl would not feel proud of having a King as a wooer, even though he wooed in so prosaic a way ? Lady Sarah Lennox was really overflowing with gratification at the thought of it, but with maiden perversity she would not take her Royal suitor at his word. When she learnt that a German wife had been found for the King, she was very annoyed with herself. In a letter to Lady Susan Strangeways she cried out somewhat incoherently in her grief : " I shall take care to show that I am not mortified to anybody ; but if it is true that one can vex anybody with a reserved cold manner, he shall have it, I promise him."

Indeed, even if Lady Sarah Lennox had said " Yes " to the oblique proposal of King George, there might still have been no wedding. Both the Dowager Princess of Wales, mother of the King, and the then Prime Minister, Lord Bute, were opposed to the marriage for different reasons, and were unitedly determined to prevent it. Princess Augusta would have regarded the alliance as one beneath the King, aye, though the bride was a daughter of an English ducal house. Royalty must marry Royalty. The proper mate of the King of England, in her opinion, was a German Princess of the Blood Royal, like herself—a caste apart and exclusive, differing almost in flesh and blood even from the highest circles of the rest of humanity. One night at a Court ball, seeing her son and Lady Sarah in intimate conversation, when the girl seemed from the look of invitation in her eyes, to be ready at once to accept another proposal that was bubbling on the thick sluggish lips of the King, the Princess rushed forward and took her son away, rudely laughing the while in Lady Sarah's face. Lord Bute, on his part, shared the feeling then rather common among the British aristocracy that the Hanoverian Royalties were a beggarly foreign lot to whom unhappy circumstances in the history of the country had given the British Throne; but he looked with jealous disfavour on a match which would bring to a particular English noble family royal influence and high precedence at Court.

Accordingly, the Princess and Prime Minister sent Colonel Graeme to Germany to look out for a wife for the King. Graeme's choice was the Princess Charlotte, the younger of the two sisters of the reigning Duke of Mecklenburg-Strelitz. She was young, barely seventeen, but could hardly be called attractive. As she is seen in Ramsay's picture in the National Portrait Gallery, she is small and slim—differing in that respect from her full-bodied predecessors—and while the upper part of her face is good, the dark eyes being particularly fine, the lower part, showing a nose with wide nostrils and a wide mouth, gives an impression of uncouthness, relieved somewhat by the expression which is bright and good-natured.

The arrangements for the marriage were quickly completed, and early in September Charlotte landed at Harwich and drove to London. Had the crowds which assembled to see the Princess to marry her themselves, they could not have been more resentful of her plain looks. Her attempts to gain their favour by laughing made matters worse only, for her expanded mouth seemed to swallow up the rest of her face. Poor girl, it was only when she was driving down Constitution Hill to St. James's Palace that the English ladies accompanying her told her that she was to be married that very night. " Mein Gott ! " she cried—she knew no English—and fainted, and a bottle of lavender water was emptied on her face to bring her round. The carriage drew up at a private door in the Friary giving admission to the gardens of St. James's Palace. As she passed through the door in fear and trembling she saw dimly a group of ladies and gentlemen waiting to receive her. What caught her eye most clearly was a splash of colour on the ground made by a scarlet cushion. Standing before it was a stout and ill-favoured old gentleman. She thought it was the King, and her heart sank within her as she went down on her knees on the cushion to do him reverence. Immediately she was seized round the waist and rising up found herself, greatly to her relief and joy, in the arms of quite a good-looking young man in rich attire. It was noticed by the company that as the King kissed her a shade of disappointment passed over his countenance. At such a moment, a pretty face is regarded as superior to any accomplishment of mind or understanding, and decidedly His Majesty's first impression of his bride was not at all favourable. Lady Sarah Lennox was in the group, and it was only human that she should have found in the encounter, and in her own superiority in feminine charm to the bride, some salve to her wounded pride.

At nine o'clock that night the marriage was celebrated in the Chapel Royal by the Archbishop of Canterbury. Lady Sarah Lennox was a bridesmaid, and so radiant was she in her loveliness that, according to contemporary records, she distracted the King even at the altar as he was being married. For it was upon her and not upon the bride that his eyes were fixed during the ceremony. The jollifications which followed were kept up until two o'clock, when the bride and bridegroom retired. At the urgent request of the bashful and very tired Queen Consort the reception in the bridal chamber was dispensed with, and it was never revived at any of the subsequent Royal weddings.

117

George III and his Consort spent a long and blameless life together and had many children. Queen Charlotte may have been physically unattractive, but she had more valuable qualities of mind and character which outlast good looks, and tend more, perhaps, to the happiness of the married state. Indeed, as she grew older she became better looking. As was said by the jokers of the Court, " the bloom of her ugliness had gone off." George III was the only Hanoverian King who did not have his favourites among the ladies of the Court. But all through his life he had a tender thought for Lady Sarah Lennox. His stupid obstinacy lost him the most flashing diadem in his Imperial Crown—the American colonies. What of that ? Not even a King in his old age could bring himself to lament the loss of so impersonal a thing as a continent. The loss he deplored with an aching heart was the youth and beauty of Lady Sarah Lennox. He always saw her in his mind's eye as she appeared, a vision in white, at his wedding.

Well, it was all for the best that Lady Sarah Lennox became not the Queen Consort of George III but the wife of Capt. the Hon. George Napier. Among the results that followed were the reign of Queen Victoria, on the one hand, and on the other, the achievements of those noble-minded brothers— Sir Charles Napier, the most gallant soldier of his age, the Conqueror of Scinde, and Sir William Napier, the distinguished author of the *History of the War in the Peninsula*. They were supremely fine characters—Kings of men.

CHAPTER II

MORGANATIC UNIONS

No member of the Royal Family under the age of twenty-five can legally marry without the previous consent of the King. His Majesty's permission must be declared by him at a meeting of the Privy Council and entered in the Privy Council's books. It must also be set out in the marriage certificate. This briefly summarises the effect of an Act for the better regulating of marriages of the Royal Family passed in 1772, by direction of King George III.

King George fell out with two of his brothers for having, unknown to him, contracted marriages with ladies who were not of the Blood Royal, and to whom personally he objected for reasons social and political. Henry Frederick, Duke of Cumberland (not the ill-famed butcher of the Jacobites at Culloden, but his nephew), married in 1771 a widow much older than himself, named Horton. Her father, Simon Luttrel, first Lord Carhampton, had aroused the hostility of the King because of his opposition in Parliament to His Majesty's wishes. At the same time the King got to know that another brother, next in age to himself, William Henry, Duke of Gloucester, had secretly married some years previously the widow of Earl Waldegrave. She was an illegitimate daughter of Sir Edward Walpole, son of Sir Robert Walpole, the famous Prime Minister. Both brothers and their wives were banished from the Court and had to go abroad. The King ultimately became reconciled to the Duke of Gloucester, but he refused to allow the Duchess to be presented at Court. And the banishment of the Duke and Duchess of Cumberland lasted to the end.

The King, moved, as he said in a joint message to Lords and Commons, by his " paternal affection to his own family and from his Royal concern for the future welfare of his people and the honour and dignity of his Crown," thereupon recommended Parliament to take into serious consideration whether it might not be wise and expedient to supply the defects in the laws relating to marriages of the Royal Family. To this Parliament agreed. "And being sensible," as both Houses declared, " that marriages of the Royal Family are of the highest importance to the State, and that, therefore, the Kings of this Realm have ever been entrusted with the care and approbation thereof" they accordingly passed the statute known as the Royal Marriage Act, 1772. It enacts that the general law that a person over twenty-one years of age requires no consent to marry does not apply to members of the Royal Family, and that " No descendant of George II (other than the issue of Princesses married or who may marry into foreign families) shall be capable of contracting matrimony without the previous consent of the King, signified under the Great Seal, declared in Council and entered in the Privy Council books." The Act goes on to declare that " Every marriage of any such descendant without such consent shall be null and void." But there is this qualification—" In case any descendant of George II, being above twenty-five years old, shall persist to contract a marriage disapproved of by the King, such descendant, after giving twelve months' notice to the Privy Council, may contract such marriage, and the same may be duly solemnised without the previous consent of the King and shall be good, except both Houses of Parliament shall declare their disapprobation thereof." The qualification does little, if anything, to remove the ban.

In cases where the King's consent is given the parties can marry in any place or at any time they please without banns, licence, or any other condition prescribed by the ordinary marriage laws, but they cannot be married by a registrar in a registry office, or according to the rites of any Nonconformist Church—a clergyman of the Church of England only being empowered to perform the ceremony. Persons celebrating or assisting at any marriage of a member of the Royal Family which is contracted without the consent of the King incurs on conviction the penalties of " præmurie," which include forfeiture of goods and imprisonment for life.

What, then, would be the position of a member of the Royal Family who, being under the age of twenty-five, entered into a matrimonial alliance without the consent of the Sovereign, or, being over twenty-five, did so without giving the year's notice to the Privy Council in a case where the Sovereign's permission was withheld? Such a marriage would be what is called " morganatic "—a term which seems to have originated in Germany to describe a union between a man who is of the Blood Royal and a woman who is not. It is known in Germany also as " a left-handed marriage," because in the ceremony the bridegroom gives the bride not his right hand but his left. A morganatic marriage fulfils the obligations of morality and religion. And of law also, save in two most important respects—the wife has no share in the rank and title of the husband, and the children, though legitimate, do not inherit their father's honours or possessions.

The legal position of the wife and children of a British Prince whose marriage was not approved by the Sovereign has been the subject of the highest judicial decision in this country. Prince Augustus, sixth son of George III, met in Rome in 1792, the Countess of Dunmore, of the Scottish peerage, and her two daughters. He fell in love with the elder girl, Lady Augusta Murray, he being then twenty and she six or seven years older. In a passionately entreating letter—it was read in the House of Lords, close on half a century later— he vowed that if she did not marry him he would starve himself to death. " I have not taken food for forty-eight hours," he wrote, " I am half dead. Good God, what will become of me ! I shall go mad most undoubtedly." He insisted that they must be married before the day was over. Then, and only then, did Lady Augusta Murray give way to his advances. She felt assured by this communication that his love for her was no passing fancy, but a genuine passion. In an answering letter she invited him to come to her lodgings, about 8 o'clock that evening when her mother would be away. " To be yours tonight seems a dream that I cannot make out," she wrote in terms of passionate yielding. " The whole day have I been plunged in misery, and now to awake to joy is a felicity that is beyond my ideas of bliss." She added—" I doubt its success, but do as you will. I am what you will; your will must be mine and no will can ever be dearer to me, more mine, than that of my Augustus—my lover, my all." That evening, in April, 1793, they were married by a clergyman of the Church of England named Green, who enjoined upon them to keep their union secret, as he would get into trouble with his ecclesiastical superiors should his part in it ever become known.

But when, towards the close of the year, the lady found that a baby was coming, she very properly sought to protect herself from the stigma of being regarded as the Prince's mistress. She asked that they should be re-married in London. Accordingly in December the ceremony was repeated at St. George's, Hanover-Square, and by banns, though the parties gave the disguised name of " Augustus Frederick " and " Augusta Murray." The birth of a son in January, 1794, led to public disclosure of their relations. The King was very angry. He got the marriage annulled by the Court of Arches, an ecclesiastical court, on the ground that it was contrary to the Royal Marriage Act. His Majesty also declared that if the Prince did not give up the lady he would not follow the usual course, in the case of a King's son, of making him a duke. The Prince bowed to his father's will in 1801 and was created Duke of Sussex, Earl of Inverness and Baron Arklow. A Royal annuity of £1,800 a year was granted to the lady, on condition that she did not use the Royal Arms, and she was allowed by royal licence to change her name from Lady Augusta Murray to Lady D'Ameland. The children of the marriage—there was a daughter as well as a son—were given the surname of D'Este, after a common Italian ancestor of both mother and father, for Lady Augusta Murray claimed to be of Royal descent.

The Duke of Sussex died in 1843. He was the most democratic member of the Royal Family. For a Prince in the first half of the nineteenth century he was a very advanced Radical, indeed. He supported in the House of Lords all the progressive measures of his time—abolition of the slave trade, emancipation of the Catholics, removal of the civil disabilities of the Jews, reform of Parliament, the repeal of the Corn laws. A few years before his death he contracted a second marriage with a widow of the name of Buggin, and as she could not legally assume the title of Duchess of Sussex, the union being morganatic, he induced the King to make her Duchess of Inverness. They had no children. The Duke was democratic in death as well as in life. He did not want any association with departed Royalty who lie in emblazoned pomp. " Bury me not in the Royal tombs at Windsor, but in the public cemetery at Kensal Green," he said in his will.

In 1844, the Duke of Sussex's son, by Lady Augusta Murray, entered a claim before the Committee of Privileges of the House of Lords to succeed to his father's peerage. He was then known as Sir Augustus D'Este, William IV having made him a Knight and given him a pension of £500 a year out of the Civil List, because of his Royal parentage. D'Este's plea was that the Royal Marriage Act applied only to marriages contracted within the British jurisdiction, and therefore that it did not affect the marriage of his parents which took place in Rome. The Judges of the High Court were called in to advise the Lords. Their opinion, read in the House of Lords by Lord Chief Justice Tindal, was that the Act applied to the marriage of a member of the Royal Family without as well as within the realm, and that the eldest son of any such marriage contracted without the consent of the King was not entitled to recover his father's title and lands. The Lord Chancellor (Lord Lyndhurst), Lord Cottenham and Lord Brougham, confirmed this opinion. Accordingly, the marriage was held void, and the claim was disallowed. Sir Thomas Wilde, counsel in the case, married the claimant's sister, Ellen Augusta D'Este. He afterwards became Lord Truro and Lord Chancellor of England. D'Este died unmarried in 1848.

In giving their judgment the Law Lords declared that Parliament ought never to have passed the Royal Marriage Act, and that the mother and children were deeply injured persons. " These observations " the newspapers of the day state, " were received with cheers."

*   *   *   *   *   *

There was one morganatic marriage in the Royal Family that was recognised as morganatic by the Sovereign and by the parties themselves. Prince George, son and heir of the first Duke of Cambridge—seventh son of George III—married in 1840 Louisa Fairbrother, a young and pretty actress. The Prince was twenty-one at the time, three years younger than his wife. Born at Hanover on March 26th, 1819—his mother being a daughter of the Landgrave Frederick of Hesse-Cassel—he was then the only living descendant of the still living George III in the second generation, and, as such, was in the direct line of succession to the Throne until the birth on May 24th, 1819, of his first-cousin, Princess Victoria, who as the child of the Duke of Kent, fourth son of George III, superseded him in the order of priority. More than that, Prince George was, in the year of his marriage to Miss Fairbrother in 1840, Heir Presumptive to Queen Victoria, and remained so until the birth in November, 1841, of Prince Albert Edward, afterwards Edward VII.

On the death of his father in 1850, Prince George became the second Duke of Cambridge, and was for many years well-known as Field-Marshal and Commander-in-Chief of the British Army—a bluff and jovial old gentleman, very industrious as head of the Army, but fond of life and its pleasures and very German in his ways. But his wife did not become Duchess of Cambridge. Queen Victoria had not given her consent to the marriage, and Louisa Fairbrother as the fond wife of the Duke and the devoted mother of his children, was known simply as " Mrs. FitzGeorge." A memoir of *His Royal Highness, the Duke of Cambridge*, compiled by the Rev. Edgar Sheppard, sub-dean of the Chapel Royal, and published in two big volumes in 1906—two years after the Duke's death—shows that such a marriage is regarded by Royalty and in Court circles as something to be hidden or glossed over. His marriage was really the one important and interesting event in the Duke's long life. Yet it is not mentioned in the *Memoir* until, in due chronological order, the year of his wife's death, 1890, is reached, and then the fifty years of his happy married life is dismissed in a couple of pages. One sentence must be quoted : " Mrs. FitzGeorge, as she became on her marriage, took up her residence in Queen-Street, Mayfair, where the Duke devoted to his wife all the hours he could spare from his public duties and private engagements." The Duke, in fact, had a separate house of his own, Gloucester House, Park Lane. He was, indeed, always very much attached to his wife as, by all accounts, he had every reason to be, as she was a most estimable lady. He says in his *Diary* that the day after his wife's death he received " a most affectionate message from the Queen which I highly appreciate and which would have been such a joy to my beloved one had she known the fact." At the funeral at Kensal Green cemetery, the Duke followed the hearse with his three sons, Colonel George FitzGeorge ; Rear-Admiral Sir Adolphus FitzGeorge and Colonel Sir Augustus FitzGeorge.

In " The Royal Lineage " set out extensively in *Burke's Peerage*, it is said that the Duke of Cambridge died *unmarried*, on March 17th, 1904, " when," it adds, " the dukedom and other honours became extinct." What a preposterous and almost incredible state of affairs ! Happily the situation during the lifetime of Mrs. FitzGeorge was somewhat relieved by one kindly touch of true human nature. Society, greatly to its credit, declined to consider the marriage as " left-handed," or morganatic, or as anything else but what was right, proper and true. Mrs. FitzGeorge was honoured as a member of the Royal Family. When she entered a room all present rose from their seats and the ladies curtsied to her. As a further testimony of his love for his wife, the Duke of Cambridge left directions for his burial with her at Kensal Green.

CHAPTER III

WIVES OF GEORGE IV AND WILLIAM IV

THE most celebrated morganatic marriage in the Royal Family was that of George IV, when Prince of Wales, to Mrs. Fitzherbert.

Maria Anne Fitzherbert came of one of the oldest Roman Catholic families of Lancashire, the Smythes. She was a beautiful and accomplished woman of irreproachable character. She was twice married and widowed, and both her husbands had been country gentlemen. The Prince of Wales met her in 1785, four years after she had been left a widow the second time, when she was twenty-nine and he twenty-three years of age. Many hard things have been written of George. It is said he was a libertine and drunkard. Even as a boy he was addicted to tippling and low company, and his word, then and always, was wholly untrustworthy. Still, George IV remains the most delightfully interesting Monarch in English history. His very name, when met with, always incites curiosity. In him, more than in any other Prince or King, Royalty showed its human side. Towards the close of his career he sought to excuse its errors by saying : " I was badly brought up." Before he met Mrs. Fitzherbert the Prince already had intrigues with ladies of easy virtue, married and single, one of the earliest having been Mary Robinson, a famous comedy actress who captivated him in her character as " Perdita " at Drury Lane Theatre. He invited Mrs. Fitzherbert to become another of his mistressses and promised to make her the favourite. But she was a woman of an entirely different sort. Being a Roman Catholic of a deeply religious turn of mind, she regarded the proposal as an insult, even though it came from the Prince of Wales and the Heir Apparent to the British Throne.

So infatuated was he that Mrs. Fitzherbert's resistance to his solicitations sent him into a frenzy of unsatisfied desire. He stabbed himself just sufficiently to draw blood without risking his life—he was always apt to temper his crude sensualism with histrionic sentimentality—and sent his cronies to bring the lady to Carlton House so that she might see him in his bleeding state of despair. She tried to comfort him, but she would not submit. On another occasion he flung himself down in her presence, tore his hair, banged his head on the floor, and howled. But all to no purpose. Then he declared his willingness to marry her. He knew that what he proposed was but a form of marriage, that any union he contracted without the consent of George III, his father, was void in law under the Royal Marriage Act, and, furthermore, that a valid marriage with a Roman Catholic would involve the forfeiture of his succession to the Throne under the Act of Settlement. Mrs. Fitzherbert was assured, however, that despite these constitutional impediments the marriage would be proper and moral in the judgment of her Church, and also in the opinion of all right-minded persons. She therefore accepted the proposal. So flattering was it that any young woman might well have succumbed to it. George was the handsomest Prince of the Hanoverian Line. He had indeed the traditional kingly bearing and presence. But, oh, what a contrast between the despicable inward character and the dazzling outward seeming. "The First Gentleman of Europe," as he was styled, could stoop to do the meanest things, especially in his dealings with the fair sex. However, Mrs. Fitzherbert consented to marry him in the hope of saving him from himself, and, incidentally, from other women.

The marriage took place in December, 1785, in the drawing-room of Mrs. Fitzherbert's house in Park-street, Park Lane. The celebrant was a clergyman of the Church of England, named Burt, of Twickenham, who received £500 for the risk he ran in performing the service. Two witnesses were present, the lady's brother, John Smythe, and her uncle, Henry Errington, both Roman Catholics. Mrs. Fitzherbert separated from the Prince in 1795, when he married Princess Caroline of Brunswick. No children had been born to them. A sealed packet was left by Mrs. Fitzherbert at Coutts' bank, under the care of her executors, Lord Stourton and Lord Albemarle, and George IV's executor, the Duke of Wellington. During the reign of Edward VII the packet was opened with the King's consent. It contained the marriage certificate.

*   *   *   *   *   *

The line of commonplace and submissive German Consorts of the Kings and Princes of England was broken when Caroline, daughter of the Duke of Brunswick, became the wife of George, Prince of Wales. Caroline was a passionate, self-willed, eccentric young creature devoid of the homely, wifely qualities of her predecessors. King George III selected her to be the wife of his scapegrace son and heir. She was the King's niece—her mother being His Majesty's sister—and therefore the first cousin of her intended husband. The Prince had never met her. At that time the Heir Apparent was not permitted to leave the Kingdom—even for the purpose of seeking a wife in the little principalities and dukedoms of Germany, which by reason of the Royal Marriage Act, had become more than ever the nurseries of princesses and princes for the Royal Family of England. The Prince, therefore, knew nothing of the looks or disposition of Caroline. His pecuniary circumstances compelled him to accept her as his father's choice. He was in debt to the extent of half a million sterling, as the result of his free living, and the Government told him that they would pay what he owed and increase his yearly allowance only when he took to himself a wife in a way that was lawful, according to the British Constitution. Parliament, in fact, agreed, on his marriage, to raise his allowance from 60,000 to £125,000 a year, to pay off his debts at once, but to deduct £25,000 a year from his allowance towards their liquidation. In addition, £26,000 was voted for the refurnishing of Carlton House, £28,000 for jewels and plate, and £27,000 for the expenses of the wedding.

Lord Malmesbury, the English envoy who escorted Princess Caroline from Brunswick to London, was a confidential servant of George III, Harris by name, and had recently been raised to the peerage. It was at the house in Cleveland Row, St. James's, of Ernest, Duke of Cumberland—one of the many sons of George III—that the Prince of Wales and Caroline met. The only other person in the room at the time was Malmesbury who gives in his *Diary* a brief but terribly poignant description of the scene. When the Prince entered the room, the Princess, acting on the instructions given to her by Malmesbury beforehand, went down on her knees to him, in token of her submission to her future King, as well as her intended husband. "The Prince," says Malmesbury, "raised her (gracefully enough) and embraced her, said barely one word, turned round, retired to a distant part of the apartment, and calling me to him, said, 'Harris, I am not well, pray get me a glass of brandy.' I said, 'Sir, had you not better have a glass of water?' Upon which he, much out of humour, said 'No, I will go directly to the Queen.' And away he went."

Caroline had used the rouge-pot freely in the hope of awakening every grace and calling forth the wonders of her face. But the Prince, scrutinising her with the experienced eye of the pampered voluptuary, saw through her artificialities. Heavens, was this the woman to whom he was to be tied down in domestic servitude, as he regarded the holy bonds of matrimony! Over and over again he had declared that it was his desire to live the free life of a bachelor with his many "favourites," and leave the succession to the Throne to some child of one or other of his many brothers. So he turned away from Caroline with disgust, and hastening to the Queen, his mother, furiously railed at the fat, commonplace and painted woman whom the King, his father, had chosen to be his wife. Her strange reception by the Prince perplexed Caroline. She gave some vent to her annoyance by reflecting on the personal appearance of her appointed husband. Calling out to Malmesbury in French, for she knew no English, she said, "My God, is the Prince always like that? I think him very stout, and by no means so handsome as his portrait." Had the Prince heard the remark, it would have cut him to the quick. A gibe at his face and form hurt him more than a slur on his character. So vain was he that he spent £10,000 a year on clothes and adornment. And just then his constitutional disposition to corpulency was on the increase.

A few days later the ill-fated marriage was solemnised in the Chapel Royal, St. James's, by his Grace the Archbishop of Canterbury. The ceremony was well in keeping with what had passed before. At all weddings in Church the bridegroom waits at the altar for the bride—a survival of the primitive custom of the bride pretending she was brought to marriage reluctantly and by force. At the wedding of George, Prince of Wales, and Princess Caroline, it was the bride, attended by her maids, who had to wait at the altar for the bridegroom; and, in further reversal of the ancient and familiar order of things, the bridegroom was actually dragged thereto by his "best men," two young unmarried dukes. His Royal Highness had taken copious draughts of brandy to fortify himself for the ordeal, with the result that he came to his waiting bride heavily under the influence, supported, literally as well as figuratively, by the two dukes, Roxburghe and Bedford. It is probable that had His Royal Highness been sober he would have run away. For in the middle of the ceremony, when kneeling with the bride, he rose unsteadily to his feet, and turned towards the door, and the Archbishop paused in pronouncing the binding words while the King, whispering to his son and pressing his hands on his shoulder, induced him to kneel down again.

A supper at Buckingham Palace followed. It must have been a ghastly festivity. At midnight the bride and bridegroom left for Carlton House, the Prince's residence. They are said to have quarrelled in the carriage as they drove through the streets in which the populace of London with huzzas and illuminations expressed their joy at the marriage. Long afterwards, when Caroline was Queen, separated from the King, she declared that George was dead drunk most of the wedding night.

*   *   *   *   *   *

Soon after the birth of their only child, Princess Charlotte, in January, 1796, they separated for ever. The Prince, in a letter to the Princess dated "Windsor Castle, April 30th, 1796," in which he addresses her as "Madam," sets forth the terms of their separation. "Our inclinations," he says, "are not in our power, nor should either of us be held answerable to the other because nature has not made us suitable to each other. Tranquillity and comfortable society is, however, in our power; let our intercourse, therefore, be restricted to that." He also makes the remarkable statement, "I will distinctly subscribe to the condition which you require through Lady Cholmondeley that, even in the event of any accident happening to my daughter, which I trust Providence in His mercy will prevent, I shall not infringe the terms of the restriction by proposing at any period a connexion of a more particular nature." He adds—" I shall now finally close this disagreeable correspondence, trusting that as we have completely explained ourselves to each other, the rest of our lives will be passed in uninterrupted tranquillity." He finishes in this elaborately formal manner : " I am, Madam, with great truth, very sincerely yours, George P." Caroline in her reply says she should not have returned any answer to the letter if it did not make it doubtful whether the arrangement proposed came from him or from her. " You are aware," she goes on to say " that the credit of it belongs to you alone." The last sight history gives us of the unfortunate lady was on the day her husband, now George IV, drove alone through the crowded streets to the Abbey to be crowned, when she appeared at the entrance to Westminster Hall and demanded admission to be crowned Queen. The doors were closed in her face.

In 1800 the Prince made urgent calls to Mrs. Fitzherbert to return to him. She appealed to Rome as to what would be her position should she consent, and being fortified by a Papal Bull declaring her to be the Prince's lawful wife, she resumed her married life with him. She took a house in Old Steyne, Brighton, close to the Royal Pavilion which the Prince had built as a seaside Palace. A subterranean passage connected the two residences, and stories are told that through it the Prince was wont to steal o' nights. The final parting came in 1806. At a great dinner given by the Prince at Carlton House, Mrs. Fitzherbert, instead of being given her customary high place at the table, was told she must sit according to her rank— as plain Mrs. Fitzherbert. She accepted this as a dismissal and went away. She survived until Queen Victoria came to the Throne. She had been given an allowance of £10,000 a year when the Prince of Wales married Caroline. It was reduced to £6,000 on the accession of William IV, but the King allowed her to use the Royal scarlet liveries, and whenever she attended his Court he treated her with the courtesy due to a dowager Royal Consort. She continued to reside at Old Steyne. Her carriage and servants in scarlet were often seen flashing along the front, and she was a much-loved old lady in the Catholic Church of St. Mary the Virgin attending Mass and telling her beads. She passed away in 1837 at the age of 81, and was buried in the Catholic Church.

When George IV died a strange and unexpected thing came to light. He hoarded everything. He never gave an old suit away. All the coats, waistcoats, trousers and hats of a lifetime were carefully retained. His extensive wardrobe fetched £30,000 after his death. Before it was sold all the pockets were searched, and in most of the suits were found, not only large sums of money in bank-notes amounting to £10,000, but also innumerable locks of women's hair, odd gloves, pieces of lace, dainty handkerchiefs, perfumed love letters—tokens of past philanderings which in his old age he often looked at and fingered with stealthy ecstasy, stirring all sorts of emotions in his withered breast. Crafty and unsophisticated, sentimental and prosaic, mean and magnificent Monarch! But of the numerous women with whom he had intrigues, the one he really loved, and loved to the very end, was Mrs. Fitzherbert. The Duke of Wellington was an executor of the dead King. On visiting the death-chamber in Windsor Palace he saw round the neck of the corpse a much-worn black ribbon. Attached to it was a jewelled locket containing a miniature of Mrs. Fitzherbert! The relic was buried with the King.

*   *   *   *   *   *

William IV had been married thirteen years when he was crowned in succession to his brother, George IV, in 1831, at the age of sixty-six. As Duke of Clarence he lived in Bushey Park, of which he was Ranger, with Dorothea Jordan, a popular comedy actress, and had so many children by her, ten in all, that she became noted for her periodical absences from the stage owing to these frequent calls of maternity. The Duke allowed her £1,000 a year. His father, George III, remonstrated with him on his extravagance, and at his suggestion he wrote to Mrs. Jordan suggesting a reduction of the allowance to £500. In reply she sent the bottom of a playbill bearing the line— " No money returned after the rising of the curtain."

Princess Charlotte, the sole issue of the union of George,

Prince of Wales, with Caroline of Brunswick, married Prince Leopold, son of the Duke of Saxe-Coburg-Saalfeld, and died in 1817, giving birth to a dead child. The direct succession to the Throne being thus broken, and as the Duke of York, next in age to the Prince of Wales, had no children, though many years married, the Government, anxious in regard to the succession, offered liberal allowances to induce the younger sons of the still reigning George III to take to themselves lawful wives and become parents of collateral heirs to the Throne. The first of the Princes to respond was the Duke of Kent, fourth son of George III. He had been living obscurely in Belgium with a French actress when, tempted by the prospect of getting his allowance of £12,000 a year increased by Parliament, he left her in 1818 and married Victoria Mary Louisa, daughter of the Duke of Saxe-Coburg-Saalfeld, sister of Prince Leopold and widow of the Prince of Leiningen, who died in 1814, leaving her with two children. In the following year a girl was born to the Duke and Duchess of Kent—Princess Victoria, afterwards Queen.

The Duke of Clarence, who in order of birth, came before the Duke of Kent, also looked out for a wife. His younger brother, Prince Adolphus, first Duke of Cambridge, then living in Germany, whom he commissioned to find one for him, selected a certain lady and wrote home in very glowing terms of her charms, too glowing, in fact, for Clarence sent him a letter saying—" You appear to admire her over warmly, take my advice and marry her yourself." And the Duke of Cambridge did. The lady was Princess Augusta, daughter of the Landgrave Frederick of Hesse-Cassell, whom we have already met, as the mother of the second Duke of Cambridge.

Ultimately, acting on the recommendation of his mother, Queen Charlotte, the Duke of Clarence selected Princess Adelaide, daughter of the Duke of Saxe-Meiningen. It was a wise choice—for him. Adelaide was a very good woman, the best, as well as the last, of the Hanoverian Queens of England. She was twenty-six, just half the age of the Duke of Clarence, and, though she was no more favoured with good looks than her predecessors, she was exceedingly amiable and kind in disposition. She arrived in London, one July evening in 1818, accompanied by her widowed mother, and put up at Grillon's Hotel, Albemarle Street. No member of the very numerous Royal Family was there to welcome her. Later on the Duke of Clarence came with the Prince of Wales. It was still another instance of Royal bride and bridegroom meeting for the first time on the eve of their marriage. Without any preliminary courtship they were married in the Old Palace at Kew. The Prince of Wales gave the bride away.

The Duke dismissed Mrs. Jordan, making her an allowance, and settled down as quite an exemplary husband. Being also a good father he kept his illegitimate children the FitzClarences with him—Adelaide also was as devoted to them as if they were her own offspring—and had them well put out in the world. On his accession to the Throne he made them lords and ladies. The eldest son, George FitzClarence, was created Earl of Munster. Other sons were given high ranks in the Army and Navy. Three of the girls married into the peerage. Two daughters were born of his marriage with Princess Adelaide. One survived but a few hours, and the other only a few months. Thus the way was clear for William's niece, the Princess Victoria, to succeed him on the Throne.

*   *   *   *   *   *

Queen Victoria was greatly distressed by the revelations of *The Greville Memoirs* (1875.) She thought the tone in which the late Clerk of the Privy Council wrote of Royalty was most reprehensible, and asked Sir Arthur Helps (the succeeding Clerk) to tell Henry Reeve, the editor of the *Memoirs*, that the book degraded Royalty. "Not at all," said Reeve, "it elevates Royalty by the contrast it offers between the present state of things and the past."

CHAPTER IV

ROYAL WEDDING ROMANCES

THE comedy and tragedy associated with the adventures in love of the Royal Family came to an end, and romance, so long banished, returned when Victoria the girl Queen married her young lover, and cousin, Prince Albert, in 1840. It was the first marriage of a Sovereign of the Hanoverian Line which was not arranged solely in the interest of the State and regardless of the feelings of the parties concerned. Albert was Victoria's personal selection. She pleased herself, and, at the same time, undoubtedly did well for the State. The union was a supremely happy one. Albert proved a most devoted husband, and Victoria doted on him. They had nine children, well mixed, boys and girls. The Queen was intensely maternal. She used to say there was only one element of married happiness that was denied her—triplets, which she greatly desired as the triumph of maternity. She sent a letter of congratulation and three pounds to every mother who had three children at a birth. Her offspring filled half the Royal nurseries of Europe. At her death she had forty grandchildren and thirty-seven great grandchildren. It is highly probable that the last of European Kings will have in his veins the blood of Queen Victoria.

*   *   *   *   *   *

A Queen regnant has the privilege of proposing. One day Victoria told her aunt, the Duchess of Gloucester, that on the morrow she was to announce to the Privy Council her engagement to Prince Albert. " Won't you be very nervous ? " said the Duchess. " Yes," replied the Queen, " but I did a much more nervous thing a little while ago." " What was that ? " " I proposed to Prince Albert." Of course, the Prince could not himself propose to the Queen of England. As Victoria said on the same occasion, " He would never have presumed to take such a liberty."

When the arrangements for the marriage were being made, the Archbishop of Canterbury waited upon Victoria to inquire whether she desired any alteration to be made in the religious service relating to the promise of the wife to " obey " her husband, having regard to the fact that Prince Albert, on being naturalised, had taken the oath of allegiance to her as Queen, and was therefore her subject. " It is my wish," said Victoria, " to be married in all respects like any other woman, according to the usages of the Church of England. Though not as a Queen, I am as a woman ready to promise all things contained in the service." Again, after the marriage, the Queen—as we are told in the *Memoirs* of the Prince Consort—was advised that as Sovereign she must be head of the house and the family, as well as of the State, and that she must never forget that her husband was, after all, but one of her subjects. Victoria met these representations by saying, " She had solemnly engaged to ' obey ' as well as to ' love and honour,' and this sacred obligation she could consent neither to limit nor refine away."

Here, at last, was a pure love match in the Royal Family, a union inspired by genuine mutual affection. Nevertheless, while the bride and bridegroom were still children in their cradles, the one in England and the other in Germany, their respective parents, the Duke of Saxe-Coburg-Gotha, father of Albert, and the duke's sister, the Duchess of Kent, mother of Victoria, had conspired to bring the match about. The children, in fact, were educated for one another. Even in its immediate preliminary stages the marriage did not differ from most of the Royal alliances in the past in being the outcome of a family arrangement. The intermediary between Victoria and Albert was the uncle of both, King Leopold of Belgium, the widower of Princess Charlotte, daughter of George IV, who died so untimely. Towards the close of 1837, Leopold wrote to Victoria urging her to make up her mind and betroth herself to her cousin. Victoria, replying in January, 1838, said she thought they were both too young for wedlock. Moreover, she added, Albert did not know English sufficiently to be the consort of the English Queen. So Leopold wrote to Albert that he must wait for a few years more, and meanwhile continue his studies. The Prince's reply, young as he was, was more indicative of the cautious man of the world than the ardent lover. " I am ready," he wrote in German to his uncle,

" to submit to this delay if I have only some certainty to go upon. But if after waiting perhaps for three years I should find that the Queen no longer desired the marriage, it would place me in a ridiculous position, and would, to a certain extent, ruin all my prospects for the future."

Even in July, 1839, Victoria still declined to come to a decision. In October Albert visited England. He had the idea that Victoria wished him to consider the understanding at an end—it was no more than an understanding, there never having been any real engagement—and he wanted the matter decided once and for all. The couple met at Windsor. They had not seen one another for three years. And, lo, what a change! Here was Albert transformed from a raw youth into a tall, slim, handsome, and charming young man, with blue eyes, clear complexion, fine mouth, shapely chin, and a most ravishing moustache. What is more, he was not a bit like a German. He looked quite an Englishman. Victoria was smitten. She wrote to Uncle Leopold : " Albert's beauty is most striking, and he is most amiable and unaffected—in short, very fascinating." She declared her love to Albert on October 15th, 1839. That very day she sent an account of the interview to Uncle Leopold, giving expression to her raptures in italics. " My mind is quite made up—and I told Albert this morning of it ; the warm affection he showed me on learning this gave me great *pleasure*. He seems *perfection*. . . . I *love* him *more* than I can say, and I shall do everything in my power to render the sacrifice he has made (for a *sacrifice* in my opinion it is) as small as I can. . . . I *do* feel *very very* happy."

The public announcement of the engagement was made at a meeting of the Privy Council held at Buckingham Palace on November 23rd, 1839. There were eighty-two members present, a large and embarrassing company of men for a young and modest girl to face in such circumstances. She was naturally very agitated in reading the momentous declaration— " It is my intention to ally myself in marriage with Prince Albert of Saxe-Coburg-Gotha." " I felt my hand shake," she says in her *Journal*, " but I did not make one mistake. I felt most happy and thankful when it was over." She was in plain morning dress. On her wrist she wore a heavy gold bracelet

with a miniature of Prince Albert. " It seemed to give me
courage at the Council," she remarks. She wore it through her
comparatively short married life, and still more through her
long widowhood. It may be seen, conspicuously exhibited, in
many paintings or photographs of her.

The marriage took place on February 10th, 1840. Queen
Victoria was almost invariably fortunate in having fine weather
on her public appearances in State during her reign. So much
so, that " Queen's weather " passed into a proverb. But as she
drove from Buckingham Palace to the Chapel Royal, St.
James's, to be married, there was a storm of wind and the rain
fell in torrents. For once, the old saying, " Happy is the bride
that the sun shines on " was belied. However, as she drove
back with her husband to Buckingham Palace, after the ceremony, the weather had cleared up sufficiently to allow of the
carriage windows to be let down, and the crowds had the
pleasure of seeing her soft, chubby, rosy face smiling happily
beneath her veil of Honiton lace and wreath of orange blossoms.

*   *   *   *   *   *

The marriage was popular with all who were sentimental,
because of the youth and comeliness of bride and bridegroom
and their exalted rank. But the politically minded were swayed
by that British insular distrust of the foreigner which has
passed into a proverb. Nothing was known of Albert, save
that he was the younger son of a German duke, and that was
not a passport to the favour of either the aristocracy or the
common people. They could tolerate their Kings and Heirs
Apparent going to Germany for wives, though they did
not quite like it. Moreover, the sphere of a wife was the
nursery, or so it was then thought. But the circumstances
were wholly different when there was a reigning Queen with a
German husband. Was it likely that Albert would confine
himself to the domestic circle ? On the contrary, having regard
to the natural subjugation of the wife to the husband—as it was
then regarded—it was probable that he would endeavour,
through her, to exercise influence in State affairs.

This racial animosity found quick expression in an outcry
against the Government's proposal to vote an allowance of

£50,000 a year to Albert, which was the annuity granted to the Consorts of George II, George III, and William IV. For a young man who had no more than £2,400 a year of his own, and who had been brought up to consider such an income as sufficient for anyone of his rank, £50,000 was certainly a most extravagant annual allowance. And the £50,000 was to be all for himself, just pocket-money, as it were, because the Queen had £385,000 a year, and also several palaces maintained at the cost of the taxpayers. Joseph Hume, noted in his day as a rigid economist in national expenditure, thought £21,000 would be amply sufficient. He made the House of Commons laugh by seriously pointing out the moral danger of setting a young man free in London with so much money in his pocket. Ultimately, the House of Commons, by 262 votes to 158, reduced the proposed £50,000 to £30,000.

That was not the only cause of vexation to Victoria. She desired that her husband should have precedence over all her other subjects, at all times and in all places. Had she not given him her heart and hand ? Why, then, should he not be allowed to share with her, as far as possible, her regal state ? So it appeared to her. At least, she contended, she was entitled to have her husband next to her in precedence whenever she appeared in public as Queen. There was a clause to that effect in the Bill brought in by the Government for the naturalisation of Albert. The Lords rose in revolt against it. What, place this younger son of a German duke, who was not even Royal, before all the English nobility ! The obnoxious clause had to be withdrawn before the Bill was passed as an Act of Parliament.

The Queen, however, took the matter into her own hands. By the exercise of her prerogative she issued Royal Letters Patent providing that Prince Albert should be styled " His Royal Highness," and " have, hold and enjoy place, pre-eminence and precedence," next to herself. And going in State to the House of Lords to prorogue Parliament, the first time after her marriage, not only was she accompanied by Prince Albert, but she had a Chair of State placed by the Throne, at her right hand, for his accommodation—greatly to the mortification of the peers to which vocal expression was afterwards given by her uncle, the democratic Duke of Sussex.

There is a remarkable difference between the state, style and title of the wife of a King and the state, style and title of the husband of a Queen. Under the Constitution, a King's wife is crowned, bears the title of Queen, and is styled " Her Majesty." The husband of a reigning Queen has no special privileges or honours conferred on him by the Constitution. Why this distinction? It is conformably with the ancient maxim that a wife receives honour from her husband, but cannot confer honour upon him. The wife of a peer becomes a peeress, but the husband of a peeress, in her own right, does not become a peer. In the same manner, the wife of a King becomes a Queen, but the husband of a Queen does not become a King.

Besides Prince Albert, there have been only two Consorts of Queens of England. The first was Philip of Spain, husband of Mary, daughter of Henry VIII. Philip and Mary were styled " King and Queen of England," and the statutes passed by Parliament during the reign were enacted under their joint names—" Philip and Mary." Though designated " King Consort " Philip was never allowed more than a nominal authority, and this, coupled with his disappointment at having no child by Mary, induced him to quit England within a year. In the case of William III, Prince of Orange, husband of Mary II (elder daughter of James II), the Sovereignty was jointly vested in both by Act of Parliament, so that William and Mary reigned as King and Queen together. The remaining example of a Consort of a reigning Queen was George, Prince of Denmark, husband of Queen Anne. The only notable thing that history has to say of George is that he was the father of eighteen children by Anne, not one of whom lived to succeed her as Queen.

Queen Victoria, who always rated her husband as superior to herself in every respect but rank, was persistent in her endeavours to get her Ministers to give him the highest possible title and dignity, and have it established by Act of Parliament. At the close of 1841 her wish was that Albert should be entitled " King Consort." " He ought to be," she wrote in her private

Journal. " He is above me in everything really, and therefore I wish that he should be equal in rank to me." She seemed at this stage to have thought and desired that making Albert a King would create a joint sovereignty, like that of William and Mary. In this, of course, she was mistaken. Had her wish been granted she would still be sole Sovereign, and her husband, though a titular king (such as Philip of Spain was) would still be her subject. Sir Robert Peel, who was then Prime Minister, set his face against the project, knowing that it would arouse racial and national resentment, and it fell through. The Prince's idea of his own position is set out in a letter which he wrote to the Duke of Wellington. He held that as Consort of the Queen he was the natural head of her family, superintendent of her household, manager of her private affairs, sole confidential adviser in politics and only assistant in her communications with the Government. Summing it all up he describes himself " Private Secretary of the Sovereign and her permanent Minister."

Sixteen years later the Queen sent a most interesting memorandum to the Prime Minister, then Lord Derby (it is given in *Letters of Queen Victoria,* 1837-1861), proposing that the title of " Prince Consort " should be conferred on Albert by Act of Parliament. " The present position is this," she says, " that while every British subject, down to Knight, Bachelor, Doctor and Esquire, has a rank and position by *Law*, the Queen's husband alone has one by *favour*—and by his wife's favour, who may grant it or not ! " Having remarked that Albert's undefined position caused her humiliation when visiting Foreign Courts, she proceeds to disclose the pride and jealousy bred among reigning Royalties by questions of precedence— who shall go first to the dining-room, or last in a procession. " When the Queen has been abroad," she writes, " her husband's position has always been a subject of negotiation and vexation ; the position which has been accorded to him the Queen has always had to acknowledge as a grace and favour bestowed on her by the Sovereign whom she visited. While last year the Emperor of the French treated the Prince as a Royal personage, his uncle (the King of Belgians) declined to come to Paris avowedly because he would not give precedence to

the Prince; and on the Rhine in 1845 the King of Prussia
could not give the place to the Queen's husband which common civility required, because of the presence of an Archduke,
the third son of an uncle of the then reigning Emperor of
Austria, who would not give the *pas* and whom the King would
not offend. The only legal position in Europe, according to
international law, which the husband of the Queen of England
enjoys, is that of a younger brother of the Duke of Saxe-
Coburg, and this merely because the English law does not
know of him."

All this, the Queen continues, is derogatory to the dignity
of the Crown of England abroad. And at home injury was done
by the fact that the Queen's husband, having no other title
than that of Prince of Saxe-Coburg, was thus perpetually
represented to the country as a foreigner. " The Queen
and her foreign husband Prince Albert of Saxe-Coburg and
Gotha ! " she exclaims. " The Queen," she adds, "has a right
to claim that her husband should be an Englishman bearing an
English title, and enjoying a legal position which she has not
to defend with a wife's anxiety as a usurpation against her own
children, her subjects and Foreign Courts." Nothing was done
by the Government to give effect to the Queen's wishes, and
again taking the matter into her own hands she, by Royal
Letters Patent, dated June 25th, 1857, gave her husband the
style and title of " Prince Consort."

The one cloud on the life of Queen Victoria was the failure
of the Prince Consort to ingratiate himself with the English
people. He was persistently disparaged. Sometimes he was
even suspected of being a traitor. Just before the Crimean War
broke out, when the Russians were objects of popular hatred,
the Prince Consort was denounced by some newspapers as a
Russian agent. It was even rumoured that he had been caught
red-handed, and that he, and possibly the Queen as well, were
to be committed to the Tower. " People," the Prince wrote on
January 24th, 1854, " surrounded the Tower to see us brought
to it." The Queen wrote an indignant letter to Lord Aberdeen,
then Prime Minister, threatening abdication. She declared that
were it not for the Prince her health and strength would long
since have sunk under her multifarious duties as Queen and

mother of a large family. "Were the Queen to believe," she added, "that these unprincipled and immoral insinuations really were those of any, but a wicked and despicable few, she would leave a position which nothing but her domestic happiness could make her endure, and retire to private life—leaving the country to choose another ruler after their own heart's content." She was heart-broken when the Prince died in 1861. "It was the first grief he caused me," she used to say in later years. As she herself lay dying, her last words were a cry for "Albert, Albert, Albert."

*   *   *   *   *   *

More romantic still was the marriage of Albert Edward, Prince of Wales, afterwards King Edward VII. He was a student at Cambridge University and in his nineteenth year, when Queen Victoria, and the Prince Consort, and Lord Palmerston, the Prime Minister, were considering his future state. Kings and Queens and statesmen are naturally always anxious to have the Heir to the Throne married and settled as early as possible, in the interest of the continued succession. Besides, the father and mother of the young Prince were alert to the danger he ran from girl admirers. It was true that the Prince could not follow the example of King Cophetua and choose to marry a healthy, handsome, bare-foot beggar-maid. The Royal Marriage Act barred out any such alliance. But there was the possibility of unpleasant entanglements. A Prince has an irresistible fascination for the more sentimental and romantic sex, and remembering the amorous escapades of the brothers and sons of George III who, apart from the Prince Regent, were not remarkable for their good looks, it was thought well to protect this handsome young Prince from the host of feminine adorers who sent him love-notes in flowers, fluttered round him when they got the chance, liked to touch him, and pined for the privilege of holding his hand.

The Times was the first to call public attention to the question of the future King's marriage. It pointed out that the Prince's choice of a wife was "positively limited" to seven ladies of the Blood Royal who were Protestants—unless, the newspaper added, his Royal Highness selected a consort

143

much older than himself. The names of the ladies were given. Six were German Princesses. It is curious that it does not seem to have entered into the head of *The Times*—that great organ of English opinion, sentiment and prejudice—to suggest the abolition of the unnatural caste system by which eligible mates for Royalty were confined to a narrow circle, not particularly remarkable for beauty, health or intelligence, and to advocate an English wife for the Heir to the Throne of England. No, apparently the Blood Royal was, even in the opinion of *The Times*, too sacred to be diluted with even the blue blood of the English aristocracy. Or, what was more probable, it was feared that the choice of an English wife by the Prince would have had two unpleasant consequences—jealousy of the favoured family among the Nobility, and the risk to Royalty of having undesirable relations—not exactly skeletons at the banquet, but shadows in the background of social life.

In any case, Queen Victoria, a rigid upholder of all the traditions, superstitions and etiquette of the freemasonry of Royalty, would never have given her consent to the marriage of her son and heir to an English lady however high her rank, who was not of the Blood Royal, and there was no English lady so endowed. Accordingly, she and the Prince Consort followed the old-established regal practice of themselves selecting a wife for their son in the person of one of the eligible German Princesses. The lady was in *The Times* list, but the Prince himself, answering the dictates of his own heart, selected the one Princess on the list who was not German by nationality, " Princess Alexandra, daughter of Prince Christian of Denmark," as *The Times* described her. Through both her parents she was descended, on the one hand, from George II—a daughter of his having married a King of Denmark—and on the other from the Danish Kings.

The Prince had seen a photograph of Alexandra in the drawing-room of the Duchess of Cambridge, who was the great aunt of both of them, and was captivated by the girl's grace and loveliness. As the young people had never met, their parents arranged a meeting between them, as if by accident to see how they would take to one another. The Prince of Wales went to Prussia to attend the manœuvres of the Prussian

Army. He was the first Heir Apparent of the Hanoverian Line to leave England on a holiday, or for any other purpose. At the same time, Prince and Princess Christian set out from Denmark with their daughter to join a family party in Germany. They visited the ancient Cathedral of Speier, capital of the Rhemish Palatinate, to see its famous frescoes, and who, of all persons in the world, should they meet there but the Prince of Wales, who had also come to see the frescoes accompanied by his tutor and equerry ! The young couple were introduced, and we may be sure that the frescoes paled into insignificance beneath the light they saw in each other's eyes, which impelled them to draw close together to the obliviousness of everything else. Alexandra was then seventeen and Albert Edward nineteen.

Owing to the death of the Prince Consort in December, 1861—premature and wholly unexpected—the engagement was not announced until November, 1862, on the eve of the Prince's twenty-first birthday, when it was published in the *London Gazette*. Its effect on the country was to plunge it into one of those unrestrained revels of emotion which only the joys or sorrows of the Royal Family can evoke. The newspapers gave dazzling pen-pictures of the bride's beauty. Would she in person fulfil the general expectation ? On that Saturday, March 17, 1863, when she came to England to be married, she appeared transfigured with the light of her radiant girlhood. Her exquisite face, delicate and refined in its outlines, sweet and gracious in its expression, won all hearts. She was as beautiful as the Princess of a fairy tale.

The Princess crossed the Channel in the Royal yacht, which, with its escort of British men-of-war, anchored in the Thames opposite the pier at Gravesend. The Prince of Wales went on board, and meeting the Princess at the door of the cabin, took her by the hand and kissed her most affectionately to the great delight of the crowds assembled afloat and ashore. She landed at Gravesend pier, where she was received by sixty fair maids of Kent in white dresses, red cloaks and straw hats, garlanded with oak leaves and acorns, and they strewed her way with violets, primroses and sprigs of myrtle. In London the decorated streets were packed with dense masses who went into raptures over her. The City Corporation had voted £40,000 for the reception.

It was provided by the Marriage Treaty, entered into between Great Britain and Ireland and Denmark and signed at Copenhagen in January, 1863, that the marriage was to take place in England " according to the laws of England, and the rites and ceremonies of the Church of England." The Princess had been brought up a Lutheran Protestant, but in fulfilment of the Act of Settlement, she joined in Communion with the Church of England. The marriage took place three days after the coming of the Princess in St. George's Chapel, Windsor. The Prince, wearing the scarlet uniform of a British General, and the rich flowing purple mantle of a Knight of the Garter, was supported by his uncle, the Duke of Saxe-Coburg and Gotha, and his brother-in-law, the Crown Prince of Prussia. The Princess was in white satin and had a wreath of orange blossom covered by a veil of Honiton lace. Eight English bridesmaids, daughters of the leading noble families, carried her train. She was given away by her father. Nine hundred representative ladies and gentlemen witnessed the ceremony. Queen Victoria looked down on the scene from the Royal Closet. She was in deep black, even to her gloves, and a widow's cap, the only colour in her attire being the broad blue ribbon of the Order of the Garter and its glittering star, which she wore across her bodice. As the bridal party were leaving the Chapel, Beethoven's " Hallelujah Chorus " from the *Mount of Olives*, was sung.

It was the first marriage of the Hanoverian Line that gave universal satisfaction. On the proposal of Lord Palmerston, Parliament unanimously voted the Prince £40,000 a year out of the Consolidated Fund which, with the £60,000 he derived from the revenues of the Duchy of Cornwall, made his annual income £100,000. A separate annuity of £10,000 was voted to the Princess, with a jointure of £30,000 a year in case of widowhood. They also got Marlborough House—the private property of the Royal Family—as a town house, and, as a country seat, Sandringham in Norfolk, which the Prince Consort had bought for £220,000 saved out of the revenue of the Duchy of Cornwall during the minority of the Prince of Wales.

*　　*　　*　　*　　*　　*

Edward, Prince of Wales, attended the dinner of the Honourable Society of the Middle Temple one evening early in May, 1893. He was to have been accompanied by his son, the Duke of York, but the " Sailor Prince," as he was popularly called, did not come. " I have no doubt," said the Prince of Wales genially explaining the Duke's absence, " that it would have afforded my son the greatest pleasure to come among you ; but as it is only two days since he has become engaged to a very charming young lady I think you will understand he is most naturally spending the evening in her company. Thus was announced the engagement of—to describe the parties in the official language of the *London Gazette*—" His Royal Highness, George Frederick, Duke of York, Earl of Inverness, and Baron Killarney, to Her Serene Highness the Princess Victoria Mary of Teck." The company were carried to their feet by a simultaneous feeling of delight, and the old hall rang with the loud and prolonged cheers.

This Royal engagement made a particularly strong appeal both to the sentiment and the loyalty of the nation. The Duke of York had come into the direct line of succession to the Throne, owing to the death, the year before, of his elder brother, Prince Albert Victor, Duke of Clarence. The late Prince had been a captain in the Hussars—a tall and slim figure with a long handsome face strikingly resembling Charles I. In December, 1891, when he was twenty-seven, he proposed to Princess Mary of Teck and was accepted. The wedding was fixed for February 27th, 1892. On January 14th, 1892, the Prince died at Sandringham of pneumonia, following influenza after less than a week's illness. On his coffin, as it was lowered into the grave at St. George's Chapel, Windsor, was a bunch of white lilies, a pathetic tribute from Princess Mary.

The deepest sympathy was felt for Princess Mary. Born and brought up in England and going about with her mother —an intensely human and kindly Princess—the girl was noted for her winsomeness and was most popular. The country had rejoiced that its future King, instead of following the old custom of contracting an alliance by marriage with a foreign Court, was to wed an English Princess. And it was the tragic disappointment of this prospect, caused by the untimely death of the Duke of Clarence, which gave an added zest to the rejoicings at the news that Princess Mary's betrothal to the Duke of York would bring about its fulfilment after all.

Prince George and Princess Mary were cousins. Both were descended directly from George III, the Prince being the great, great grandson, and the Princess the great grand-daughter of that monarch. Princess Mary's mother, the Duchess of Teck, was the daughter of Prince Adolphus (youngest son of George III, and the first Duke of Cambridge) by Princess Augusta, daughter of the Landgrave Frederick of Hesse. The Duke of Teck, father of Princess Mary, was the son of a German morganatic marriage. His father, Duke Alexander of Wurtemburg, son of a Sovereign of that King-dom, married a Hungarian countess. As she was not of the Blood Royal, she did not take the rank of her husband, and the only son of the marriage was excluded from the succession to the Royal dignities and property of his father. The son was called after his mother, Count Hohenstein. He served in the Austrian Army, and because of his good looks was known in Vienna as " the handsome Uhlan." In 1873 the King of Wurtemburg conferred upon him the title of Prince Teck with the style of Serene Highness, and in 1871, five years after his marriage to Princess Mary Adelaide of Cambridge, he was created by the King of Wurtemburg, Duke of Teck.

The Duke of York and Princess Mary of Teck were married at the Chapel Royal, St. James's, July 6, 1893, by the Arch-bishop of Canterbury. Queen Victoria, who, it was announced, had gladly given her consent to the union, attended in State. The bridegroom wore the uniform of a captain of the Royal Navy. He was supported by his father, the Prince of Wales, and his uncle, the Duke of Edinburgh. Her father, the Duke of Teck, and her brother, Prince Adolphus (afterwards Marquis of Cambridge), were the bride's supporters. She was in silver white brocade, with clustered shamrocks, thistles, and roses, and her veil was of old Honiton point.

All the maids of the bride were Princesses of the Royal Family. At the end Mendelssohn's *Wedding March* was played. In London the marriage was marked by an extraordinary outburst of popular sympathy, enthusiasm, and loyalty. It was celebrated likewise in every town, village, and hamlet throughout the country.

Few things set the heart-strings of the nation more athrobbing to the tune of a sentimental song than a Royal wedding. Thousands of a particularly soft nature weep over it, but their tears are the exquisite tears of joy. It all shows the human appeal of a marriage in any circle. But a Royal marriage is a romance splendidly enacted on a golden stage, with panoply and pomp. It is regarded as an enactment in real life of the fairy tale that countless generations have heard, and that the world never grows tired of : " And so she married the Prince, and they lived happily ever after." They really do—sometimes, as this history shows.

It is said that sexual selection, sentiment, and romance only infrequently enter into the marriages of Kings and Queens. Even so, the matrimonial records of the English Throne contain love stories which are as ideal as any to be found among mediæval knights and ladies, and simple peasants. In Macaulay's *History* there is not much love-making, high or low. But when illness compelled the historian to put aside his great work unfinished, the very last sentences he wrote tell of the end of a Royal romance. William III was no more. " When his remains were laid out," Macaulay says, " it was found that he wore next to his skin a small piece of black silk riband. The lords in waiting ordered it to be taken off. It contained a gold ring and a lock of the hair of Mary."

END OF BOOK III

BOOK IV

THE REPUBLICAN MOVEMENT IN ENGLAND

CHAPTER I

ITS RISE

ONE night in 1872 the House of Commons lost its habitual self-control and became angry almost to the point of hysterics. Well it might. Because for the first time perhaps in its history the substitution of a Republic for the Monarchy was being advocated. Not infrequently one side of the House, or the other, is swept by passion on some party question. But that night in 1872, the Liberal Ministerialists and the Conservative Opposition were equally scandalised by this affront—as they regarded it—to what Shakespeare movingly designates, " The supreme seat, the Throne majestical, the sceptred Office," and unitedly they gave clamorous expression to their loyal indignation.

The working-man had not yet appeared in the House. Membership was still exclusively confined to the gentry, mine-owners, manufacturers, financiers, and barristers-at-law. The Commons might be divided on the public question of the hour, according to the orthodox principles of the two political parties which for generations had turn about in governing the country; but they moved together along the deep-trodden footmarks; they were as one in guarding the ancient traditions. Above all, the Throne was reverenced by them as the centre and symbol of the organic national life. Accordingly, the rise of republicanism was to them a most hateful pheno-menon—foreign and decidedly un-English. There were, how-ever, only two professed republicans among them, but they were particularly odious for the reason that one was a baronet, and the other a younger son of a notable aristocratic family—" Citizen Dilke " and " Citizen Herbert," as they were called at republican assemblies displaying red caps and singing the *Marseillaise* in Trafalgar Square or in Hyde Park, London, or at meetings of ardent-eyed artisans in republican clubs in provincial manufacturing towns.

A strange episode, indeed, was that republican outburst which startled the country in the 'seventies of the nineteenth century. It blazed up unexpectedly, attracting widespread notice throughout an astonished world; quickly burnt itself out, and left not even a smouldering spark behind. For some reason or other it has been ignored in history books. But anyone who turns to the files of the newspapers of the time cannot fail to be struck, first, by the prominence given to the movement in the current records of the day, and, next, by the complete oblivion into which it fell in the course of a few years.

*   *   *   *   *   *

All classes of the cummunity were more or less affected by the republican spirit, though the force of the movement, in its outward manifestation, at least, was supplied by the working-classes. Among the middle-classes hitherto all references to the Monarchy were in the nature of a combination of platitudes and beatitudes. When the anti-corn law agitation in the 'forties appeared to be threatening social order and political institutions, the Marquis of Lansdowne was sent by his Whig supporters to Manchester to counsel moderation. At his conference with the central committee of the Anti-Corn Law League, Lansdowne said it was apprehended in London that if the movement were pushed too far it might lose its moral weight through excesses, and, what was worse, assume a revolutionary form. " No fear of that, my lord," said Wilson, the president of the League, " here in England we are all loyal subjects." " More than that," broke in Richard Cobden with his ironic smile, " we are flunkeys from first to last."

The atmosphere of a republican movement was created later on by Thackeray who, in the 'fifties, went about the country delivering to crowded audiences his lectures on " The Four Georges," in which he held up the Hanoverian Sovereigns to ridicule and contempt. In his character sketch of George IV, as Prince of Wales, he says the biographers of His Royal Highness state that when he began housekeeping in Carlton House he had projects of having assemblies of literary characters and societies for the encouragement of geography, astronomy, and botany. Thackeray, the scoffer, then goes on:

Astronomy, geography, and botany! Fiddlesticks! French ballet-dancers, French cooks, horse-jockeys, buffoons, procurers, tailors, boxers, fencing-masters, china, jewel and gimcrack merchants—these were his real companions. At first he made a pretence of having Burke and Fox and Sheridan as his friends. But how could such men be serious before such an empty scapegrace as this lad? Fox might talk dice with him, and Sheridan wine, but what else had these men of genius in common with their tawdry young host of Carlton House? That fribble, the leader of such men as Fox and Burke! That man's opinions about the Constitution, the India Bill, justice to the Catholics— about any question graver than the button for a waistcoat or the sauce for a partridge—worth anything! The friendship between the Prince and the Whig chiefs was impossible. They were hypocrites in pretending to respect him, and if he broke the hollow compact between them, who shall blame him? His natural companions were dandies and parasites. He could talk to a tailor or a cook; but, as the equal of great statesmen, to set up a creature lazy, weak, indolent, besotted, of monstrous vanity and levity incurable —it is absurd!

The lectures were first given in the United States. When the reports reached this country, angry charges of disloyalty were levelled at Thackeray. But he was not out at all to upset the Constitution. The lectures were delivered in the way of his trade. He wanted to supplement his earnings as a writer, and the purpose was achieved, for he got £50 every time he spoke. Still, the lectures are salted with remarks which show that at heart Thackeray was a republican. He mentions that the French memoirs of the seventeenth century are full of such squabbles as who should carry Louis XIV's candle when he went to bed; what prince of the blood should hold the King's shirt when His Most Christian Majesty changed that garment. " The tradition is not yet extinct in Europe," he says, and proceeds:

Any of you who were present, as myriads were, at that splendid pageant, the opening of our Crystal Palace in

London, must have seen the two noble lords, great officers of the Household, with ancient pedigrees, with embroidered coats, and stars on their breasts and wands in their hands, walking backwards for near the space of a mile, while the Royal procession made its progress. Shall we wonder, shall we be angry, shall we laugh, at these old-world ceremonies? View them as you will according to your mood; and with scorn or with respect, or with anger and sorrow, as your temper leads you. Up goes Gessler's hat upon the pole. Salute that symbol of sovereignty with heartfelt awe, or with a sulky shrug of acquiescence, or with a grinning obeisance; or with a stout rebellious No; clap your own beaver down on your pate, and refuse to doff it to that spangled velvet and flaunting feathers. I make no comment upon the spectators' behaviour. All I say is that Gessler's cap is still up in the market-place of Europe, and not a few folks are still kneeling to it.

It was in answer to a challenge that he dare not repeat the lectures here that Thackeray decided to go on tour through Great Britain. " Is it," he asked, " disrespectful to a good Sovereign to speak the truth about a bad one? " At a public dinner given in his honour in Edinburgh he said: " The mere slaverer and flatterer is one who comes forward, as it were, with flash notes and pays with false coin his tribute to Cæsar." Subsequently the lectures were published in the *Cornhill Magazine*, of which Thackeray was then editor, and had a big circulation. Queen Victoria so bitterly resented the sneering, sarcastic tone of them that when Thackeray died she discountenanced, it is said, the proposal to pay him the honour of burial in Poets' Corner of Westminster Abbey.

The spread of republican sentiments among the working-classes of Great Britain arose out of the fermentation of ideas caused by the fall of the French Empire in 1870, following on the surrender of Napoleon III to the victorious Germans at Sedan, and the establishment by France of her third and final Republic. The working-classes had not previously shown in their manifestations of political and social unrest any desire to change the form of Government. The most levelling of all their movements, the one that caused the aristocratic and propertied classes the greatest apprehension, was the Chartist agitation from 1838 to 1848. Yet, though it frequently made a parade of physical force, it wanted nothing more extreme than universal suffrage, vote by ballot, the abolition of the property qualification for membership of the House of Commons—all of which have come to pass in the course of time without even an uneasy flutter in Society. To demand a Republic did not enter into the minds of those of its leaders who were most advanced in thought and boldest in action. In the 'sixties the political emotion of the working-classes found vent in a campaign for household suffrage. They pulled up the railings of Hyde Park in July, 1866, because the gates were closed to a great demonstration in support of Reform. The deed was looked upon as almost revolutionary. But it was very far off from an attempt to pull down the Throne.

*　　*　　*　　*　　*　　*

Sunday, September 19, 1870, should have a place among at least our minor historical dates, for it was on that day that the red cap of republicanism was first hoisted on poles to the singing of the *Marseillaise* in Trafalgar Square, and that from the broad base of the Nelson Column, flanked by Landseer's four gigantic bronze lions, speakers hailed the coming of the " Republic of England." Following on this demonstration, republican clubs were formed in London and here and there in the provinces.

There were two distinct elements in this working-class movement. One was anarchical. Its adherents, in their rage against the inequalities of Society, the disproportionate distribution of the good things of life, were vindictively destructive. Their model was the Commune of Paris. Far from being content with the crumbs which fell from the rich man's table, they wanted to kick the rich man out of his house and sit themselves down at the feast. As for what they would do with Monarchs, they were of the same mind as John Thelwall, the English political orator of the time of the French Revolution, who, as he blew off the head of a frothing pot of porter, used to exclaim, " This is the way I would serve all Kings."

Conspicuous in this element were Russians and Frenchmen from the East End of London. The other element was entirely English. There was no flavour of Socialism, much less of Communism, in their aims. They would abolish rank and privilege, but not private property. Their model for the British Republic was the Republic of the United States, where —as they put it—all men were equal, and position was the reward not of birth or blood, but solely of merit and service. All they wanted for themselves in the way of social better-ment was a little shortening of their long day of labour, and a little raising of their low rates of wages, and these they agitated for in their separate trades union movement. Be-tween these two sections of republicans there was opposition rather than co-operation.

The leader of the British element was Charles Bradlaugh, then notorious as a public preacher of atheism. He was a typical demagogue, herculean of frame, with large hands, short nose, long upper clean-shaven lip over a wide mouth which gave him an appropriate bull-dog look, and a voice that was loud and rather blatant. He had been a trooper in the Army before he became a solicitor's clerk. " The Icono-clast," he called himself, and he would destroy Christianity and the Monarchy ; but he was against the use of violence in doing so. " If we cannot win by reason I will not try to win by force," he declared, as president of the London Re-publican Club, founded in February, 1871, at a meeting at-tended by 15,000 men and women, and held at the Hall of Science—the temple of Secularism—in Old Street, St. Luke's. There never was a stouter opponent of Socialism, and defender of the rights of private property, than this atheist and re-publican. The weapons he used against the Church and the Throne were ridicule and contumely. He compared the Three Gods in One to a monkey with three tails. He wrote a pamphlet of 104 pages called *The Impeachment of the House of Brunswick*, which had a large circulation in America as well as in Great Britain. It aimed at doing for the working-classes what Thackeray's *Four Georges* had done for the middle-classes about twenty years earlier—presenting to them past generations of the Royal Family in a ridiculous light, but doing it in a coarser and more ribald way. Bradlaugh, like Thackeray, played up to the English hatred of the Germans. It was due somewhat to this racial animosity that the sympathy of this country was so largely on the side of France in the Franco-Prussian War of 1870. " I hate those small German breast-bestarred wanderers," says Bradlaugh in the *Impeachment*. " In their own land they vegetate and wither unnoticed ; here we pay them highly to marry and perpetuate a pauper prince-race. If they do nothing, they are good. If they do ill, loyalty gilds the vice till it looks like virtue."

Still, the mass of the workers were staunchly loyal, and the republican movement had but a fitful existence in the obscurity of the clubs, which met mainly in the bar-parlours of public-houses, until it was lifted into extraordinary newspaper prominence by the announcement that it had gained an ad-herent of good social position, some political standing, and considerable wealth. Sir Charles Dilke, M.P., proclaimed himself a republican at a public meeting held at Newcastle-on-Tyne, November 6th, 1871. Shortly before that he had in-herited from his father a baronetcy, and the proprietorship of *The Athenæum*, which for many years was the leading and most prosperous literary journal of the country. Chelsea had returned him to Parliament as a Radical in 1868. He was twenty-eight, tall, and athletic, with a bearded face in which it was not easy to detect the dreaminess it wears in Watt's contemporary portrait of him—now in the National Gallery (though the expression was open, manly, and smiling), when he set out on his great adventure to establish a Republic on the ruins of the Monarchy. The chair, at the Newcastle-on-Tyne meeting, was taken by Joseph Cowen (his father was Sir Joseph Cowen, a wealthy fire-brick manufacturer, and Radical member for Newcastle-on-Tyne), who was noted at the time for the countenance and aid which he gave to all republican unrest on the Continent. Dilke reckoned up the cost of the Monarchy in pounds, shillings, and pence, and declared it was not worth the money. He also indulged in sarcastic comments on the Royal Household—the kitchen scullions, the flunkeys, the lords-in-waiting, the lord grand falconer, the portrait painter, the lithographer-in-ordinary, and the numerous physicians, surgeons, and apothecaries, in ordinary and in extraordinary. All this gave great offence to the middle and upper classes. In their opinion it was a personal attack on Queen Victoria, of a particularly low and wicked kind coming as it did from a man whose father—so it was said at the time—got his baronetcy in reward for assiduous and obsequious attendance on the Prince Consort. What Dilke's father had done was to help the Prince Consort in the organisation of the Great World Exhibition of 1851—which His Royal Highness had fondly hoped would inaugurate the era of universal peace—and on that account Wentworth Dilke was undoubtedly a favourite at Court. "The Queen cannot forget," her Majesty wrote to him in 1862 when she made him a baronet, "for how many years you have been associated with her beloved husband in the promotion of objects which were dear to his heart." When Queen Victoria read Sir Charles Dilke's republican speech she recalled that she had stroked his hair on meeting him as a boy with his father in the Exhibition Grounds, Hyde Park. "I suppose," she added, "I stroked it the wrong way."

The Times denounced Dilke's speech in an article that was characteristic of its usually apt expression of the common-sense and reasonableness of the British people. It admitted that "meddlesome obstructiveness like that of George III, or a private life such as that of George IV" would not now be tolerated. "Englishmen," it went on to say, "know that Monarchy is an expensive institution, but they know also that a Republic, ostensibly cheaper, may really be dearer. Still more do they know that Revolution is the dearest alternative of all. They like economy in small things, but they do not count half-pence in great things." Chiding notice was also taken of Dilke's action by the Prime Minister at the Lord Mayor's Banquet on November 9th. "Our great ambition with respect to the Monarchy under which we were born," said Gladstone, "is that we may see its strength improved and not impaired, and that our lot may be amongst those labourers who deepen its foundations in the heart and understanding of the British Nation!"

But Dilke was not in the least intimidated. He went on

with his campaign, addressing crowded meetings in large industrial centres. His audiences were not all sympathisers with republicanism. On the contrary, it is probable that the snobbery of the average human being was the motive which induced many to go to hear him. The fascination of Royalty is in no small degree due to the privacy with which it has protectively surrounded itself. Accordingly, if anyone was expected to throw open the windows of Buckingham Palace or Windsor, and exhibit the Royal Family in the domestic circle to the public gaze, crowds would be certain to flock to see what was to be seen. Dilke also encountered opposition from what he called " organised Tory roughs." At Bolton there was a riot and a man was killed.

Among the letters of sympathy and support which Dilke received was one from a personage who then had a great local reputation in Birmingham, and afterwards became a renowned parliamentarian and statesman—Joseph Chamberlain. " The Republic must come," he wrote, " and at the rate at which we are moving it will come in our generation." At a public meeting held in Birmingham in the autumn of 1870, to rejoice that France had " established the Republic after a century of sacrifice for freedom," Chamberlain made a declaration of his republicanism. " I do not feel any great horror," he said, " at the idea of the possible establishment of a Republic in our own country. I am quite certain that sooner or later it will come." At this time he was in business as a screw manufacturer. About thirty-six years old, tall and slim, with a smooth waxy face and intensely black hair, he used to wear a soft, broad-brimmed hat, a single eye-glass, a velvet coat, a red tie, drawn through a gold ring, and—as if further to emphasise the outward seeming of his revolutionary tendencies—a red camellia in his button-hole. Thus arrayed, and with his air of conscious affectation, Chamberlain must have presented an appearance more in keeping with musical-comedy than with these little gatherings of artisans in the smoky back-parlours of public-houses, where he cultivated by the advocacy of radicalism and republicanism, that clear reasoning and icy intensity of expression which he was to employ long after in the House of Commons—in

161

defence of the Crown and Imperialism. In 1871 he was Mayor of Birmingham. He invited Dilke to address a public meeting in the town hall in December, and had the entire police force present, or in reserve, to deal with any opponents of republicanism—a precaution which events showed was wise, for several hundreds of objectors had to be singly ejected by the constables.

* * * * * *

Soon afterwards the republican movement received a staggering blow, a powerful set back, when it was announced in December, 1871, that the Prince of Wales was lying dangerously ill of typhoid fever at Sandringham. This was, perhaps, the kind of check which the republicans least expected. It so happened that the Royal Family was under a cloud of popular disfavour. Queen Victoria was still in the retirement in which she sought refuge with her grief on the death of Prince Consort. She had ceased to be a part of the public life of the nation. She was almost an unknown figure. It was whispered that she had become mentally incapable. That was a wholly unfounded suggestion. Even a quarter of a century later (as we now know from the revelations of her Ministers) she was as clear-brained and as strong-willed as ever, concerned for the welfare and eager for the good wishes of her people. Nor can the Prince of Wales be said to have been popular at the time. He had not yet developed the fine qualities which distinguished him in his middle age. He was regarded as a young man of pleasant manners, highly esteemed in his own narrow and exclusive set, but, from the public point of view, of no great parts, and promising, by reason of his convivial habits, to be but the making of a second George IV.

But now the life of the Prince was in danger, and at the thought there was a most remarkable outburst of sorrow and anxiety. It was national in the fullest extent. All classes shared in it, the lowest as well as the highest. Loyalty to the Throne was revivified. Was not the Throne, after all, the solid rock upon which the national existence was built ? And what a terrible thought, that the regular and ordered succession to its occupancy should now be threatened by death ! So the public argued, and helping to swell this tide of poignant feeling in a race which has glorified the home more than any other, was the pride in the domestic side of Royalty—the devotion of the Queen in her still more exalted role of wife and mother. The Prince, as we know, recovered. On February 27th, 1872, there was a thanksgiving service at St. Paul's. Both Houses of Parliament attended it. Queen Victoria and the Prince and Princess of Wales drove through the thronged and decorated streets amid demonstrations of unbounded affection and loyalty.

John Richard Green, the popular historian, writing in December, 1871, to a friend, sneered at the constant repetition in the newspapers of the statement that the Queen was an admirable mother, as was seen in her attentions to her son stricken with typhoid, and said it would not settle the question of republicanism. " One remembers," he added, " that all France went mad with anxiety when Louis the Well-Beloved fell sick in his early days, and yet, somehow or other, '89 came never the later." Green, in fact, was convinced that Victoria would be the last of the English Sovereigns. Dilke was of the same way of thinking, and he gave it public expression once more. Three weeks after the thanksgiving service he, greatly daring, re-opened the republican campaign in the House of Commons. On March 19th he moved for an inquiry into the Civil List, which was paid to Queen Victoria for the maintenance of the state and dignity of the Monarchy. This amounted to £385,000, of which £60,000 was for the Queen's own personal use, or Privy Purse, and the rest for the salaries and expenses of the Royal Household. Rising from the front Ministerial bench below the gangway, Dilke was received with a faint cheer from a few Radicals who sat near him, and with loud and prolonged groans from the Government and Opposition parties. The speech was long and dreary, full of lifeless figures. Dilke was always a well-informed but most ineffective speaker. He was incapable of illuminating his knowledge with imagination. He had no fervour or passion of delivery—no quality whatever to excite in his hearers that kind of support or antagonism which finds vent in outcries. He put as little heart into his opponents as into his friends.

After the first shouts of anger had died down, he unfolded his case to the listless Commons. His main argument was not so much that a Republic was a good thing, as that the Monarchy was a dear thing. " I have no hesitation in saying in this House as I have said out of it," he declared, " that I consider the republican form of Government a better and more reasonable form of Government than the Monarchy." For the rest, the speech, like the speech at Newcastle, dwelt on the cost of the Court to the Nation ; urged the necessity of a parliamentary inquiry on account of the popular belief that Queen Victoria had amassed an enormous private fortune for herself out of the Civil List—her savings were said to amount to £5,000,000—and the impossibility of ever ascertaining the Sovereign's financial position otherwise than by an inquiry because of the secrecy maintained in regard to Royal wills. Gladstone, the Prime Minister, rose at once to end the matter. In the course of a spirited reply he pointed out that the committee of the House which had, at the beginning of the reign, according to custom, made a careful investigation into the Civil List, fixed an annual sum for the Queen which showed a very large reduction on the sums granted in the two former reigns. He asked the House to reject the motion without further discussion, in order effectively to mark their condemnation of Dilke's speech and their loyal and grateful duty to the Sovereign. The appeal was loudly cheered. But it could not be acted upon. For Auberon Herbert, another professed republican—scion of the ancient house of Herbert and Howard, his father being the Earl of Carnarvon, and his mother a niece of the Duke of Norfolk—rose from beside Dilke to support the motion.

Herbert was the most notable of the intellectual republicans, because of the originality or eccentricity of his opinions. It was not on account of any evil in the English Monarchy peculiar to itself, and still less on account of its cost, that he wished to pull it down. He was an anarchist, and as such was opposed to all forms of government. " I do not think it possible," he said, " to find a perfect moral foundation for the authority of any Government, be it the Government of an Emperor or of a Republic." Government, in a word, was tyranny. It was a barrier to complete self-realisation. It compelled him to do many things he disliked, and to refrain from doing many things he had a mind to. He supported republicanism because it was at the moment the only public movement which, as he regarded it, was a declaration of the right one had to shape one's life uninfluenced by authority, rank, custom, or habit.

Herbert's social position gave an added piquancy to these unorthodox views. He was educated at Eton and Oxford, and was a Fellow of St. John's College, lecturing on history and jurisprudence, before he took to soldiering as an officer in the 7th Hussars. He first tried to get into Parliament as a Conservative, and failed. He was returned for Nottingham as a Radical at a by-election in 1870. It sometimes happens that a member of a noble and historic family makes a violent break with the traditions of his house in religion, politics, or social ideas, but it occurs so rarely that the fact that Herbert was of the aristocracy, and held views so antagonistic to the prepossessions of his class, made him the most outstanding figure of the movement. There was nothing of the fierce fervour of the reformer about him. But he had a quizzical expression of face, an ironic jauntiness of manner, and a railing voice, which made him far more provocative than Dilke, and aroused in his opponents the most violent resentment. Though he was a very sincere man, there was something about him which suggested that he was merely frivolous and mischievous in his unconventionality—an impression that was strengthened by the impish arrogance of his admission that he was willing to allow Queen Victoria a lease of the Crown for life. The House tried to overwhelm him in a storm of uproar. He sent Dilke out to fetch him a glass of water in sign of his determination to say what he proposed to say, whether he was heard or not.

An attempt was then made to " count him out," to deprive him of the quorum of forty members, without which no business can be done in the House of Commons. The Conservative Opposition, with the exception, says a contemporary report, " of a few of the more elderly who occupy the front benches," left the Chamber, and were followed by a considerable number of Liberals from the Government side. Three times, during Herbert's speech, the Speaker's attention was called to the absence of forty members, but the count on each occasion showed that a quorum was present. Many of the Radicals below the gangway, on the Ministerial side, stayed in their places so that a House might be kept, not that they agreed with Herbert, but that for the sake of freedom of opinion they thought he should be heard. The Conservatives then returned to the Chamber, more exasperated and noisier than ever, and mustered behind the Speaker's Chair. By calling attention to the fact that " strangers were present," they had the Reporters' Gallery cleared, as well as the other public galleries, thus preventing the publication of Herbert's remarks in the Press. When the division was taken, it was found that the motion had only two supporters, in addition to the tellers, Dilke and Herbert. The numbers were —ayes 2, noes 276. One of the two was George Anderson, a Scottish Radical, the other was Sir Wilfred Lawson, a Cumberland baronet. It was Lawson who, having a turn for humorous verse, composed the following epitaph in ridicule of the hereditary principle :

> " Stay, traveller, for there lies below
> The noble Duke of So and So,
> Obedient to the heavenly will,
> His son makes laws for England still."

This sudden emergence of republican sentiment genuinely perplexed and alarmed Queen Victoria. To her it was inexplicable and monstrous. She consulted Selborne, the Lord Chancellor, as to what it implied, and to her consternation she found that he took a most serious view of the situation. He was bold enough to tell her that if the new French Republic held its ground, it would influence British public opinion in a republican direction.

CHAPTER II

ITS FALL

Most of the intellectuals of the time were Radicals, with leanings towards republicanism. They included a group of able young men who afterwards rose to high distinction in public life and letters. One was Henry Fawcett, the blind Professor of Political Economy in the University of Cambridge. He was in Parliament at the time, but he gave no support to Dilke, as he thought the lofty moral issue of republicanism was degraded by being mixed up with a miserable haggle over the cost of the Royal Household. And, indeed, to the individual taxpayer the matter was only a farthing affair. Another was Frederic Harrison, afterwards head of the British Positivists. In 1872 he described the Sovereign as nothing more than " a hereditary grandmaster of the ceremonies "—a thing of no national utility, ministering only to the unamiable weaknesses of human nature, and he protested that the establishment of a Republic was as certain as the rising of to-morrow's sun. The most stern of them all in his republicanism was John Morley, then well known as the author of a fine study of Edmund Burke—his own guiding star of conduct, if not entirely of opinion, in politics. Morley was highly disdainful of what he called the demoralising habit of accommodation—the doctrine of practicability in politics —of the necessity of adapting theories to facts. If he could not transform the Monarchy into a Republic at a blow, or, rather, at a stroke of the pen, he, at least, would avoid any debasing compliance with Royalty and Courts.

These men, and others like them, gave some literary distinction to the movement by their writings and speeches. But the middle class generally met the attempt to permeate them with " the republican spirit " in a mood of exasperated disapprobation, and slammed their dining-room doors in the young men's faces. This the youthful apostles welcomed rather than deplored. As republicans they enjoyed the felicity of looking down disdainfully upon Kings; and a slight boycott by Society gave them, in addition, a delicious and not too painful sense of martyrdom. But whatever real force the movement possessed was imparted to it by the working-classes. Their interest in republicanism was revived and widened by the scene in the House of Commons. Bradlaugh was assisted in his propaganda by a man of considerably greater influence among the artisans—George Odger, a London shoemaker who was then the leading trade unionist. A man of short stature, but massive frame, all head and trunk, with a powerful voice, and a talent for public speaking, Odger brought about a federation of the trade unions and led them to take political action on the radical and republican side, as well as working for shorter hours and higher wages. Thus it was that in 1872 there arose a definite and organised agitation for the Republic. It had its organ, *Reynolds's News-paper*, a weekly with a big circulation. The movement had made so great an advance in the provinces that a conference was held in Sheffield one Sunday in December. Over seventy delegates, representing republican clubs, attended. A National Republican Brotherhood was formed. Its flag was unfurled—a tri-colour of green, white, and blue, with the white star of freedom on the blue ground. Green denoted fertility ; white, purity ; blue, the sky under which all men were equal, " so long," to quote the official description— " as they are guided by purity of action and thought." What an idealistic revolution ! The anarchist element had by this time entirely disappeared. Even the first President of the Republic was nominated. This was John Bright, the demo-cratic orator and tribune who, among politicians, had first place in the hearts of the populace. Bright undoubtedly was of republican sympathies. These are reflected particularly in his speeches in support of the North, during the American Civil War. The United States, he was fond of declaring, was the home of freedom, and a refuge for the oppressed of every race and every clime. Its greatness was largely due to the happy circumstance that it was a Republic, that it had neither Emperor nor King, nor Prince or Princess, nor a State Church, " which lends to the crimes of Monarchs and Statesmen the sanction of the simulated voice of God." Bright had effected a profound change in the ancient constitutional relations

168

between Parliament and the constituencies. By his exaltation
of the Platform he brought Parliament under the influence of
the pressure of outside opinion, with the result that the old
deference of the electorate to Parliament gave place to the new
deference of Parliament to the electorate. There Bright was
content to stop. He was but a theoretic revolutionary. Any
disturbance of the established order of things would be
destructive of his political ends, as one of the founders of the
Manchester school of commercialism—peace, plenty, and
profit.

Indeed, the most touching vindication of Queen Victoria's
seclusion was made by Bright at a meeting of trade union
delegates held in London in 1866 in support of the enfran-
chisement of the working classes. The chairman, Ayrton, a
London Radical M.P. of republican sympathies, condemned
the Queen's prolonged retirement from public life as an
injury to business. Bright immediately interposed. He said
he was not accustomed to stand up in defence of the wearers
of Crowns, but he felt bound to say that a great injustice had
been done to the Queen in her widowed and desolate position.
" A woman," he added, " be she Queen of a great realm,
or the widow of a labouring man, who can keep alive in her
heart a great sorrow for the lost object of her life and affection
is not at all likely to be wanting in great and generous sympathy." The Queen, he declared, was a good woman, doing
her best to keep Court life pure, and now that she was in
sorrow it was the duty of her subjects to comfort her rather
than condemn. All the delegates sprang to their feet, and,
after cheering loudly, sang " God Save the Queen." Next
day one of the private secretaries of the Prince of Wales
waited on Bright with the message that His Royal Highness
would be greatly pleased if he would call to see him at Marlborough House. Bright did call, and the Prince thanked him
for his kind references to his mother. At the parting the
Prince, as he shook hands with Bright, said, " May I have the
pleasure of counting you among my personal friends ? " It
was the beginning of an intimacy which lasted until Bright's
death.

The offer of the Presidency of the Republic was, as might

have been expected, declined by Bright. He humorously remarked that those who proposed to make him President could not be very desperate characters. Anyway, the time was not yet. " I would suggest that you and I," he said, " should leave any further decision to our posterity." He seemed to reject the position for the sensible reason that those who offered it to him had it not to give. Bright would have looked, at any rate, the President of the British Republic. His solid massiveness of figure, his uprightness of carriage, the determined curve of his mouth, the heavily moulded jaw, were all typically English, as was also the conservatism that was the foundation of his character.

* * * * * *

It may be asked, What were the authorities doing? In truth the republicans had no need to be apprehensive of a State prosecution. " Seditious intent," as laid down in numerous decisions of the High Courts, meant bringing into hatred or contempt the King or the Constitution, or inciting the King's subjects to attempt, otherwise than by legal means, an alteration of the form of Government as by law established. The trades-union republicans did not contemplate violence. They had no notion of going down into the streets, erecting barricades, and shedding their own blood, or anybody else's, for the realisation of their dream. They would not even throw a stone at the windows of Buckingham Palace. They were determined to keep well within the law. Recognising that public opinion was not ripe for so profound a constitutional change being suddenly affected, they, with that common sense which is so characteristically English, were content to postpone the setting up of the Republic until the death, or abdication, of Queen Victoria, and then to effect it only by Act of Parliament—if they could.

The position of the intellectual leaders was defined by Joseph Chamberlain at a dinner given by him in December, 1872, to his supporters in a contest for the municipal corporation, in the course of which the charge that he was a republican had been brought up against him. It was done in proposing the toast of " Her Majesty Queen Victoria." Chamberlain said he was one of those who held—and he thought there were very few intelligent and educated men who did not hold—that the best form of government was a Republic. Moreover, it was the form of government to which the Nations of Europe were surely and not very slowly tending. " At the same time," he said, " he was not at all prepared to enter into an agitation to upset the existing order of things in order to destroy the Monarchy and to change the name of the titular ruler of the country." He thought that was a matter of not the slightest importance. What was of real importance was that the republican spirit should spread among the people, and this spirit he defined as—" that merit should have its fair chance and not be handicapped in the race, and that all men should be equal before the law."

But the Prince of Wales had really no reason to fear any interference with his right to the succession. More remarkable even than the unexpected rise of republicanism was its sudden collapse. The last republican conference was held at Birmingham in May, 1873. Fifty-four accredited delegates from clubs in England and Scotland were said to have been present at the conference, and 5,000 people attended a public meeting held in the town hall. Chamberlain did not put in an appearance. The leading figures were Bradlaugh and Odger. John Bright declined an invitation to send a word of encouragement. He now emphatically declared that he had no sympathy with the movement. " It is easier," he wrote, " to uproot a Monarchy than to give a healthy growth to that which is put in its place, and I suspect the price we should have to pay for the change would be greater than the change would be worth." A Republic had just been proclaimed in Spain, and Bradlaugh was deputed to go to Madrid, the bearer of a message of sympathy from British republicans to Castelar, the republican orator, who had been elected President. The fearful confusion into which Spain was plunged, and the atrocities committed by both sides in the internecine struggle, gave point to Bright's words of warning, which was not lost on that quality of the British race—the recognition of hard facts. The movement which only the year before seemed to have had reality and some element of permanency, exciting the utmost astonishment in foreign lands, and some apprehension at home, passed out of sight and notice. Its last cry for the Republic was heard at Birmingham.

As is the nature of things, the decay of the republican movement was due in no small degree to the allurements of Royalty. *The Times*, in a leading article on the recovery of the Prince of Wales, suggested that His Royal Highness would rise from his sick bed as a new character, in, as it were, a new life. An undercurrent of mild and guarded reproof of the Prince is noticeable in the article. " The British public," it was said, " cannot be called unduly exigent in their loyalty, but they have an ideal, and, as becomes a practical people, they expect Royalty to be and do something." " Even a Prince has to make a career of his own," the article added. The Prince did appear in a new role, that of " Prince Charming " (as it was called) in which, with his geniality and good humour, supported by his beautiful Princess, he invested Royalty with a glamour that endeared it more than ever to the populace. As the Prince and Princess were travelling to Scotland their train stopped at Sheffield, and they were told that the redoubtable Anthony John Mundella, the Radical member for the borough—he who, opposing in the House of Commons annuities to the Royal Family, had sneeringly referred to "the pinchbeck and tinsel Monarchy "—was on the platform and was to address his constituents that evening. Mundella came to the carriage at the invitation of the Prince and, having first presented him to the Princess, addressing him as " my dear Mr. Mundella " in his most winning manner, asked him to tell the good people of Sheffield how sorry the Princess and he were that they were unable to break their journey for a few days' stay in the town, and that they always looked back with the greatest pleasure to the loyal and warm-hearted welcome they had received on their last visit to Sheffield. When the enchanted Mundella rose to address his constituents he astounded them by his opening sentence : " I have been commissioned by Their Royal Highnesses, the Prince and Princess of Wales, to communicate to you the following gracious message." The announcement put the meeting in the greatest good humour. They and Royalty were one for a little while, and " Rads " though they were, they were highly pleased with themselves. Royalty is regarded by the populace as a mysterious and veiled figure, whose secret they would like to penetrate and understand, and, when Royalty comes forth and shows a shining human face, they are hugely delighted.

Even Chamberlain fell under the spell of Royalty. As Mayor of Birmingham he received the Prince and Princess of Wales when they visited the town in 1874 to open the new municipal buildings. Great public interest was taken in the affair. The attention of the whole country was concentrated upon it. Would the Mayor flavour the proceedings with the rue and wormwood of republicanism ? In London political circles bets were taken that he would refuse to shake hands with the Prince. Chamberlain acted the courtier—not in the snobbish meaning of the word, but in its best sense of tact, consideration, and courtesy towards the Royal guests. He wore the red tie drawn through the gold ring, but not the velvet coat. Whatever apprehension the Prince may have felt as to the reception he would get, he must have assured himself that all was well when he first caught sight of the Mayor in tall hat and frock coat. For no man in these stiff ceremonious garments could contemplate mischief, even though he had in his button-hole what might have been regarded as a danger signal—the red camellia. On their part, the Prince and Princess delighted everybody. To what was the popularity of the Royal Family due ? Chamberlain, answering the question in his speech at the luncheon, was the democratic leader as well as the courtier. " It is based," he said, " quite as much on their hearty sympathy and frank appreciation of the wishes of the Nation, as on their high position and exalted rank ! " Never afterwards was republicanism heard from the lips of Joseph Chamberlain.

John Morley and Joseph Chamberlain were on terms of the closest friendship, warmed by perfect agreement on political questions, for Morley also wore a red tie drawn through a gold ring. Yet it cannot but have been Morley's opinion that his comrade-in-arms had fallen from grace. In that very year, 1874, Morley brought out his famous book

On Compromise, in which he raises his voice in austere repre-
hension of the sacrifice of principle to expediency. He insisted that if there were those who believed that in the stage
of civilisation to which England had reached in other matters,
" the Monarchy must be either obstructive and injurious, or
else merely decorative, and that a merely decorative Monarchy
tends in divers ways to engender habits of abasement, and to
nourish lower social ideals, to lessen a high civil self-respect in
the community," they should lose no opportunity of putting
these convictions to the proof. They were bound " to abstain
scrupulously from all kinds of actions and observance, public
or private, which tend ever so remotely to foster the ignoble
and degrading elements that exist in a Court and spread from
it outwards." Brave words these, but when he wrote them,
Morley could not have foreseen the days when he himself—
as well as Chamberlain, Dilke, and Fawcett—would, as a
Minister of the Government, kneel to Queen Victoria and kiss
her hand on receiving from her the seals of his office; and,
later, having been made a peer of the Realm, obey the Writ of
Summons of King Edward VII to take his place in the House
of Lords. The logic of events proved more powerful than the
logic of opinion.

* * * * * *

So the " slump " in republicanism continued. At the general
election of 1874, Dilke was returned again for Chelsea, but he
disclaimed being a republican candidate. He had already
declined to attend republican meetings or to subscribe to
republican funds. He seemed like a mischievous boy to have
let off a " squib " in the public street, and to have run away
frightened by the flash and the report and the scowls on the
faces of peaceable passers-by. Henry Fawcett lost his seat for
Brighton. It was brought up against him that he had founded
at Cambridge University a republican club which declared
itself hostile to the hereditary principle as exemplified in the
Monarchy and the peerage. He got back into the House of
Commons again as member for Hackney and was made
Postmaster-General by Gladstone. Auberon Herbert did not
stand for Parliament again. Joseph Cowen who succeeded his

father as member for Newcastle-on-Tyne became an ardent Imperialist. He supported in an eloquent speech, made additionally fervent by his Northumbrian burr, the Royal Titles Bill of 1876 embodying Disraeli's idea of making the King of England also Emperor of India.

Of all the defections, the most remarkable was Dilke's. In 1882 he publicly recanted his republicanism. Two years earlier he was made Under-Secretary for Foreign Affairs in Gladstone's Government. It was said at the time, in the political gossip of the newspapers, that his capacity entitled him to a higher post, and that he would have got it had not Queen Victoria objected to the appointment to office of Cabinet rank of a man who had avowed himself a republican. Later developments showed that this journalistic surmise was well-founded. Dilke, addressing a meeting of his constituents in 1882, said, " There were opinions of political infancy which, as one grows older, one might regard as unwise, or might prefer not to have uttered " ; and he went on to sweep them away with the admission that when he professed them he was " rather scatter-brained." The speech was naturally the subject of much comment, especially as soon afterwards the announcement was made that Dilke had been appointed President of the Local Government Board with a seat in the Cabinet.

In the official *Life of Dilke* the whole story is told. Gladstone advised Dilke to take some action that would tend to assuage the suspicion and distrust with which the Queen continued to regard him. For the sake of his future career—and Gladstone is said to have looked to him as his successor as Liberal leader —he should try to establish confidence and co-operation between himself and the Sovereign. Dilke then assured Gladstone that he would make a public statement on his change of mind in regard to republicanism. One gathers that Gladstone conveyed this intimation to the Queen, for in a letter written to Dilke he says Her Majesty " looked with some interest, or even keenness to the words of explanation as to the distant past," which, as Gladstone cautiously put it, Dilke had himself proposed " not in any way as a matter of bargain but as a free, tender." So, to appease the resentful Queen, Dilke appeared before his constituents in sackcloth and ashes !

Writing in his *Diary*, Dilke records his visit to Osborne for the meeting of the Privy Council at which he was to be sworn in and get his seals of office. He says : " I was rather amused by the punctiliousness with which, after I had kissed hands on being sworn a member of the Council, the Queen pointed out to the Clerk of the Council that it was necessary for me again immediately to go through precisely the same ceremony on appointment as President of the Local Government Board." " A curious point of strict etiquette," he calls it. Perhaps it was more than that. Perhaps the knowing Queen desired to make assurance of his loyalty doubly sure by the kissing of hands—the prescribed form of fealty—twice over.

John Morley's later attitude towards the republican ideal was in practice (as we have seen) that of compromise—a wholly unexpected position for a man who had so strenuously preached disregard for convention and authority in matters of principle. To have adhered rigidly to his original position would have meant his exclusion from public life. As things developed, he had what was a strange experience for a one-time republican. As we have already seen, during the visit of King George and Queen Mary to India for the Coronation Durbar in 1910-11, Morley as Secretary of State for India was one of three who were vested with Royal authority during the absence of their Majesties. But in his *Recollections* (published in 1919), Viscount Morley, as he then was, and retired from public life, testifies that his mind had not lost its force, nor his blood its fire, in relation to republicanism. He has first a passing reference to " that great idol of the world which has been glorified under the name of Republic," then, in a later passage, quoting the saying of Dr. Johnson : " I would not give half a guinea to live under one form of Government rather than another : it is of no moment to the happiness of the individual," he makes the comment, " The strange undying passion for the word Republic, and all the blood and tears that have been shed in adoration of that symbolic name, give the verdict of the world against him."

The only one of the republicans of '72 who remained staunch to his opinions was Auberon Herbert. He formulated a system called Voluntarism. It recognised the necessity of a slight

modicum of restraint by the policeman, just sufficient to protect the individual from force and fraud, and that while taxation was to be abolished each individual might voluntarily
contribute something towards defraying the expenses of the
policeman. Carlyle happily described it " Anarchy *plus* the
street constable." Not only was there to be no King, but there
was to be no Legislature to make law or Judicature to interpret
law. All caste was also to be abolished. Herbert carried his
levelling principles into practice, to the extent of shaking hands
with his servants and giving, once every summer, at " The Old
House " in the New Forest, a tea to all comers. On one
occasion they numbered thousands. Frederic Harrison, in
his *Last Words*—published in 1920, when he was 90 years
old—bears testimony to the value of a hereditary Monarchy,
which he qualified only by the fantastic suggestion that the
title " King " should be abolished and that of " Hereditary
Chief " adopted in its place. It is certain that the great memories which the British Monarchy calls up, those ancient
loyalties which unite the Empire and make its people one,
would soon be dissipated if " the King " were to disappear in
" the Hereditary Chief." As for Joseph Chamberlain, speaking
in the House of Commons in 1889, he declared, " We enjoy
the fullest measure of political liberty under a Constitution
which is more democratic than any Republic of Europe or of
the world." He was defending the provision the Government
were proposing to make for the children of the Prince of Wales.
He had already broken with his old Radical comrades, and
turning upon them now he charged them with aiming at
making the Monarchy unpopular, so as to prepare the way for
its destruction—a thing horribly wicked, frightful to contemplate. Outside Parliament not a word was heard of the
republican movement. The working-classes had come to the
conclusion that neither their economic interests nor their
political freedom were affected by the Monarchy. The great
protagonist of republicanism, Charles Bradlaugh, took
to advocating the lowering of the birth-rate by artificial
checks. When next his *Impeachment of the House of Brunswick*
was heard of, it was in a bitter speech by Lord Randolph
Churchill, opposing the admission of Bradlaugh to the House

of Commons in 1881, which he brought to a finish by throwing the pamphlet on the floor in condemnation of its impiety and sedition, and trampling it underfoot. " Thus perish all sedition-mongers and traitors," cried the noble lord. And the Commons expressed their loyalty in rounds of tremendous cheering.

*   *   *   *   *   *

Since then the working-classes have shown that they are indifferent to republicanism. They are wholly concerned with social and industrial reform. They look to the United States and France, the two triumphant Republics of the World, and they see that instead of republican institutions offering greater protection from economic oppression, or even from political wrong, they enjoy under a Monarchy considerably more political freedom and industrial justice, and also, it may be added, better opportunities for the realisation of every human aspiration and ambition. There was not the slightest clash between Labour and the Monarchy when Labour was in power in 1924. King George acted with the same absolute Constitutional impartiality towards Labour—so its Prime Minister testified—as he had acted towards Liberals and Conservatives. On the defeat of the Conservatives at the general election the King sent for Ramsay MacDonald, the Leader of the Opposition in the House of Commons, and appointing him Prime Minister, entrusted him with the duty of forming a Government. The Labour Ministers, on their part, acted precisely as Liberal and Conservative Ministers had done in like circumstances. They waited on the King and " kissed hands " on receiving the seals of their offices. They even appointed to the political office of the Household which, being held by members of the Administration, change with each change of Government. They attended Courts and Levees and appeared at those functions in all the glory of blue coats richly laced with gold, and having lots of buttons down the front, knee breeches, silk stockings, cocked hat and sword. The King, as is customary, commanded the Prime Minister and his daughter, Miss Ishbel MacDonald, " to dine and sleep " for a week-end at Windsor, and the command, we may be sure, was loyally and gladly accepted.

The Labour Party is committed to Socialism, but it is not committed to republicanism. It happened that at the annual conference of the Labour Party held in the preceding year, 1923, a resolution was moved : " That the Royal Family is no longer necessary as part of the British Constitution." It was opposed by the Executive. There are, of course, many republicans in the Party. It was stated that opinion also in the Executive was divided on the question. But it was not regarded as practical politics. The issue was put as plainly as it could well be—" Is Republicanism the policy of the Labour Party ? " and by 3,694,000 to 386,000 the Party declared that it was not. The Monarchy has proved itself essential to the British political system so far, and there is no reason to suppose that it would be out of place even under Socialism. Indeed, it might be that Socialism would but open for the Monarchy new horizons of service.

END OF BOOK IV

BOOK V

THE SOVEREIGN AND PARLIAMENT

CHAPTER I

THE KING ON HIS THRONE

WHERE is the Throne of England?—or of Great Britain, if that term be preferred. We have already had a good deal about the Throne in the historical sense, or as the symbol of the Monarchy. But is there a material Throne on which the King sits with all the attributes of sovereignty to transact regal business? Apart from the Chair of State used at the Coronation in Westminster Abbey, in which—as we have seen—the King is enthroned after he has been anointed and crowned in Edward's Chair, there are, in fact, several Thrones. There is one in Buckingham Palace, the town house of the King. There is another in St. James's, which is still officially the habitat of the British Court—known as the Court of St. James. That Throne is the oldest of all. Its canopy of crimson velvet is embroidered with crowns set with fine pearls. In Windsor Castle, there is also a Throne—a strange but very modern structure composed entirely of carved ivory inlaid with precious stones, mostly emeralds. It was presented to Queen Victoria by the Maharajah of Travancore, and is characteristically Indian. No doubt any seat in which the King sits in his regal capacity for the transaction of business of State may be called a Throne. But the Throne that is best entitled to claim the exclusive style of " The Throne of England "—or of Great Britain—is surely the Throne in the House of Lords which the King occupies when he opens Parliament and reads to the Lords and Commons the " Speech from the Throne " announcing the Government's programme of legislation.

The Throne in the House of Lords looks—as a Throne should look—magnificent and imposing under its great gilt canopy at the upper end of the Chamber. The first Sovereign to use it was Queen Victoria in 1847—the year the Chamber was first occupied by the Lords in place of the temporary meeting-place provided for them after the burning of the Houses of Parliament in 1834. All through the reign of Victoria only one Chair of State stood on the canopied platform of the Throne. A second Chair was added by King

Edward VII, on his accession, for Queen Alexandra. This second Chair is an exact replica of the old, save in one significant particular—it is an inch and a half lower. Both Chairs, the King's to the right and the Queen's to the left—looking down the Chamber—are superbly carved, gilt with English gold leaf, and studded with egg-shaped crystals, and their crimson velvet backs are embroidered with the Royal Arms. By the side of the Throne to the right is a small Chair for the use of the Prince of Wales at the opening of Parliament. It was on February 14th, 1901, when King Edward opened his first Parliament, that for the first time in history a Queen Consort accompanied the King in equal State for the ceremony. Even in the reign of William and Mary who were joint holders of the Sovereignty, William sat alone on the Throne in the House of Lords. Each of the Queen Consorts, of the second and third Georges and William IV, always preceded her Lord and King to Westminster, and sat in a low chair at the foot of the Throne. Queen Mary, like her predecessor, Queen Alexandra, sits by the side of her Lord and King, but an inch and a half lower, just to indicate that she is a Queen Consort and not a Queen Regnant. It is a sight I have frequently seen in the reigns of Edward and George.

*　　*　　*　　*　　*　　*

The opening of Parliament by the King gives the most impressive expression to the exalted position of the Monarchy in the Government of the land. It is also one of the few splendid ceremonies associated with the Monarchy which still survive to remind us of the perfection to which the Middle Ages brought the art of investing State occasions with stately pageantry and a certain humane and refining grace. The King and Queen ride from Buckingham Palace to Westminster in the old painted State Coach drawn by eight bay ponies. They are attended by the lords and ladies of the Royal Household. They are escorted by Life Guards, in shining breastplates with tossing plumes and drawn swords and magnificently mounted on prancing horses. They are surrounded by the King's bodyguard of the Yeoman of the Guard, on foot—the old bearded soldiers of long service, popularly known as " Beefeaters," in

Tudor uniforms and muslin ruffs, and carrying halberds. The route is lined by the Foot Guards, in scarlet and big bearskins ; and their bands of music, placed at intervals, entertain the waiting crowds with national airs.

The lofty Chamber of the Lords richly decorated in gold and blue, red and silver, is filled by a brilliant assembly of both sexes. In the centre are the peers in their scarlet robes trimmed in ermine, or white fur, and displaying the collars and stars of various Orders of Knighthood. On the back benches are the peeresses, dainty and exquisite, attired in dresses of delicate hues and glittering with jewels. The Judges of the High Court form a group near the Throne—the Lords Justices in black and gold, the Judges of Assize in red. To the right of the Throne, in an enclosure by themselves, are the Ambassadors and Ministers of foreign Powers and countries, wearing uniforms which, like the peoples they represent, are marked by the widest divergencies in style and colour. Immediately below the enclosure are the Bishops' Benches, where the spiritual peers are distinguished by their State robes of crimson and long ermine hoods. The assembly and its setting form a spectacle which leaves an ineffaceable impression of historic significance and dignity.

Yet the central figures in the pageant, the King and Queen, are yet to come. The time appointed is at hand. So still is the assembly in its expectancy that in the deep silence can be heard the muffled thunder of the salute of forty-one guns fired in Hyde Park by a battery of the Royal Horse Artillery, announcing the arrival of Their Majesties at the Houses of Parliament, which has been signalled from the lofty Victoria Tower. A few minutes later, the doors to the right of the Throne—on the left of the spectator who is facing the Throne—are flung open.

Across the large ante-room outside, known as the Prince's Chamber, is seen an extended line of tall soldierly figures in scarlet and gold uniforms, plumed helmets and long white gauntlets. They are another of the King's Bodyguards—The Honourable Corps of Gentlemen at Arms, composed of old Army Officers, as the Yeoman of the Guard are composed of men of the rank and file. In another moment the head of the Royal procession appears at the door. Immediately the clusters of electric lights in the groined and painted ceiling are turned on, flooding the Chamber with a brilliant white radiance, and peers and peeresses stand up with a simultaneous movement—the ladies dropping their wraps, baring their white shoulders and arms, while diamonds and pearls sparkle and glow from brow and throat and bodice.

At the head of the procession are pursuivants and heralds, whose old-world titles, such as, for the pursuivants, Rouge Croix, Blue Mantle, Rouge Dragon, Portcullis, and for the heralds, Chester, Windsor, Richmond, Somerset, York, Lancaster, and whose quaint tabards of silk are woven, back and front, with the Royal Arms, in gold and crimson, recall the romantic age of chivalry, its jousts and tournaments, and sounding trumpets. They stand before the Throne, two by two, and bow low to it, before passing on and ranging up in the open space on the left. They are followed by equerries-in-waiting, gentlemen-ushers, and grooms-in-waiting, all in Court costumes, and by the chief permanent officials of the Royal Household in a variety of uniforms—Private Secretary to the King, Keeper of the Privy Purse, Silver Stick in Waiting, Gold Stick in Waiting, and the Queen's personal attendants, Women of the Bedchamber, Lady in Waiting, Mistress of the Robes. They also pass the Throne with many a bow and group themselves on the left. Pursuivants, heralds, officers of the Royal Household—they all contribute to the pageant memories half forgotten, but still romantically potent.

Great Officers of the State come next—members of the Government who are peers. There is the Lord Chancellor, wearing the scarlet and ermine robes of his peerage and his big grey wig, and carrying in his hand a richly embroidered satchel containing the Great Seal. In this part of the procession are three noblemen carrying ancient symbols of regal authority and power. They are preceded by Garter King of Arms—the principal of Herald's College—who seems in his embroidered tabard of velvet and cloth of gold to be enveloped in a rich vivid pattern of the Royal Standard. The first symbol is the Sword of State, a long heavy weapon in a scabbard of crimson velvet encircled with gilt metal rings. The peer carrying it holds it aloft before him, its pommel grasped by his two hands,

as he walks in his heavy robes with slow and measured tread.
The next is the Imperial Crown. It is carried on a cushion of
crimson velvet supported by a chord round the neck of another
peer. Its circles and arches of gold are encrusted with diamonds
and pearls and are surmounted by a golden globe and cross. A
thing alive it seems, so many are its sparkling points of light.
The third symbol is the Cap of Maintenance—a quaint, low-
crowned head-dress of crimson velvet, with a high peak in front
and its turned-up brim lined with white ermine—which is
carried by a third peer on the top of a short white staff.

*   *   *   *   *   *

Then enter the King and Queen, walking side by side and
hand in hand—the right hand of the Queen being held in the
left hand of the King. The long trains of their State robes are
held up by dapper young Pages of Honour in scarlet doublets
and white knee-breeches, under the direction of the Groom of
the Robes. The Robe of the King is a wide flowing garment
of silk-velvet of a deep crimson colour, edged with gold lace
and ermine, and hanging behind is a long deep mantle of
ermine, the snowy whiteness of which is flecked with innumerable tiny spots of black fur. His Majesty is crowned.
King Edward VII did not follow his predecessor's practice of
wearing the Crown at the opening of Parliament—the last
King to do so being William IV—but George V, in his later
years, wore his Crown when he opened Parliament. The robe
of the Queen is also of deep crimson silk-velvet edged with
ermine, but it is not so ample and flowing as that of the King ;
nor is its train so long, nor its ermine cape, spotted with black
fur, so deep. Over her hair Her Majesty wears a miniature
crown of diamonds. Standing before the Throne, the King and
Queen bow to it together, and still hand in hand, ascend the
three steps to the platform. The King stands while the Queen
takes her seat and gentlemen-in-waiting bring her a footstool,
and adjust her robe over the back of the chair. Before she
parts with the hand of the King she stoops and kisses it. His
Majesty then sits down to the right of the Queen, and throwing back his robe discloses the blue and gold-braided uniform
of an Admiral of the Fleet (King Edward used to wear a Field

Marshal's uniform) its breast a blaze of jewelled insignia of many Orders. Beneath the robe of the Queen, and across her left shoulder is seen the broad blue sash of the Order of the Garter, around her throat glows a necklace of pearls, and conspicuous for its lustre among the jewels on her breast is that rarest and most precious of diamonds—the Koh-i-Noor.

" Pray be seated," the King says, and the peers and peeresses sit down. But the picture, crowded though it be, is not yet complete. The Commons are still to come. Through the Lord Great Chamberlain the King's Command is conveyed to " Black Rod "—the messenger of the Lords—to summon the Commons to " attend His Majesty immediately in the House of Peers." Having made a low bow at the foot of the Throne, " Black Rod," holding up his ebony staff, ringed in gold, makes his way through the mass of ermine and scarlet on the floor, and crosses the corridors to the House of Commons, where he has to knock three times on the closed doors before he is admitted to deliver his message. In a few minutes he returns with the Speaker and the Commons. The Speaker wears his State robes of black satin damask trimmed with gold, over his Court suit of black velvet. He is attended by the Sergeant-at-Arms and Chaplain, accompanied by the Prime Minister and the Leader of the Opposition, and followed by a crowd of members of all parties. The place of the Commons is the Bar, a sort of pen enclosed by carved oak barriers, at the end of the Chamber, directly facing the Throne. The Speaker reverently bows to Their Majesties three times. And now are gathered before the King the three Estates of the Realm—the Lords spiritual, the Lords temporal and the Commons. There is a movement among the brilliant and illustrious group which surround the Throne. The Lord Chancellor emerges to the right of the Throne, close to the King, and kneeling with his right knee on the higher step of the platform, hands a printed paper to His Majesty. It is the Speech from the Throne. His Majesty rises and reads the speech to the standing assembly. The King in all his regal state is revealed to the representatives of his people.

*　　*　　*　　*　　*　　*

It is one of the oldest, as well as one of the most national of our State spectacles. In all essentials it is the same as was witnessed at the opening of Parliament four or five centuries ago. The statesmen of the past are but shadows, and Time has disentangled and put aside all the questions that perplexed them. The Constitution has been almost entirely transformed. But this splendid assembly of the Sovereign and the three Estates of the Realm, Lords spiritual and temporal and Commons, has remained stable through all the changeful history of the Nation, and is still, as much as ever, an organic part of our system of Parliamentary Government.

CHAPTER II

GIVING THE ROYAL ASSENT TO ACTS

THE Sovereign is the beginning and end of Parliament. He summons it, he prorogues it at the close of a Session; he dissolves it. It cannot meet until he has issued a Proclamation. "We do, by and with the advice of Our Privy Council, hereby proclaim and give notice of Our Royal intention and pleasure that Our said Parliament shall assemble and be holden for the despatch of divers urgent and important affairs." The Sovereign is constitutionally bound to summon Parliament on the advice of his Ministers. The phrase in the Royal Proclamation, "by and with the advice of our Privy Council" will have been noticed. The Privy Council in this connection is His Majesty's Ministers. But should he refuse to act on their advice there is no statute or precedent by which Parliament could legally convene itself.

The only contingency which enables Parliament to come together without the summons of the King is the death of the King. Parliament meets forthwith on the demise of the Crown, but solely for the purpose of swearing allegiance to the new Sovereign. Parliament is all powerful once it has met on the summons of the King. But it can only meet on the King's summons. It is also by the exercise of the Royal Prerogative that Parliament is dissolved. The Proclamation is issued by the King, in like manner "by and with the advice of Our Privy Council." The dissolution of Parliament may technically come about without the exercise of the Royal Prerogative—that is by the expiration of the five years to which the maximum duration of a Parliament is limited by the Parliament Act, passed in 1911 by the Liberal Government. The term was previously seven years. But no Parliament has hitherto been allowed to continue for its full term, save during the Great War, when the Parliament then in existence prolonged its life by statute until peace was declared, and that Parliament also, like all its predecessors, was finally dissolved by Royal Proclamation.

*　　*　　*　　*　　*　　*

One curious disability the King labours under in regard to Parliament. He may not attend a sitting of the House of

Commons. Parliament is summoned by him that the representatives of the people may advise him in the government of the country. The advice is tendered in the form of Bills which, having passed both Houses, are submitted to him for approval, or the Royal Assent, as it is called. But it would be unconstitutional for the King to go down to Westminster to hear the arguments advanced by the Commons for or against any particular Bill. Queen Victoria never saw the Commons at work during her long reign of sixty-three years.

The presence of the Sovereign would, it is supposed, so over-awe members as to make them afraid to give full expression to their opinions. For much the same reason, it is out of order to mention the King's name in debate, with the object of influencing the decision of the House—such as saying that His Majesty was known to look with favour or disfavour on the Bill or motion under discussion. These objections were probably valid in years long gone by, but they hardly count to-day. And yet they remain. It has almost become a settled principle that the only occasion on which the King may appear in Parliament is at the State opening of a new Session. The Sovereign may, if he pleased, also attend in person at the end of the Session to give the Royal Assent to Bills and to prorogue Parliament, but so long a time has elapsed since any Sovereign made such an appearance that the custom is now regarded practically as a thing of the past.

Nevertheless, according to the theory of the Constitution, it is from the King all legislation proceeds. Every statute opens with what is called " the enacting clause," as follows :

Be it enacted by the King's most excellent Majesty, by and with the advice and consent of the Lords spiritual and temporal, and the Commons in the present Parliament assembled, and by the authority of the same.

It would seem as if the three Estates of the Realm in Parliament, the Lords spiritual and temporal, and the Commons, simply agreed to or authorised the legislation initiated by the King. That was the position long ago in the days of arbitrary Kingship when petitions were presented to the King praying that he might be graciously pleased to pass this law or that, and he granted or refused the prayer as his will or pleasure dictated. But it has not been so for many centuries. In the course of the Session the King has submitted to him dozens of Bills, which have passed both Houses. Some of them he may not have even heard of, not to speak of knowing their contents. His Prerogative in regard to legislation is constitutionally limited to the expression of his assent to it.

During the excitement aroused by the Home Rule Bill of the Liberal Government in 1913 and 1914, the right of the King to refuse the Royal Assent was raised by a section of the Unionists. In some of the principal streets of London and large provincial towns might be seen placards in shop-windows inviting passers-by to step in and sign a petition to the King, praying His Majesty to insist upon the Bill being submitted to the judgment of the country before he assented to it. The view that the King had the power which he was thus to be asked to exercise was backed by the authority of the leader of the Ulster Unionists, a gentleman highly learned in the law. " The King," he said, " has a right to be assured by constitutional means before he signs the Home Rule Bill that he has behind him the great body of his subjects." Perhaps Sir Edward Carson was bemused in giving this opinion by his political principles. For it is utterly unconstitutional.

No King has ever suggested, much less insisted, that a Bill submitted to him for his assent should be put to the test of a general election. It has been enough for any King that it is a Government measure which has the approval of his Ministers, who are supported by a majority of the House of Commons, and that it is a measure also which has passed through Parliament. For a King to withhold his assent to a Bill—passed according to the law of the land—would be a revolutionary act, even though he personally thought it a bad Bill. The Monarchy can be worked upon no principle but this—that the King's actions are the actions of his Ministers and not his own, and, therefore, that for them he has no responsibility.

* * * * * *

The Royal Assent is necessary to give a Bill the sanction of law. It is the final stage in the long process of legislation, the crowning touch which imparts authority and power to the provisions which statesmanship has embodied in the Bill. But Bills are not now laid before the Sovereign that he may dispose of them as he thinks fit, rejecting some and approving others, according to his prejudices and predilections, or even according to his unbiased and sagacious judgment of what is good or bad for the nation. He is bound by the spirit of the Constitution, if not by its theory, to be guided entirely by the advice of his Ministers. Even so long ago as the days of George III—a King who endeavoured to rule as well as to reign—the giving of the Royal Assent to Bills that had passed through Parliament was regarded simply as a matter of form. There is an amusing story by Lord Eldon, the Lord Chancellor—a Tory with sympathy for the doctrine that Kings ruled by divine right— of what happened when he went out to Kew to obtain the assent of George III to a number of Bills. He was reading the titles of the Bills from a sheet of note-paper, and explaining their provisions briefly in his own words, when the King interrupted him with the exclamation :

"You are not acting correctly. You should do one of two things—either bring me down the Bills for my own perusal, or say, as Thurlow once said to me on a like occasion. Having read several of the Bills, Thurlow stopped and said to me : 'It is all damned nonsense trying to make you understand them, and you had better consent to them at once.'"

Thurlow was an earlier Lord Chancellor who had gained the esteem and confidence of George III for his devotion to his interests. Yet even he contended in 1788, during one of the King's attacks of insanity, that the King's personal assent was of such little account that he could himself, if necessary, put the Great Seal to a Royal Commission empowering him to give the Royal Assent to Bills which had passed through both Houses. This was, in fact, done in 1811, when George III again became incapable of expressing any rational intention. A Commission was sealed for the purpose of giving the Royal Assent to the Regency Act, the object of which was to enable the Prince of Wales to exercise all the duties of sovereignty during the illness of the King.

What actually happens now is that the titles of Acts, which have passed through Parliament and await the Royal Assent, are first submitted to the King by the Clerk of the Crown, and then Letters Patent, signed by His Majesty, are issued under the Great Seal, appointing a Royal Commission, consisting of three or more Peers, publicly to signify to both Houses of Parliament, on behalf of the King, the giving of the Royal Assent to such Acts the titles of which are set out in this document or instrument. The ceremony—a very curious one—takes place in the House of Lords. The Lords of the Commission are seated, in scarlet robes and cocked hats, all in a row, on a bench beneath the imposing Throne. The centre figure is the Lord Chancellor. In front of them is the scarlet Woolsack—like a comfortable lounge—on which rests the glittering Mace and the richly-embroidered purse or sachet of the Lord Chancellor, which is supposed to hold the Great Seal. At a nod from the Lord Chancellor, "Black Rod," goes out to summon the Commons, as both Houses must be present at the ceremony. The Lords Commissioners keep their seats when the Speaker and the Commons appear at the Bar, but raise their hats in acknowledgment of the profound bow which the Speaker makes to them as the representatives of the King.

Then the Reading Clerk at the table reads the terms of the Royal Commission. The document is engrossed on parchment, and has attached to it by silk ribbons an impression of the Great Seal, as large and round as a bread-plate. It sets forth, with much quaint circumlocution, in the name of the King, that His Majesty has appointed "our most trusted and well-beloved Councillor" the Lord Chancellor, and "our most dear cousin and Councillor" or "our well-beloved and faithful Councillor," naming the other Commissioners—each peer lifting his hat at the mention of his name and title—to signify the Royal Assent by Commission to Bills. At the end the Reading Clerk says—"By the King himself, signed by his own hand."

Presently, the Clerk of the Crown and the Clerk of the Parliaments appear, one on each side of the table. The Clerk of the Crown, standing on the Opposition side with a list of the Acts which have received the Royal Assent, bows to the

Commissioners and reads out the title of the first of the Acts. Then comes the turn of the Clerk of the Parliaments, standing on the Government side. His part in the ceremony is the more important. He first bows to the Commissioners, then turns round and bows to Mr. Speaker and the Commons at the Bar, and announces to them the Royal Assent in the ancient Norman-French phrase. " Le roy le veult " (" The King wills it.") Accordingly, that Act has become part of the law of the land. The antiquity of the ceremony is testified by this use of Norman-French—the one surviving memento of the Conqueror who came over so long ago as 1066. The Clerk of the Crown again bows to the Commissioners, reads the title of the next Act on the list, and bows once more ; and the Clerk of the Parliaments, bowing to the Commissioners and then to the Commons, again declares " Le roy le veult." And so on till the list of the Acts is exhausted.

There is, however, heard now and then a change in the form of words in which the Royal Assent is announced. Should the Act be one for granting subsidies to the Crown—for instance, the Finance Bill, in which the Budget is embodied—the Clerk of the Parliaments says : " Le roy remercie ses bon sujets, accepts leur benevolence, et ainsi le veult." Or if it be a Private Bill—one empowering a town council or company to supply gas or water or build a railway—the term used is : " Soit fait comme il est desiré."

If the Royal Assent were refused to a Bill it would be declared in the mild fashion of " Le roy s'avisera," or " The King will consider it." But these words have not been heard in the House of Lords since 1707, when Queen Anne withheld her assent to a " Bill for the Settling of the Militia of that part of Great Britain called Scotland." In that case, however, the Royal veto was not exercised by the Sovereign because she was personally opposed to the provisions of the Bill. She was advised by her Ministers not to give her assent to the Bill for the reason that, since it had passed through Parliament, a Jacobite movement in Scotland for the re-establishment of the Stuart dynasty made the enactment of the Bill perilous to the Hanoverian succession. It will thus be seen that the Royal veto has its constitutional uses. Just as the assent of the Sovereign is really the assent of the Ministers by whom the Bills have been introduced or supported in their passage through Parliament, so the veto of the Sovereign, should it ever be exercised, would really be the veto of the Ministers. The veto affords to Ministers the means of dropping a Bill after it has gone beyond the control of Parliament. If it were found to be undesirable at the twelfth hour to place a Bill on the Statute Book, the Sovereign need only say, " nay," on the advice of the Ministers, and the measure would be as dead as if it had been rejected on a division in the House of Commons or the House of Lords.

Queen Elizabeth " quashed "—as Sir Simon D'Ewes expresses it in his *Journal*—" forty-eight several Bills " because she disliked them. At that time, and indeed until the coming of the Hanoverian Georges, it was the custom for the Sovereign to sit on the Throne in the House of Lords and personally give or refuse the Royal Assent. As the title of Act after Act was read out by the Clerk of the Parliaments, Elizabeth said in Norman-French she would take time to think about it. And her Ministers made no remonstrance. They knew their Queen.

The last instance of the veto of the Sovereign being exercised in opposition to the wishes of Parliament was in 1693, when William III refused his assent to a Bill for limiting the duration of a Parliament to three years. Resentment of the King's action was manifested throughout the country. In order to appease it he caused the explanation to be given out that he was indisposed to part with the Parliament while the nation was at war. In the following year the Triennial Bill was again carried through Parliament and received the Royal Assent.

* * * * * *

An impressive sense of the antiquity and continuity of the Monarchy, as well as its stability, in its relations with the Legislature, is imparted by these ceremonies of the opening of Parliament and the giving of the Royal Assent. They are indeed rooted in the historic past. In form and substance the opening of Parliament is exactly the same in the twentieth century as it was in the sixteenth, despite all the incursions of the modern spirit since then. The King is now, as he was then, the central figure. He keeps his State in Parliament unaffected by political changes and innovations. From him emanates all the splendour of the spectacle, and all the power and authority it suggests. The Monarchy still has its purple, its Crown and sceptre. Changeless amid time's changes the Monarchy would appear to be; affording in that respect a striking contrast with Parliament which is peculiarly susceptible to change, which in each era adopts different customs and practices. It is true that the great framework of Parliament remains, but in the matter of procedure there are constant changes in detail and often changes of importance. Take up any book on the Constitution which purports to show how the mighty machine works, and, as one reads, if one is at all familiarly acquainted with the institution, one feels that the work is already out of date. It may have been true of Parliament yesterday, it is not true of Parliament to-day. But the Monarchy remains the same—an impressive symbol of Government, its continuity and authority.

The King, reading the Speech from the Throne, uses the personal pronouns " I " and " My." The plural phraseology, " We," " Us," " Our," so commonly used and accepted as fittingly representing the august majesty and power of the Sovereign, is said to have been first adopted by King John, after his crowning in the year 1199. Accordingly, it has had the sanction of over seven centuries of usage. The first person singular of the Speech from the Throne suggests that the legislation foreshadowed is, as it was of old, laid down by the King. But we know that it is not so. Among the members of the House of Commons at the Bar listening to the Speech, as it is being read by the King, may be seen the man who actually wrote the Speech—none other than the Prime Minister, and the " I " and " My " are really his, as the spokesman of the Cabinet.

That being so, it is inevitable, perhaps, that the spectacle in the early decades of the twentieth century should be found wanting in reality—as it appears, at least, in the eyes of those who pride themselves on being logical and rational. So overwhelmed were the Lords and Commons of the sixteenth century with the power and authority inherent in the ceremony, that they fell on their knees when Henry VIII or Elizabeth began to address them from the Throne. Elizabeth, in the course of her last speech to Parliament in November, 1601, interrupted the flow of her discourse to say, " Mr. Speaker—I would wish you and the rest to stand up, for I fear I shall yet trouble you with a longer speech." In that speech it was that she made the famous remark, " To be a King and wear a Crown is a thing more glorious to them that see than it is pleasant to them that bear it."

Other times, other men. Labour representatives of Socialistic tendencies appeared for the first time in considerable numbers in the Liberal Parliament of 1906. At the opening of that Parliament by King Edward a Labour member, standing with the Speaker at the Bar of the House of Lords, remarked quietly to a colleague—" A wonderful sight! It will take a lot of undoing." Obviously, he was a modernist, but was touched by the antiquity and charm of the spectacle. Sixteen years later, at the opening of the Unionist Parliament of 1922, when there was a still larger incursion of more extreme Labour men from the Clyde, one of them on returning to the House of Commons after seeing the pageant—one evidently who was unfamiliar with history, or cold to its appeal, one who had no poetry in his soul—exclaimed in a pronounced Scottish accent, " That scene yon," jerking his head in the direction of the House of Lords, " Wasn't it a terrible scandal." He would eliminate—unchivalrous man!—the lovely and sparklingly jewelled peeresses. He would strip the peers of their scarlet and ermine. " Ah, what avails the sceptred race! Ah, what the form divine!" This anti-mediævalist would have Parliament opened by a man in a Tall Hat. But how many would he get to agree with him? Certainly the Tall Hat as a symbol of Governmental authority would excite the hilarious laughter of the average English working man and woman. For them, the Golden Crown.

The ceremony is not an anachronism. In its exact purport of meaning to-day it expresses the whole inheritance of English ideas of constitutional liberty. In its own way, it is as English as another quite different and very familiar scene—also expressive of the national greatness—a cricket match on the village green, the players in flannels, the umpires in long white coats, on a sunny Saturday afternoon in June.

END OF BOOK V

BOOK VI

GOVERNMENT AND ADMINISTRATION

CHAPTER I

THE WAY OF VICTORIA WITH HER MINISTERS

THE paradoxes of the British Constitution, arising out of the clash between modern political practice and old legal theory, are most strikingly illustrated in the relations between the King and his Ministers. In theory, Ministers are appointed by the King; in reality, they are the selected leaders of the Party in power in the House of Commons. In theory, the King is master, and the Ministers are his servants; in practice, it would be unconstitutional for the King to do anything affecting the State without the advice of his servants. Yet the system works with admirable smoothness. All the apparent contradictions are logically harmonised by the principle that the King reigns but does not rule. Whether it be due to accident or design—whether the result of those wayward and uncertain agencies summed up under the name of chance, or the result of pervading and overruling law operating through the seeming chaos of human affairs—England is pre-eminent among the lucky or providentially most-favoured nations in having evolved a constitutional Monarchy of the highest and sanest type—in its outward form, conservative, in its animating spirit, progressive.

The country is ruled by the Ministry, in the name of the Crown. But the King is free of responsibility for their acts. If we survey the political situation at any time, we find it a complex struggle of interests, opinions, aims and desires, and it is thus reflected, ever raging and ever changing, in the House of Commons. The King is enthroned above it all, safe from the shocks and changes of party strife. As Head of the Nation he is stable and permanent. His Ministers are fugitive. Representing, as they do, the shifting opinions of the millions of the electorate, they are frequently replaced. The King stands for the common and permanent cause, the State as a whole, to which all citizens, whatever their politics, pay allegiance.

It is not quite true what some historians say, that personal government by the Sovereign was entirely abolished by the Revolution of 1688. The seed was then sown, but no more.

Not for nigh two hundred years afterwards did it really burgeon
and blossom. Even in the last decades of the eighteenth century the Radicals, under the influence of French revolutionary
principles, used to vow their intention to plant the Tree of
Liberty on the political wastes of England. But they failed to
do so. The system of personal Government prevailed under
George III, and in fact the Crown had then as much power as
it possessed even in the time of the Stuarts. One of the means
by which George III made himself the strongest Monarch
since Elizabeth, in personal ascendancy and dictatorial power,
was the election of a large number of place-men as members for
close boroughs. In the House of Commons they were known
as " the King's friends." They were men who were not even
in the Ministry of the day, men who had only a nominal
connection with Party, but their votes were always available
to defeat anything that the King wished to have defeated, and
to carry anything that he wished to have carried.

The first staggering blow was given to the individual
dominance of the Sovereign in parliamentary politics when
George IV was compelled by Wellington, then Prime Minister,
to give the Royal Assent to the Catholic Emancipation Act,
against his religious and political convictions, and his interpretation of the obligations personally imposed on him as King
by his Coronation Oath to defend the Established Church.
Personal rule declined under the pressure of ministerial
responsibility. It finally collapsed when William IV agreed
in 1832, also against his conscience, to the proposal of the Whig
Ministry of Earl Grey to create sufficient peers to swamp the
House of Lords should they dare to reject the Reform Bill a
second time. The King, at first, drew back, alarmed at the
democratic and revolutionary consequences of such an act
which his imagination bodied forth. Grey therefore resigned.
Wellington was sent for. He told the King there was nothing
for it, in the temper of the country, but to recall the Whigs and
pass the Reform Act. " How can I, as a gentleman, so humili-
ate myself," protested the King. " Sir," said Wellington,
" you are not a gentleman, but King of England."

*   *   *   *   *   *

The reign of Queen Victoria, the longest in English history, is remarkable also for this—that during it there steadily set in the tendency of the Monarchy to acquire its present constitutional definiteness of purpose, and of the Sovereign's place and influence in the system of Government to be definitely assigned. This is best disclosed by an exposition of the relations between the Queen and her Ministers in the actual work of Government and administration. It shows that she was able to exercise but little influence in really great and vital affairs of State. We see her not so much controlling as criticising the work of her Ministers.

If Victoria had any politics on her accession to the Throne in 1837 they were Whig. The atmosphere of her home, as far as it was political, tended to give her opinions a bias in favour of that Party. Her father, the Duke of Kent, was a Whig, like his brother, the Duke of Sussex, thus widely differing in politics from the other sons of George III—the Prince of Wales (he quickly abjured the Whiggery of his youth) the Duke of York, the Duke of Clarence (afterwards William IV) and the Duke of Cumberland, who became King of Hanover, all of whom professed high Protestant and Tory principles. The Duke of Kent was prominently associated with the Whig Opposition of his day. He made a public profession of his politics at a Whig banquet in London. " I am a friend of civil and religious liberty all the world over ; I am an enemy to all religious tests," he said. " All men are my brethren, and I hold that power is only delegated for the benefit of the people. Those are the principles of myself and of my beloved brother, the Duke of Sussex. They are not popular principles just now, that is, they do not conduct to place or office. All the members of the Royal Family do not hold the same principles. For this I do not blame them. But we claim for ourselves the right of thinking and acting as we deem best, and we proclaim ourselves with our friend, Mr. Tierney, 'Members of His Majesty's loyal Opposition.' " The Duke of Kent died a few months after the birth of his daughter, the Princess Victoria, but the Duchess sympathised with the Whig principles of her late husband, which, as she was German, she understood only to the extent that they meant opposition to the wicked Tories who wanted—so it was believed at the time—to displace her daughter and put forward the ugly Duke of Cumberland as Heir to the Throne. Accordingly she taught the Princess Victoria to regard the Tories as her personal enemies.

The fact that the Whigs were in office when Victoria ascended the Throne must also have tended to influence the young Queen, not so much in her political views, for she can hardly have had any, as in her political friendships. At that time the law providing for the dissolution of Parliament at the demise of the Crown was in force. During the general election the Queen took the warmest interest in the success of the Whig candidates. The Whigs, indeed, did not scruple to make use of Victoria's name as a Party cry. They boldly declared that she was on their side. One member of the Whig Administration, Sir Henry Parnell, said in a speech that she had definite and firm opinions on all the political questions of the day. " What ! " exclaimed young William Ewart Gladstone—the rising hope of the Tories—at Manchester, " does Sir Henry Parnell conceive that amidst the shades of Kensington Gardens the Princess Victoria has been studying the question of the Irish Municipal Corporations ; that she has taken her morning walks with the division list in her hands ; and has over her evening tea discussed the probability of Tory or Whig ascendency ? " Despite those jaunty words, the Tories well knew, to their mortification, that Victoria regarded them with disfavour and suspicion. She rejoiced that the result of the general election confirmed the Whig Administration in office.

From Lord Melbourne, her first Prime Minister, the young Queen got her first lessons in constitutional duty. She had for him the affection of a girl for her father. That interesting gossip, Charles Greville, Clerk to the Privy Council, records in his *Journal* that the Queen and the Prime Minister passed " if not in *tête-à-tête* yet in intimate communication, six hours every day." " If Melbourne should be compelled to resign," Greville adds, " her privation will be the more bitter on account of the exclusiveness of her intimacy with him. Accordingly, her terror when any danger menaces the Government, her nervous apprehension at any appearance of change, affects her health, and upon one occasion during the last Session (1838) she actually fretted herself into an illness at the notion of their going out." The Whigs having been defeated in the House of Commons, May, 1839, decided to resign. "The Queen had not been prepared for this catastrophe, and was completely upset by it," writes Greville. "Her agitation and grief were very great. In her interview with Lord John Russell (then Leader of the House of Commons) she was all the time dissolved in tears, and she dined in her own room and never appeared on that evening."

Sir Robert Peel was sent for by the Queen with a view to the formation of a new Government. In their discussion of the situation the Queen was told by Peel that the ladies of the Court, appointed by Melbourne, must resign with the Whig Ministry. It was the custom then, as it is now, when a change of Government takes place, for the holders of what are called the political offices of the Royal Household, filled by Members of Parliament, Lords or Commons, to go out with the Ministry—of which indeed, they form a part—but usually, at that time, the ladies of the Court were left undisturbed by the new Government. Victoria objected to being deprived of her ladies. "They are my personal friends," she said, "and not party politicians. Why should I be required to part with them?" Peel pointed out that the state of Ireland was the chief difficulty with which he would be confronted as Prime Minister, and argued that he could not be satisfied he was having "fair play" as long as the wife of the Whig Viceroy of Ireland (Marchioness of Normanby) and sister of the Whig Chief Secretary (Duchess of Sutherland) were in the most intimate daily intercourse with the Queen as Ladies of the Bedchamber. But Victoria would not consent to have ladies, strangers to her, brought into her Court, and Peel, baulked of his first chance of becoming Prime Minister, left Buckingham Palace in a huff.

At a meeting of the outgoing Ministers held the next day, Melbourne read a letter which the Queen had sent him : "It was written," remarks Greville, truly enough, "in a bitter spirit and in a strain such as Elizabeth might have used." In it Victoria said, " Do not fear that I was not calm and composed. They wanted to deprive me of my ladies, and I suppose they would deprive me next of my dressers and my house-maids. They wished to treat me like a girl, but I will show them that I am Queen of England." The Whigs, out of sympathy with the Queen, and to relieve her from an embarrassing situation, acceded to her wish to resume office. On Melbourne's advice the Queen sent the following note to the Tory leader— " The Queen having considered the proposals made to her yesterday by Sir Robert Peel to remove the Ladies of her Bedchamber, cannot consent to a course which she considered to be contrary to usage and repugnant to her feelings." The episode caused a sensation. It would seem as if the Queen was something of a revolutionary in the eyes of the Tories. The great Society ladies of the party went about declaring that when they composed the Court they would see to it that the young thing was kept in her proper constitutional place. There was a discussion in both Houses of Parliament. Peel adopted quite a tragical vein. Was it fitting, he asked, that one man should be a Minister, " responsible for the most arduous charge that can fall to the lot of man," and that the wife of another man— " that other being his most formidable political enemy "— should, with his consent, hold office in immediate attendance on the Sovereign ? " Oh, no," he exclaimed. " I felt it was impossible. I could not consent to this."

If it is referred to at all in the history books, this dispute has been treated as a sort of comic interlude. It is called " The Bedchamber Plot." Certainly, it had its ludicrous side. Peel, of a dignity almost chilling in its austerity, prevented from forming a Government of the great British nation because of the insistence of a girl Queen to retain in her service two ladies who superintended her dressing in the morning and her undressing at night ! But it also had a serious side, which has been lost sight of. What a testimony to the personal power of the Sovereign, and the extent to which party ends were served by Court intrigues, even as late in the nineteenth century, that a whisper in the ear of Queen Victoria, by her lady attendants, while she was having her hair done, should be regarded as fraught with trouble for a Tory Ministry !

* * * * * *

There was a marked change in the attitude of Queen Victoria

towards her Ministers after her marriage with Prince Albert in 1840. The Conservatives could no longer complain of her bias in favour of the Whigs, which, had it really found expression in the conduct of affairs, would, of course, have been decidedly unconstitutional. She ceased to be a partisan, and became, instead, the critic and counsellor of her different Ministers, irrespective of politics. The first of the private advisers of the Queen and Prince Albert, the German physician, Baron Stockmar, recommended that the Queen should resist being reduced to " a Mandarin figure " which had " to nod its head in assent, or shake it in denial, as Ministers please." Prince Albert in order to fit himself for the position which he regarded as properly his, that of "permanent private secretary and adviser to the Queen," entered upon an exhaustive study of English constitutional law and history, under the guidance of the best authorities, and Victoria shared in his readings and reflections. The Prince was whole-heartedly devoted to his adopted country, and it was undoubtedly his constant endeavour to bring the Monarchy into harmonious co-operation with the British system of Party Government, favouring neither Whigs nor Tories, but exercising by advice and suggestion a steadying influence on each when in office.

In a private memorandum, found among Prince Albert's papers, on the duties of an English Monarch, he asks :

" Why are Princes alone to be denied the credit of having political opinions, based upon an anxiety for the national interests, their country's honour, and the welfare of mankind ? Are they not more independently placed than any other politician in the State ? Are their interests not most intimately bound up with those of their country ? Is the Sovereign not the natural guardian of the honour of his country ? Is he not necessarily a politician ? "

In other words—a King was a King, however democratic the system of which he was the Head. Why should he not rule, as well as reign ? Why should he not have, at least, a supervision of affairs ? Moreover, his was the most highly specialised as well as the most exalted of callings. He could not so divest himself of his professional pride and spirit as to allow himself to be reduced to a cipher. He could not be expected to let Kingship down. Frederick the Great was urged by Benjamin Franklin, having regard to that Monarch's declared liberal sentiments, to help the revolted Colonists of North America in shaking off the grip of King George III. " Born a prince and become a King," answered Frederick, " I must not employ my power to ruin my own trade."

The upshot of the studies of Queen Victoria and Prince Albert was that they came to the conclusion that the least the British Sovereign was entitled to from his Ministers was full and early knowledge of all public affairs, and of the proposed decisions of the Cabinet in regard to them, before they were laid before Parliament, so that he might criticise them—suggest amendments, raise doubts, propose alternatives, or, it might be, back them with his entire approval. This, they held, the Sovereign was well qualified to do, by reason of his dispassionate aloofness from the Party conflict in the bewildering details of which Ministers were immersed. Queen Victoria guided her conduct in public affairs along these lines in her earlier years. She was fairly impartial as between parties, but she approved or condemned certain lines of policy more than others, and she had her likes and dislikes among the Ministers.

In 1841 the Melbourne Government were defeated in the House of Commons, and having been beaten also in the general election they resigned. This time Peel got a most cordial reception from the Queen when he came to receive her commission to form a new Administration. The Whig Ladies of the Bedchamber departed with the willing consent of their Royal mistress. " My relations with the Queen are most satisfactory," Peel wrote to a friend. " The Queen has acted towards me not merely (as everyone who knew Her Majesty's character must have anticipated) with perfect fidelity and honour, but with great kindness and consideration. There is every facility for the dispatch of public business, a scrupulous and most punctual discharge of every public duty, and an exact understanding of the relation of a constitutional Sovereign to her advisers."

The failure in 1845 of the potato crop of Ireland—the chief

food of the peasantry—and the starvation which followed, forced Peel, as Prime Minister, to the conclusion that the Corn Laws, which he was pledged to maintain, must be repealed if the people not only of Ireland, but of Great Britain also, were to have, as they ought to have, the security of an abundant and cheap supply of food. In this momentous change of opinion he had the sympathy and support of the Queen. Having heard from him of the opposition which his proposal to repeal the duty on corn from abroad was meeting from some of his colleagues, she wrote from Osborne, November 28th, expressing her regret at the news. " At a time of impending calamity," she said, " it is more than ever necessary that the Government should be united. The Queen thinks the time is come when a removal of the restrictions upon the importation of food cannot be successfully resisted." Peel was unable to conciliate his divided Cabinet, and resigned in December. An attempt by Lord John Russell to form a Whig Government failed. The Duke of Wellington then induced most of the wavering Tory leaders to support Peel. This he brought about by his famous declaration that while he was personally in favour of the Corn Laws, he thought their maintenance a matter very subordinate to the necessity of carrying on the Queen's Government.

When Peel, in January, 1846, presented to the House of Commons his Bill for the abolition of the Corn Laws, Disraeli, expressing the feelings of a large section of the Tories, fiercely assailed him as a traitor to his party. On February 4th, the Queen wrote to the Prime Minister, " She is sure that Sir Robert will be rewarded in the end by the gratitude of the country. This will make up for the abuse he has to endure from so many of his Party." She sent him another encouraging communication a few days later. " Sir Robert Peel has the confidence of the country, and she need not add that he has hers, as he knows that well enough." These letters of sympathy and approval were, of course, strictly private at the time. Not until the later years of her reign did Queen Victoria disclose her personal views in a political crisis to other than her constitutional advisers. Prince Albert, who shared the Queen's opinion that Peel's action was right and proper in the circumstances, went to the House of Commons to hear Peel's speech introducing the Bill for the repeal of the Corn Laws. On the twelfth night of the debate, Lord George Bentinck, leader of Tory revolt, thus referred to the Prince's appearance in the House: " I cannot but think he listened to ill advice when, on the first night of this great discussion, he allowed himself to be seduced by the First Minister of the Crown to come down to the House to usher in, and, as it were, by reflection from the Queen, to give the semblance of a personal sanction by Her Majesty to a measure which, be it for good or for evil, a great majority at least of the landed aristocracy of England, of Scotland, and of Ireland, imagine fraught with deep injury, if not ruin to them." That was the last visit of Prince Albert to the House of Commons. As his presence in the Peers' Gallery was thus liable to arouse Party animosity and misrepresentation he decided to go there no more.

Peel carried his Bill, despite violent opposition to it in both Houses; but on the very day it received the Royal Assent, June 26th, 1846, he moved in the House of Commons a Bill to put down coercively the disorder then prevailing in Ireland, and was defeated on it by a strange combination of Tory Protectionists and Irish Repealers with the Whig Opposition. The Queen was much grieved by the fall of Peel. He was sustained amid the loss of power, the wreck of his Party, the disruption of his private friendships, by the sympathy of his Sovereign. A letter written by Victoria to her uncle, the King of the Belgians, shows how her first dislike of Peel had given way to regard and confidence. " Yesterday was a very hard day for me," she said. " I had to part with Sir Robert Peel and Lord Aberdeen, who are irreparable losses to us and to the country. They were both so overcome that it quite upset me, and we have in them two devoted friends. We felt so safe with them. Never during the five years they were with me did they ever recommend a person, or thing, that was not for my or the country's best, and never for the Party's advantage only."

* * * * * *

There are two remarkable instances of the reality of Queen

Victoria's influence in non-political affairs, and its beneficence. One relates to the Indian Mutiny. After the suppression of the Mutiny, an outcry for vengeance arose. Lord Canning, the Governor-General for India, writing privately to the Queen on September 25th, 1857, said : " There is a rabid and indiscriminate vindictiveness abroad, even amongst many who ought to set a better example, which it is impossible to contemplate without a feeling of shame for one's countrymen." In the reply sent by the Queen to Lord Canning she said she shared " his feelings of sorrow and indignation at the un-Christian spirit shown, alas, to a great extent here by the public towards Indians in general, and towards Sepoys *without discrimination*." This attitude was due, she explained, to the horror of the " unspeakable atrocities perpetrated on innocent women and children " and for these " stern justice must be dealt out to all the guilty " ; but to the faithful natives the greatest kindness should be shown. " They should know that there is no hatred to a brown skin—none ; but the greatest wish on their Queen's part to see them happy, contented, and flourishing."

After the passing of the Act of Parliament transferring the government of India from the old East India Company to the Crown, a Royal Proclamation to announce to the natives the change in the situation was prepared and the draft submitted to the Queen. She was in Germany at the time, on her first visit to the home of her daughter, the Princess Royal, who had married the Crown Prince of Prussia. Lord Malmesbury was the Minister of the Crown in attendance on the Queen—at that time the Sovereign when out of London was always accompanied by a Cabinet Minister—and to him she strongly objected both to the spirit and the words of the Proclamation. " The Queen would be glad if Lord Derby would write it himself in his excellent language," she said in a letter to the Prime Minister, " bearing in mind that it is a female Sovereign who speaks to more than a hundred millions of Eastern people on assuming the direct government of them, and after a bloody war, giving them pledges which her future reign is to redeem and explaining the principles of her government. Such a document should breathe feelings of generosity, benevolence, and religious toleration, and point out the privileges which the Indians will receive in being placed on an equality with the subjects of the British Crown, and the prosperity following in the train of civilisation." It is easy to trace in this communication the hand of Prince Albert.

Lord Malmesbury's memorandum, sent with the Queen's letter to the Prime Minister, explained in more detail the faults Her Majesty found in the draft Proclamation. The statement that she had the "power of undermining" the native religious customs of India was particularly distressing to her. "Her Majesty would prefer," Lord Malmesbury wrote, "that the subject should be introduced in a declaration in the sense that the deep attachment which Her Majesty feels to her own religion, and the comfort and happiness which she derives from its consolations, will preclude her from any attempt to interfere with the native religions, and that her servants will be directed to act scrupulously in accordance with her directions." The document was rewritten "entirely in the spirit of Your Majesty's observations," as Lord Derby informed the Queen. To the new draft she added in her own handwriting, as its last sentence, the words : " May the God of all power grant to us, and those in authority under us, the strength to carry out those wishes for the good of our people." The Proclamation, in its final form, gave the greatest satisfaction to the Governor-General of India. " To the good effect of the words in which religion is spoken of," he wrote to the Queen, " Lord Canning looks forward with very sanguine hope. It is impossible that the justice, charity, and kindliness, as well as the true wisdom which mark those words, should not be appreciated." Certainly in this case the Queen proved herself a better statesman than her Ministers.

On the second notable occasion the tact and judgment of the Queen and the Prince Consort probably averted the calamity of a war between England and the United States. In November, 1861, during the American Civil War, the British Mail Steamer *Trent* was boarded by the *San Jacinto*, a vessel of the Federal Navy, and delegates of Southern States, Messrs. Slidell and Mason, who were on their way to England, were seized. This affront to the British Flag naturally aroused indignation in England, and Lord Palmerston, then Prime Minister, decided to send the United States a stiff demand for the prompt release of the envoys. The fiery despatch was, in the usual course, submitted to the Queen. Her Majesty took the document to the Prince Consort, then lying in his bed, sick unto death, and got him to soften its tone and modify its terms. It was the last service the Prince rendered to the State. He said to the Queen as he gave her the memorandum on the despatch which he wrote for the Cabinet, " I am so weak I could hardly hold the pen." A facsimile of the document was published after the death of the Prince. It shows that the Queen, in turn, altered some of its expressions. The Prince referred to the subject of the despatch as " a quarrel," and for that phrase the Queen substituted " a question of dispute." The despatch, rewritten in the spirit and language suggested by the Prince Consort, was presented by Lord Lyons, the British Ambassador at Washington, to Seward, the American Secretary of State. Before he opened it Seward remarked, " Everything will depend on the tone of it." Happily it smoothed the way to peace instead of provoking war.

When the pacific settlement of the dispute was communicated to the Queen on January 6th, 1862, about three weeks after the death of the Prince Consort, she wrote to the Prime Minister : " Lord Palmerston cannot but look on this peaceful issue of the American quarrel as greatly owing to her beloved Prince, who wrote the observations on the draft to Lord Lyons in which Lord Palmerston so entirely concurred. It was the last thing he ever wrote." We may be sure that the widowed Queen gave way to a passion of tears as she penned this note to her Prime Minister, thinking of her lost husband and the misrepresentation he had had to endure. For twenty-two years he had been to her, in her own words, " Husband, father, lover, master, friend, adviser, and guide." Lord Palmerston, in his reply, said : " There can be no doubt that the alterations made in the despatch to Lord Lyons contributed essentially to the satisfactory settlement of the dispute. Those alterations were only one of innumerable instances of the tact and judgment, and the power of nice discrimination, which excited Lord Palmerston's constant and unbounded admiration."

The death of the Prince Consort changed the current of the Queen's life, to the extent that she retired from Society for many years and shunned, as far as possible, appearances in public. But during all this long isolation, though deprived of the advice and aid of her husband in the discharge of her constitutional duties, her close attention to State affairs was unabated.

She was one of the most remarkable of British Sovereigns in the attributes of personal force and ability. She had a mind that seized the bearings of a question, however complicated, and an understanding of character which shrewdly appraised the motives of her Ministers. But she was narrow in her ideas and strong-willed and dictatorial in maintaining them—characteristics which strengthened as she grew older. Tory in politics, Broad Church in religion, puritanical in morals—she sought more and more to find in the narrow and stern creed thus composed a guiding light for her actions as Queen. She had the highest sense of duty and was a strict disciplinarian of herself. These were qualities which she thought not only that everyone should possess, but that everyone could possess, if they only tried to ; and she held firmly to the opinion that if they were so deliberately wicked as not to try to, they should be punished. She had intense and practical sympathy with what she regarded as unmerited misfortunes. Her letters to sufferers from coal mine explosions, shipwrecks, and railway accidents, bespoke a tender and compassionate heart. But she had no sense of pity for those innate defects of human nature with which some of us are cursed more than others by powers outside ourselves. For, according to her philosophy, the failings which spring from such weaknesses of character are assumed with deliberate evil intent ; and could be cast aside by only a slight exercise of the will.

*　　*　　*　　*　　*　　*

All matters affecting the Navy and Army gave her a concern that was curious in a woman. In 1869 she wrote to Childers, then First Lord of the Admiralty in Gladstone's first Government, suggesting a modification of the rule of clean shaving in the Navy, because of the discomfort and also the danger of using the razor at sea, and enclosed a letter from Prince Leiningen, Captain of the Royal Yacht, supporting the suggestion. " There is," the Prince wrote, " more bad language made use of during the quarter of an hour devoted to shaving than during any other part of the day." The sailor's face was made as hard as iron by his long hours of daily exposure to sea air and sun. He had a bad razor, a small bit of broken looking-glass, very often a wet deck to stand on, and at all times a rolling or pitching ship. " Such," added Prince Leiningen, " are the difficulties under which the British seaman shaves."

Childers found that all the Admirals, and the entire Board of Admiralty, with two exceptions, were against the growing of beards in the Navy. He decided, nevertheless, to issue an Order in conformity with the Queen's wishes. " The Queen thanks Mr. Childers very much for his communication on the subject of beards. She thinks the Order will do extremely well. Her own personal feeling would be for the beard without the moustaches, as the latter have rather a soldier-like appearance, but then the object in view would not be obtained, viz. to prevent the necessity for shaving. Therefore, it had better be as proposed—the entire beard, only it should be kept short and very clean." She was determined to secure to the Army the copyright in the moustache. Writing to Childers a few days later she said : " The Queen wishes to make one additional observation respecting the beards, viz. that on no account should moustaches be allowed without beards. That must be clearly understood."

When the Liberals were again returned to power in 1880, Childers was appointed Secretary of State for War. It happened that in the last Session of the preceding Conservative Parliament flogging in the Army was prohibited except for offences on active service. Feeling in the new Liberal Parliament against corporal punishment in any circumstances soon manifested itself, and the Queen showed the puritanical, or hard side, of her nature by conveying to Childers her hope " that officers on service may not be deprived of the only power they possess of keeping young troops in order, viz., by inflicting corporal punishment in the extreme cases of cowardice, treachery, plundering, or neglect of duty on sentry." She added : " The Queen hates the system of flogging, but sees no alternative in extreme cases or cases on active service. Her Majesty trusts you will listen to the opinion of officers recently returned from the War." Childers replied that it would be impossible to maintain flogging against the sentiment of the House of Commons. So flogging in the Army for any offence was abolished.

As Queen Victoria regarded herself in spiritual as well as in temporal affairs head of the Nation, she was naturally concerned about morals. She endeavoured to lift the moral tone of England not only by excluding misdemeanants from the Court and from honours, but also by severely punishing criminals. She remonstrated with Sir William Harcourt, the Home Secretary, for his undue tenderness in his exercise of the prerogative of mercy. He had reduced sentences on juvenile offenders. " She would like to whip them, but it seems that cannot be done." Harcourt's frequent exercise of the prerogative of reprieve in cases of criminals condemned to death also seriously disturbed her. There were more of such remissions than formerly, she wrote. Harcourt explained at length that these were cases in which public sentiment would not support the carrying out of the extreme sentence. She had as much tender consideration for animals as for men and women and children. In 1883 her private secretary wrote to Harcourt : " I am commanded by the Queen to ask if men who are cruel to dogs cannot be more severely punished than by a fine of £2." She was vehemently opposed to vivisection. In a letter to Harcourt she denounced it as " horrible, brutalising, un-Christian." She was annoyed when Maclean, who fired a pistol at her as she was entering her carriage at Windsor station, was declared mad. " The Queen thinks the verdict an extraordinary one, and it will leave her no security for the future." An instance of leniency in a subsequent Home Secretary, White Ridley, led to an odd remark by the Queen. A burglar disturbed by the woman who occupied the house tied a handkerchief round her mouth to keep her quiet. She was found dead in the morning. Her false teeth became dislodged,

and suffocated her. The burglar was tried for murder and convicted, but White Ridley, satisfying himself that the man had
not intended to kill the woman, advised the commutation of
the death sentence to penal servitude. The Queen was not
satisfied with the reason advanced by the Home Secretary.
" I maintain," she said, " that old ladies who wear false teeth
are entitled to the protection of the law." All the same, it was
as an arbiter of morals that Victoria was perhaps most successful. She neither led nor followed the fashion. That she left to
the Prince and Princess of Wales. But she wrought a revolution in customs, manners, conduct in social affairs, family life,
sexual relations—at least in the great middle class.

    *   *   *   *   *   *

    Queen Victoria's almost implacable adherence to her own
personal opinions were displayed in relation to the last great
political question that vexed her reign, and was carried unsettled into the reigns of her son and grandson, disturbing
them likewise—Home Rule for Ireland. The Queen developed strong Conservative predilections, and was always a
staunch Unionist. Disraeli, as Prime Minister, gained an
extraordinary influence over her. Her feeling for Gladstone,
as Prime Minister, was one of dread of him as a statesman,
and not, as has been said, one of dislike of his manners as
a man. Gladstone, in all his relations, was always a fine and
gracious gentleman. The Queen seemed rather to think that
as a statesman Gladstone was the subject of demoniacal
inspiration. Certainly, his scheme for curing the political
distempers of Ireland by giving her a dose of self-government
could have come, in the opinion of the Queen, only from such
a source. Her vehemently partisan indignation overflowed
even into her private correspondence in 1886, when Gladstone's first Home Rule Bill furiously engaged the public
mind—for and against. Sending her sympathy to Tennyson,
whose son was ill in India, she added : " I cannot in this
letter allude to politics, but I know what your feelings must
be." The Poet Laureate, in his reply, said : " Our latest
telegram from Colombo, ' No improvement ' ; but in this
pause, as it were between life and death, since Your Majesty
touches upon the disastrous policy of the day, I may say that

I wish I may be in my grave beyond sight and hearing when an English Army fire upon the loyalists of Ulster."

In political circles of the time, a story was current of a dramatic scene at Osborne when details of the proposed Home Rule scheme were laid before her by Lord Spencer. It culminated in a threat that she would abdicate should the Bill be accepted by Parliament. The story has not found its way into any of the biographies of either the Queen or Gladstone—though we learn from both that Victoria was passionately opposed to Home Rule. But, as it was told at the time, the Queen interrupted the recital of the proposals of the Bill by exclaiming, " This is treason—utter treason," and at the end she cried out, with that fierce intensity which made those around her so often tremble : "Go back to the Cabinet, Lord Spencer, and tell them that if this Bill passes Parliament, I will abdicate rather than give it the Royal Assent."

She was as violent as ever against Home Rule in 1893 when Gladstone, again in power, brought it forward a second time. In her letters to the Ministry her warnings and rebukes were quite denunciatory. They were " playing with fire." She agreed with the Unionist Opposition in the House of Commons that the Bill tended to " the disruption of the Empire," and justified the extreme obstructive tactics with which they fought it. To Sir William Harcourt, the Chancellor of the Exchequer, who, as was the custom at the time, sent her nightly a parliamentary letter, she wrote :

The Queen thanks Sir William Harcourt for his full and regular reports of the proceedings in the House of Commons. She does not like to enter on controversial subjects, but as Sir William Harcourt so often refers with apparent indignation to the " obstructiveness " of the Opposition, she must observe that nothing could equal the obstructiveness of the Liberal-Radical Party when *they* were out of office, and that they have not much right to expect similar tactics not being pursued now. Besides which, Sir William Harcourt must remember what a very strong and growing repugnance there is to Home Rule, and what a dread there is of the Bill passing, and how this feeling is increasing in Ireland. Can the Government then wonder if great efforts are made to resist it—especially to resist the attempts to force it through in so great a hurry ?

Harcourt was moved to protest, not to the Queen directly, but to Ponsonby, her private secretary. " I have done my best," he said, " to give a fair and impartial report and tell an unvarnished tale—and often sat up half the night when I was tired to death to accomplish the task. But I find that is not at all what is wanted, and that if I don't chant a high Tory anthem on all occasions I only give offence—and that your pure Tory atmosphere does not tolerate the intrusion of any light but that to which it is accustomed. I am sorry for it, as I think it is sometimes an advantage even in the most august stations to hear both sides and to learn what are the views and sentiments of the majority of the House of Commons and even of the responsible Government." Writing to the Queen personally, Harcourt could be as tactful and adulatory as Disraeli—almost. " Sir William trusts," he writes, " that he will have the Queen's forgiveness for endeavouring to show that, even if mistaken in his views, in the character of one of the most loyal and devoted servants of her person and Crown he is incapable of promoting any policy which in his conscience he believes would be injurious to her Empire or her Throne."

The second Home Rule Bill was thrown out by the Lords. A movement for the reform of the House of Lords was contemplated by the Liberal Government. " Mend them or end them," said Morley. The Queen opened her mind on the subject to Campbell-Bannerman, then—November, 1894— Minister in attendance at Balmoral Castle, with her characteristic frankness and sincerity. " Mr. Campbell-Bannerman forgets the danger of increasing the power of the House of Commons, and having no force to resist the subversive measures of the so-called Liberals—but better called ' destructives.' " . . . " She could never agree to taking from the Lords their power to alter or reject measures. This might be obtained from a President, not from her." . . . " She thinks it cruel that after her long reign, at her age, with her many cares, she should be obliged to refuse her assent to proposals of her Ministers when it would be her greatest pleasure to support them." Victoria, in her dealings with Ministers, always showed great force of personality. She was outspoken and decisive. There were no equivocations on her part. She stuck to her point with fixedness of opinion and will. Statesmen with proposals that were not altogether to her taste approached her with some trepidation, and felt rather uneasy while they were in her presence. They might be embarrassed by the free expression of her feelings, but what of that ? She had little, if any, of the feminine weakness of liking to appear agreeable in the sight of men. The one thing she was concerned with was the carrying of her point.

*   *   *   *   *   *

When Gladstone, after the defeat of the Home Rule Bill in 1894, went to the Queen to tender his resignation as Premier and take leave of her for the last time, after fifty-three years of membership of Parliament and four terms of service as her Prime Minister, and in age well past 80, she let him go— so intense was her distrust of him—not only without regret, but without a word of thanks. " The same brevity," said Gladstone in a pathetic record of the interview, " perhaps prevails in settling a tradesman's bill when it reaches over many years." It cut him to the heart ; it clouded his life to the end. Lord Gladstone, in his book in vindication of his father, *Thirty Years After* (1928), charges Disraeli with having poisoned the Queen's mind against his father in order to establish his own ascendancy as her favourite Minister. No evidence in support of this charge is to be found in the book ; or in the *Life of Disraeli* or in *Queen Victoria's Letters*. The Queen distrusted the statesman rather than disliked the man. In no circumstances would she hesitate to show her political bias, or pretend to feelings of attachment and regard which she did not feel for Ministers who thwarted her. In the same spirit she always asserted her position as Queen, and, as her correspondence with her different Ministers shows, not infrequently disputed their proposals, and in the end only reluctantly gave way. Perhaps in the case of Home Rule also—the measure to which, above all others, she was most determinedly and, as it seemed, immovably opposed—her instinct as a Constitutional Sovereign would have marked out for her a line beyond which she could not flout the advice of a Ministry backed by a majority in the House of Commons. And yet it is within the bounds of probability that had the Act been presented to her for the Royal Assent she would have abdicated rather than sign it, or, as a less extreme measure, have dismissed Gladstone and sent for a Unionist Prime Minister, which, by a straining of her Prerogative, she could have done in the circumstances. For in her self-willed and stubborn old age she had not the hesitation which cannot decide, nor the feebleness which fears to act. Even so, personal government would have been found, in the long run, to be as dead as George III. I cannot find any instance of Ministers, Conservative or Whig, altering their course, on any question which in their view was of supreme importance, solely because of the wishes or opposition of Victoria.

One sees it frequently said that Queen Victoria had unrivalled opportunities for acquiring the experience and knowledge that are necessary to the wise conduct of political affairs. But from whom? She was an old lady, leading an isolated and secluded life, rarely seeing anyone but her Maids of Honour. Her Ministers, on the other hand, whether Conservative or Liberal, were able and upright men in the closest touch with affairs, having the confidence and support, each in their turn, of more than half the people. " A King, after a reign of ten years," said Sir Robert Peel, " ought to know much more of the working of the machinery of government than any other man in the country." Yes, of the machinery of government. Queen Victoria had an unsurpassed experience of the working of the machinery of government, and to her duties in that respect she gave a devotion that burned to the very end like a fierce flame. But a statesman must keep his ears to the ground, and that is a thing which their high office and station do not allow Sovereigns to do.

CHAPTER II

" EDWARD THE PEACEMAKER "

It is true that one of the drawbacks of Kingship in a constitutionally governed country like Great Britain is that the
Sovereign is hindered in putting such talents as he may
possess to good uses for the welfare of his Nation. Success
in public life is due, like success in all other spheres of life,
to two things—natural ability and circumstances favourable
to its effective use. In Kingship opportunity is lacking. Exceptional qualities may be repressed in a King by reason of
his high office, as they are in lesser mortals by poverty and
the drudgery of the struggle for existence, and by his constitutional obligation to act solely on the advice of his Ministers.
This obligation, on the other hand, may have the still better
result of restraining arbitrary propensities in an able and
strong-minded Monarch.

King Edward VII found in the relations of Great Britain
with foreign Powers a sphere of influence in which he thought
he could exercise his particular personal gifts for the good of
the country with only the slightest danger, if any, of coming
into conflict with the political opinions that dominated home
affairs. He constituted himself, with the approval of his
Ministers, and the applause of his people, an apostle of amity
among Nations. As Prince of Wales he was always disposed
to interest himself in foreign affairs. But even in the early
'eighties, when he was over forty, Queen Victoria still per-
sisted in refusing to allow him to have " official knowledge " of what was going on, " for fear he would let it out,"
as was said by Lord Granville, Foreign Secretary at the time.
However, Sir Charles Dilke, the Under-Secretary, who had
become very familiar with the Prince, kept him privately
informed of all important movements in diplomacy. The
Prince was more of a cosmopolitan, or less insular, than most
Englishmen. He greatly enjoyed foreign holidays and the
visiting of foreign Courts. In the reigns of George I and
George II there were constant complaints that these Sovereigns
spent far too many of their days in their ancestral Hanover.

"Edward the Peacemaker"

Edward, as Prince of Wales and as King, was more frequently out of England and for a far greater length of time, than all his Hanoverian ancestors put together. As Prince of Wales he was familiarly known as "The Uncle of Europe," on account of his blood relationship with most of the Royal Families. In the earlier years of his reign he was called "The Commercial Traveller of Peace." Finally, he was given the proud title of "Edward the Peacemaker."

* * * * * *

Indeed, foreign affairs was the one department of State in which each British Sovereign had always claimed a right of action—not wholly independently of his Minister, but with greater freedom than is allowed in the more controversial field of domestic concerns. Was he not the official representative of his country in all dealings with foreign Powers relating to treaties, engagements, understandings? Did not his intimate social intercourse with other sovereigns afford him opportunities of usefulness in the interest of his people? Into this claim there entered the spirit of the trade union of Kings which existed—irrespective of the contending policies of Governments and the national animosities of peoples—before so many Thrones disappeared in the World War. They regarded themselves as a singular, separate, distinct caste, and they were intensely caste conscious. To do each other harm as kings was outside their tribal customs. Above all, they must maintain the regal dignity. At the opening of every new reign it was the custom of the Sovereign to send to other reigning monarchs a personal message by Special Envoys announcing his accession. It was done by George V when he succeeded in 1910. This act of State courtesy was of a dynastic, not of a political nature, and, therefore, was confined to hereditary and crowned Heads. The Presidents of France and the United States, being but elected for a term of years, were out of it. But the employment of the British Sovereign as an active agent in diplomacy was a new departure in the functions of Monarchy. It was sanctioned by the tendency which set in, in Edward's time, of all responsible men to treat foreign affairs and international relations as outside the domain of party controversy, such is their complexity, delicacy, and gravity.

The assumption of this role by King Edward led to a remarkable change in the relations between the King and his Ministers—an abrogation of the rule and practice that the Sovereign at home, and, still more, abroad, must be attended by a Cabinet Minister. When Queen Victoria was out of London, whether at Windsor, Osborne, or Balmoral, or on the Continent, she invariably had a Minister of the Crown in attendance. Newspaper readers in Victorian days were very familiar with the announcement, so often found in the Court Circular, " Mr. So and So was Minister in attendance on the Queen." As every act of the Sovereign in State affairs must have the sanction of a Minister, the attendance of a Minister on the Sovereign while he was away from London was necessary for the speedy transaction of public business. Gladstone used to say that when the Court resided at Buckingham Palace during the parliamentary session the Sovereign could keep a better and more constant hold on the work of government than was possible at Balmoral or Osborne, and even Windsor was considered by him as inconveniently far from the centre of State affairs. One of the Principal Secretaries of State was always in attendance on the Sovereign, at home and abroad—as a Secretary of State was then regarded as the constitutional channel of communication between the Sovereign and the Cabinet—till about the middle of the nineteenth century, when the rule was relaxed to the extent that the duty was undertaken by each member of the Cabinet in rotation.

There was an additional reason for a Minister to be in attendance on the Sovereign when he was on a visit to a foreign Court. That reason is set out by Sir William Anson in his book on *The Law and Custom of the Constitution*. " The Sovereign," he says, " does not constitutionally take independent action in foreign affairs ; everything that passes between him and foreign Princes or Ministers should be known to his own Ministers who are responsible to the people for policy and to the law for acts done." Anson states that George III " never had private communications with foreign Ministers," and mentions, on the authority of Stapylton's

George Canning and His Times, that the new practice of George IV to hold private communications with foreign Ministers was stopped by Canning, who insisted, as Prime Minister, on his constitutional right to be present at all such interviews.

It is an old and settled rule of the Constitution that letters and reports from private persons or public bodies on home affairs must not be sent to the King personally but to his Minister, the Home Secretary. Such documents relating to grievances, or matters of any kind, which are sent direct to the King by private persons or public bodies are forwarded to the Home Secretary to be dealt with. It is also contrary to the spirit and practice of the Constitution for any communication on State affairs to pass between the King and a foreign Sovereign or Minister except through the medium of a Minister of the Crown. The Duke of Wellington, writing as Prime Minister to the Secretary of State for Foreign Affairs, Lord Aberdeen, in 1829, says : " It is not usual for the King of England to receive from other Sovereigns letters which had not passed through the hands of his Minister. Indeed, I have known instances of letters having been returned because copies were not sent with the sealed letter, the copy being intended for the information of the Minister." In 1847, the King of Prussia wrote a letter to Queen Victoria on European affairs, and his ambassador, by his command, delivered it to Her Majesty at a private audience. This irregularity was corrected by Prince Albert. The Foreign Secretary, Lord Palmerston, having been summoned, the letter was opened and read by the Queen in his presence, and her reply to it was approved by him. We learn from the *Life of the Prince Consort*, written by Sir Theodore Martin and edited by Queen Victoria, that the Queen always in her communications with foreign potentates acted on the advice and with the approval of the Prime Minister and Secretary of Foreign Affairs, and that she gave them every letter touching on any public matter which she received from abroad. In some cases, indeed, letters she got from Kings or Princes were returned because copies directed to the Foreign Secretary had not been sent at the same time.

Queen Victoria was also regularly attended by one of the

principal Secretaries of State on the rare occasions she visited a foreign Court. It was suggested in the House of Commons on one such occasion that the old custom of appointing Lords Justices for the administration of the functions of Kingship during the Sovereign's absence abroad should be revived. The reply of the Government was that a Minister of the Crown was with Her Majesty and was in constant communication by telegraph or otherwise with the Cabinet. At that time it was impossible to conceive of the Sovereign being unattended by a Minister at home, and, still less, abroad. In the reign of King Edward it became the common practice to dispense with the attendance of a Minister. Usually the King was accompanied abroad by but a few officers of his Household, and only important visits by a high official of the Foreign Office. Perhaps the rule had become really obsolete constitutionally. It certainly was inconvenient to both Sovereign and Ministers. By limiting its observance the King was saved from having in attendance upon him a Minister who might personally be uncongenial; and Ministers were relieved of a duty that often was irksome because of the formality of Court observances, or the inconvenience of having to go abroad. Still, it was an innovation. The King got greater freedom and more responsibility.

*   *   *   *   *   *

Yet with all this fixing of the bounds of the Sovereign's right of interference in foreign policy, and the care and circumspection with which that admitted right was exercised, it was international relations that led on two occasions to most grievous conflicts between Queen Victoria and public opinion. As is well known, she was in constant controversy with the Whig Government from 1849 to 1851 over Lord Palmerston's management of the Foreign Office. He would persist in taking decisions of high importance in foreign affairs without consulting her, though she had told him over and over again that she must see beforehand every despatch of any significance that he sent abroad, and have all his important conversations with foreign ambassadors reported to her without delay. Even so, Palmerston—the wicked old man!—was incorrigible.

He was impatient of the Sovereign's interference in foreign affairs. And what made his conduct all the more annoying to the Queen and Prince Consort was that, holding that England's mission abroad was to aid political liberty and put down political oppression, he was rather contemptuous of Crowned Heads and sympathetic with revolutionary feeling in Italy, Hungary, and Poland. In the end, Lord John Russell, then Prime Minister, yielding to the complaints of the Queen, dismissed Palmerston.

By and by the Crimea War broke out, and in the Coalition Government formed by Lord Aberdeen to conduct it Palmerston was Home Secretary. He soon resigned in disagreement with the extension of the franchise proposed in a Reform Bill brought in by Lord John Russell. Prince Albert wrote to his friend Baron Stockmar at Coburg : " The great Liberal braggart, who wanted to press free institutions on every country, finds the Reform measure which Aberdeen approves, too Liberal ! What mischief that man has done us ! " But it was openly stated in political circles that the real reason why Palmerston left the Government was his detection of Prince Albert in the betrayal of State secrets to Russia ! " The stupidest trash is babbled in public," the Prince said to Stockmar, " so stupid that (as they say in Coburg) you would not give it to the pigs for litter." Two London morning papers actually announced that the Prince had been arrested for high treason, by order of the Government, and was about to be sent to the Tower. An immense crowd assembled that day at Tower Hill to gloat their eyes on the Prince, a captive in chains, and shout their execrations at him. They were disappointment of the spectacle, but an explanation was forthcoming. It was said the Government had changed their mind because of the determination of the Queen to share her husband's prison cell !

The other unhappy adventure of Queen Victoria in foreign politics arose out of her interference on Germany's behalf in the conflict between Denmark and the Germanic nations, Prussia and Austria, over the two duchies of Schleswig and Holstein in the early 'sixties. The duchies were incorporated in Denmark, but they were rather more German than Danish by race and sympathy, and they rose in arms in 1863 to fight for their independence. In 1864 Germany interposed in the conflict and compelled Denmark to cede the duchies to her. Palmerston was Prime Minister, close on eighty years old, and as bellicose as ever. He wanted to support Denmark. His declaration in the House of Commons—made before the actual interference of Germany—that if the Germans were to attack Denmark, it was not the Danes alone they would have to meet, was endorsed by loud and prolonged cheers. Lord John Russell (at this time he was Earl Russell in the House of Lords), Secretary of State for Foreign Affairs, was, like his chief, strongly anti-German. But Queen Victoria was vehemently pro-German. War between England and Prussia would have been fatal to the two international ideals on the realisation of which the Queen was then bent—the unity of the Germanic peoples under Prussian domination, and the closest and friendliest relations between England and Germany.

During the crisis the Queen—deprived only a few years before of the help and sympathy of her husband—made a confidant of Lord Granville (Foreign Secretary in different Liberal Administrations), who was a member of Palmerston's Cabinet, as President of the Council. She wrote to Granville one of the boldest and most outspoken letters a British Sovereign has perhaps ever addressed to a Minister in condemnation of the Government's policy. She vowed that she would make a stand against war even should it cause the resignation of the Government. " There are duties and convictions so strong that they outweigh all other considerations," she declared, adding, " but the Queen will not say this till Lord Granville tells her there is danger of anything of the kind ; but she is quite determined upon it, solely from a regard to the safety of this country and of Europe in general," and intimating, in conclusion, that " Lord Granville is quite at liberty to make use of her opinion on this subject when speaking to his colleagues." The views of the Queen having got abroad, there was a startling outcry in the House of Lords, of all places, and—most unexpectedly also—by a leading Tory statesman, Lord Ellenborough, who had served as a Minister in succeeding Governments of Wellington, Peel, and Derby. One of the most eloquent and powerful speakers of his day, he backed on behalf of the Tories Palmerston's policy of standing by Denmark, and protested against what he called "the natural prejudices of a great personage" deciding the issue. He recalled that though George III was supposed to be influenced by German feeling, he was always a supporter of true British policy. Had His Majesty not said in noble words: "Born and educated in this country, I glory in the name of Briton"? Would that his descendants followed his example, despite their German prepossessions. Lord Russell, who followed, thought this attack on the Queen wholly unwarranted. He said that however much Her Majesty, like other persons, might be influenced by private affection—married as she had been to a German Prince, and allied as she was to the Royal Family of Prussia by the marriage of her daughter with the Crown Prince—her object always was to maintain the honour and interests of England, and, moreover, she ever most willingly yielded to the counsels of her constitutional advisers. Nevertheless, a vote of censure on the Government was carried in the House of Lords, and in the House of Commons they escaped defeat only by a small majority.

General Grey, the Queen's private secretary, wrote to Granville that he had never seen the Queen " so completely upset " as she was by this attack. To add to her distress, she sent to the Prime Minister a letter of grateful thanks for his defence of her, and had a reply, insinuating, in what Grey described as Lord Russell's " coldest and hardest style," that the Queen might have used unguarded expressions which, being misrepresented or misunderstood, gave occasion for the hostile feeling shown in both Houses of Parliament. The Queen herself sent tearful protests to Granville. " Oh," she exclaimed, " how fearful it is to be suspected, uncheered, unguided, and unadvised ; and how alone the poor Queen feels ! Her friends must defend her." And again : " Alone and unaided, she writes to Lord Granville as a faithful friend and not as a Minister, to hear from him his opinion as well as that of the Cabinet generally." She was truly in a most pitiable state of mind. In a subsequent letter which she tells Granville she wrote at half-past eleven at night, she says " she fears she has written quite illegibly, but she is so tired and unwell she can hardly hold up her head or hold her pen."

The Queen had her way. Denmark was left to the spoiler. England was saved from a war with Germany on a question which appeared at the time hardly to affect her interests. It is a striking example of the resisting power of the Monarchy. On other occasions when Victoria disagreed with her Ministers she used to define her position by saying : " I sanction the measure, but I do not approve of it." In this case she said to her Ministers : " I think your advice is bad advice. Therefore I shall not follow it." It is also one of the rare instances of Ministers yielding to the Sovereign. There are historical writers who contend that this abandonment of Denmark was a turning point in European history. To it may be traced the rise of Germany to the position of the one powerful autocracy in Europe, and also the undisputed sway of material force in international relations, leading inevitably to the World War at the cost of frightful suffering to the human race.

*   *   *   *   *   *

It is curious to contemplate how King Edward's foreign policy, with the support of his Ministers, carried England in an entirely opposite direction to that in which her face had been turned by the success of the determined stand his mother made forty years previously against the intentions of her advisers. Whether this change in policy was due to deliberate design, or to an irresistible development of events, it is not easy to determine, but more probably it was the latter. When King Edward ascended the Throne in 1901 the feelings entertained of this country by other nations were jealousy, dislike, and barely concealed antagonism. The war which that mighty Power was waging upon the little farming communities known as the Dutch Republics of South Africa, seized the imagination of all peoples—ignorant as they were of the facts of the controversy—as an unparalleled act of aggression. Perfidious Albion was more perfidious than ever. And there were other reasons. The Great Powers of the Continent were divided into the Triple Alliance of Germany, Austria, and Italy; and the Dual Alliance between France and Russia. Owing to long-standing and manifold differences where their territorial and commercial interests clashed at various points of the globe, France and Russia on the one side, and England on the other, regarded one another as natural enemies, scowling and showing their teeth and expecting to come to blows any day. Germany, as a Power, was fairly friendly but there was among its people a good deal of dislike of England. This country, in fact, was completely isolated—a very dangerous position to be in, perhaps, having regard to her far-flung possessions and her immense sea-borne commerce.

King Edward set himself to turn enemies into friends. What were his qualifications? Behind his pleasant, smiling manner there were certain innate opinions. Sir Charles Dilke, who knew him well, said he was a strong Conservative and a still stronger Jingo—like Queen Victoria—" wanting to take everything everywhere in the world, and to keep everything if possible." These opinions, however, were not consistently entertained as a guide to conduct. According to Dilke, the King was " a good deal under the influence of the last person who spoke to him," when he was Prince of Wales, at least, " so that he would sometimes reflect the Queen, and sometimes reflect me or Chamberlain, or some other Liberal who had been shaking his head at him." Anyway, the King's efforts to convince other countries of England's goodwill were attended with wonderful success. In 1904, when Balfour was Prime Minister and Lord Lansdowne was Foreign Secretary, the *Entente Cordiale* with France was established. In 1908, when Asquith was Prime Minister and Sir Edward Grey was Foreign Secretary, the understanding with Russia was arrived at. Suspicion and enmity were replaced by friendliness and confidence. Popular opinion gave the main credit for those happy endings of international strife to King Edward's diplomacy, tact, and charm of manner. The Liberal Government, however, refused to admit, when questioned in the House of Commons, that the King's visits to Heads of States, and his interviews with Ambassadors, were diplomatic or ambassadorical, or that the fact that His Majesty was unaccompanied by a Secretary of State marked any real infraction of constitutional usage. The questions were inspired by the suspicion that Heads of States were determining foreign policy between themselves and that the Foreign Secretary had become more the servant of the King and less the agent of Parliament. " In the transaction of all affairs of State," said Asquith, the Prime Minister, " the practice of the Constitution is adhered to, and the responsibility of Ministers of the Crown is fully maintained." " The assumption that when a foreign Sovereign stays with the King, or the King with a foreign Sovereign, they should never meet, though staying in the same house, or, if they do meet, should only converse in the presence of a Cabinet Minister is," he said, " unreasonable." Sir Edward Grey gave a more detailed answer to a question addressed to him as Foreign Minister in reference to the King's interview with the Czar of Russia at sea off Reval. " Any conversations which have an official character are recorded. The King transacts official business in the constitutional way," Grey said, " through his Ministers." " If it is supposed that I have advised His Majesty to go abroad and transact official business with foreign Sovereigns or Ministers direct and not through a Minister of the Crown, the answer is that I am not prepared to justify such advice, because I have not given it, and the thing has not occurred." He added : " I am responsible for seeing that foreign affairs are transacted through the Foreign Minister, and that responsibility has been preserved unimpaired. But, in view of the enormous amount of the business, I must claim the right to exercise discretion as to how much of it is transacted through Ambassadors or officials of the Foreign Office, who act under instructions from the Secretary of State for Foreign Affairs. Unless I am allowed that discretion, I cannot, nor could any other human being, discharge the responsibility."

It is evident, even from these necessarily guarded replies, that the Government, while desiring to shield the King from any accusation of unconstitutional action, were availing of his influence to have things done in foreign affairs which were beyond the competence of the regular officials of the Foreign Office. But information which has since come to light, and particularly the disclosures of Sir Sidney Lee—

based on private papers which King George allowed him to consult for the purposes of his official biography of King Edward—establishes that the Liberal Government aided and abetted the King in these diplomatic missions, accepted responsibility for them, and prompted him to undertake others. " Before long," Sir Sidney Lee writes, " the King's Ministers recognised the benefits which the international relations of the country derived from King Edward's foreign tours, and from 1906 onwards, when Sir Edward (now Viscount) Grey was Foreign Minister, the Government not merely encouraged the foreign expeditions, but often suggested times and places with a view to strengthening the bases of European peace. The Ministers assumed responsibility for the King's exercise of pacifying influences in the manner which he had himself inaugurated."

All this, by the way, modifies statements made by Sir Sidney Lee in the earlier account of the career of King Edward which he wrote for the *National Dictionary of Biography*, discountenancing the exaggerated importance given in the Press, foreign and domestic, to King Edward's " public activities abroad." " He cannot be credited with bold diplomatic vision, or aptitude for technical negotiation," says the *D.N.B.* " Foreign statesmen and rulers," says the *D.N.B.*, " knew that no subtler aim really underlay his movements than a wish for friendly social intercourse with them and the enjoyment of life under foreign skies quite unencumbered by the burden of diplomatic anxieties." In the tributes paid by the Houses of Parliament to King Edward at his death, this view of his services was emphasised. Lord Crewe, a Liberal Minister in the Lords, and Balfour, Leader of the Opposition in the Commons, brushed aside " the strange misunderstanding " which represented the late King as " a dexterous diplomatist." That, said Balfour, was to belittle the King. We know better now.

Largely through the influence of King Edward, the old policy of " splendid isolation " in Continental affairs, the policy of friendly co-operation with all nations in works of peace, but military alliances or understandings with none, was brought to an end. The desire and aim of Government and

King was to maintain the peace of Europe. But Sovereigns and Ministries are judged, historically, not by what they aim at, not by what they accomplish even, but by their failures, and they failed to prevent the Great War.

*   *   *   *   *   *

Testimony to Edward's official absorption in foreign affairs is afforded by Lord Morley in his *Recollections*. In the autumn of 1908 Morley was Minister in attendance on the King at Balmoral. He dwells on the King's " intense interest " in the European situation, and goes on to say : " He made me take the long journey with him up to London alone in his special compartment ; red boxes with new supplies of diplomatic points at each of the few stations at which we stopped." Morley adds the characteristic comment : " It would have been bad taste to remind him of Bismarck's excellent saying that not even the worst democrat has any idea how much diplomacy conceals of nullity and charlatanism." It is a pity that Morley did not make the remark, for the sake of seeing, and telling us, how the King took it by word or look.

King Edward's reputation abroad was prodigious. He paid rounds of visits to Courts, fraternised with Rulers and Statesmen, went to fêtes, banquets, receptions, race meetings, and whether he travelled in state as King, or incognito as the Duke of Lancaster, he was attended everywhere by special correspondents of the Press of the world, who invested all his doings in a blaze of publicity. Was he not regarded as the dominant and all-powerful figure in diplomacy ? Europe was for years noisy with his name in praise and blame. In France he was worshipped. He dearly loved to visit her, being temperamentally so much in accord with her brightness and gaiety. Crowds of peasants left the fields and gathered at the railway stations to see dash by the express train of " Le Roi," the protector of France. Some even believed he sympathised with the deeply cherished French desire of revenge on Germany for the defeat of 1870. The wish was father to the thought. In Germany King Edward was woefully misunderstood. There he was looked upon as a deliberate enemy working outside the proper channels of diplomacy.

Had he not isolated Germany ? Had he not helped, by casting the power and influence of England on the side of France and Russia, to strengthen the net spun round her in which—so it was contended in Germany—she would be entangled and rendered helpless in the certain event of war ? It cannot be denied that King Edward's success in appeasing the animosities of France and Russia against England put Germany in this position, but it was hardly done of malice aforethought. It came about indirectly, caused by that incalculable element in human affairs which, when it makes a mess of things, is called Fate.

King Edward desired to be at peace with Germany as well as with France and Russia. At a meeting with the Kaiser at Cronberg in 1906, he exclaimed : " May our two flags float beside one another to the most distant time, as they float to-day, for the maintenance of Peace, and for the well-being not only of our own countries, but of all Nations." But the Kaiser was irritated and incensed. " Peacemaker ? " he is reported as having cried out on one occasion when the role generally ascribed to King Edward was mentioned. " Mischief-maker, rather ! " he snarled. He himself was known as " The War Lord," and with the aid of a bristling moustache that had its ends defiantly turned up, he filled the mighty role with an appropriate air of Imperial and imperious command—and a touch of absurdity. So it came to pass that on the Continent, at any rate, it was supposed that a great game of chess for the control of the international situation was being played between uncle and nephew, the two commanding rivals in European politics. A mutual effort at reconciliation failed. The German Emperor visited Windsor in the winter of 1907. King Edward paid his return visit to Berlin in the spring of 1909. He was accompanied by Lord Crewe, one of the Secretaries of State, as it was the custom for a Minister to go with the King to Germany. But nothing came of these visits. The Governments of the two potentates (that of " The Peacemaker," as well as that of " The War Lord ") entered into a mad competition to outdo one another in naval strength.

* * * * * *

The antagonism of Germany was not the only cross which

235

King Edward had to bear in his mission to preserve the world's peace. He came under a brief cloud of unpopularity at home. Arising out of the signing of the Anglo-Russian *entente*, in September, 1907, there was an exchange of ceremonial visits and hospitality between the Czar and the King. In June, 1908, the King, accompanied by the Queen, met the Czar and other members of the Russian Imperial Family at sea off Reval. The visit was historic as it was the first ever paid to Russia by a British Sovereign. The King was accompanied on this occasion, not by a Secretary of State, but by the permanent Under-Secretary of the Foreign Office, Sir Charles Hardinge, who had previously been Ambassador at St. Petersburg. The Czar and Czarina came in their yacht, the *Standart*, to Cowes in August, 1909, where they were received by the King in his yacht, the *Victoria and Albert*. A few weeks earlier, in July, an acrimonious debate was raised in the House of Commons by Labour and Radical members—a repetition, in fact, of a discussion in 1908, when the King went to Russia. It was said that the proposed Royal welcome to the Czar—" the bloody tyrant and merciless oppressor of his people," as he was called—grated on the feelings of the liberty-loving community of Great Britain. His Imperial Majesty did not land in England. Had he done so, and came to London, the metropolis would have added to its varied and extraordinary experiences quite a novel one—that of yelling its condemnation of the Czar of Russia in his very ears. The Lord Mayor and Corporation of the City had to present to him at sea the address of welcome they voted.

In June, 1908, on his return from his visit to the Czar, the King gave a garden party in the grounds of Buckingham Palace. Thousands were invited, including both Houses of Parliament. To mark his displeasure at the parliamentary attack His Majesty cancelled the invitations that had already been sent to two Labour members, Keir Hardie and Grayson, and a Radical, Arthur Ponsonby, who were conspicuous in the debate. It was the only occasion on which King Edward publicly showed his resentment of criticism. But it was a particularly unfortunate one, because in it was involved the constitutional principle of freedom of debate in the House of

Commons on a legitimate topic of public interest. Besides, the debate was free from any note of personal hostility to the King. What annoyed him was the suggestion that the Royal visit was tantamount to a condonation of the " atrocities " of the Czar's Government. He was particularly incensed against Ponsonby (son of Sir Henry Ponsonby, for many years Queen Victoria's Private Secretary) " because,"—to use the words of Sir Sidney Lee,—" he had been born and bred in the purple." The Labour Party passed a resolution denouncing the affair as an " attempt by the Court to influence Members of Parliament," and requesting the Lord Chamberlain to remove all their names from the official list of Royal guests until Keir Hardie's name was restored. Ultimately the King withdrew the ban. The fact that he gave no garden party in the following year, after the visit of the Czar to Cowes, showed that His Majesty's irritation had not subsided. He avoided having to invite the Radical and Labour men by giving no garden party at all.

*   *   *   *   *   *

King Edward's habit of spending his holidays on the Continent led him into making one constitutional mistake. While the King was at Biarritz in the early months of 1908 he was informed that the Prime Minister, Campbell-Bannerman, was seriously ill, and might have to resign any moment as his incapacity to discharge the duties of his office was causing inconvenience to the Government. The King intimated his desire that the Prime Minister should not resign until the Easter recess, and stayed on at Biarritz. In April Campbell-Bannerman felt compelled to send his resignation. The King, departing from the constitutional practice of returning to London at a Government crisis, sent a letter to Asquith, Chancellor of the Exchequer, inviting him to form the new Government, and commanding him to attend him at Biarritz. Asquith accordingly went to Biarritz to resign the Chancellorship and kiss hands on his appointment as Prime Minister. There was a general feeling—to which *The Times* gave expression in a leading article—that the King should have returned to England, and not have appointed a Prime Minister on a foreign land. Indeed, some constitutional purists expressed a doubt whether, in the circumstances, Asquith's appointment was legal. And yet it was King Edward who gave the Prime Minister a place in the Constitution, by issuing a Proclamation in 1903, recognising the office for the first time and vesting it with precedence before all peers except the Lord Chancellor.

But one great sorrow King Edward was spared. The war for which the Powers of Europe were preparing during his lifetime—knowing not the moment when they would be precipitated into it—did not come until he was dead and gone. So he bore to the end, without question, that title of which he was so proud—" Edward the Peacemaker." Speaking at the Universal Congress of Peace held in London in July, 1908, he said : " There is nothing from which I derive more sincere gratification than the knowledge that my efforts in the cause of international peace and goodwill have not been without fruit, and the consciousness of the generous appreciation which they have received, both from my own people and those of other countries." One of his last public utterances was on the subject he had so sincerely at heart. This was in February, 1910— a few months before he died, when at the first *Levee* of the season he received from the Archbishops of Canterbury and York, addresses of congratulation voted by the two Convocations on his success in promoting mutual good understanding and cordial friendship among the nations. " I feel convinced," said the King in reply, " that as civilisation advances the influence of Christian teaching on the minds of men, will tend increasingly to inculcate a love of peace," and he added—" The concord of Christendom is unbroken, and rarely in history has the idea of war seemed more repulsive, or the desire for peace more widely cherished, throughout my Empire."

Once again the evil turn so frequently given to good intentions by the indifferent hand of Fate was strikingly exemplified. Just as the dream of King Edward's father, " Albert the Good," that the Universal Exhibition held in Hyde Park, in 1851, was to inaugurate an era in which peaceful rivalry in arts and industries would be substituted by the Nations for hostile competition in armaments, was followed almost immediately by the cruel and purposeless war between England and France against Russia in the Crimea, so the hope and belief of " Edward the Peacemaker," that he had established on an enduring basis the friendship of Nations was brought to nought, four years after his death, when the youth of mankind, and its mothers and wives, were subjected by Kings, Rulers and Statesmen, to the most horrible and excruciating ordeal the world has ever known. It has even been said, in speculations on the causes of the catastrophe, that the very precautions King Edward had taken to avoid war helped to bring about the most terrible of wars : that Germany, in sheer desperation, availed of the chance to burst the cerements which he had helped to weave round her. Perhaps King Edward himself had some misgivings on the point. It is significant that in 1909, for the first time since his accession, he urged his Ministers to take into consideration " the possible event of a European War." He was moved to this searching of heart by the Lloyd George Budget of that year, which imposed new burdens on landed and other property. " The income-tax, which has always been regarded as a war tax," the King continued in his letter of admonition to Asquith the Prime Minister, " now stands so high for unearned incomes over a certain amount that any great increase would have a most disastrous effect on land generally, more especially if the war lasted a considerable time." He was made uneasy by the vast increase of German armaments. More than that, he saw the division of Europe, once again, into two hostile camps.

And think of the national monument to King Edward in York Place, Pall Mall ! He might have fancied that in the form his memorial would take he would be seen bringing, at last, to fulfilment, that poignant aspiration of war-stricken humanity —the turning of the sword into a ploughshare. Bearing in mind the World War, such a presentation would have been incongruous. But the actual monument is as wholly out of keeping with Edward's character, and his mission as King, as the one which perhaps he fancied would have been out of keeping with his achievement. Whatever King Edward was, he certainly was not a militarist. He wore military uniform on ceremonial occasions, but he was far from being militant in spirit. In his heart of hearts he was a pacifist. Had he been alive when the Great War threatened, he would have moved the earth and assailed Heaven with his petitions to avert it. Yet he is presented in a Field-Marshal's uniform, mounted on a prancing charger, as if he were proudly leading his people into war ! If that were the end of the story of " Edward the Peacemaker," it would be a satiric and sorry end indeed.

CHAPTER III

MONARCHY IN A DEMOCRATIC GUISE

KINGS do not say much : they are particularly reticent about what they think of their office, its duties and responsibilities. No Sovereign has been so frank on the subject as George V. At the annual meeting of the Miners' Federation of Great Britain, that was held in July, 1922, a delegate mentioned that having been presented to King George on the occasion of his visit to an industrial centre, His Majesty, discussing with him the housing question, said : " My heart bleeds when I read of the conditions in which so many of my people are housed." " Would not Your Majesty bring the matter to the notice of the Government ? " said the delegate. The King's reply was— " I never interfere in the affairs or with the policy of the Cabinet." This statement by the King of his constitutional position finds support in everything relevant to it that has come to light. His Majesty stands absolutely neutral in party controversies. He abides strictly by the advice of his Ministers, as he is constitutionally bound to do.

In the *Life and Letters of Walter Page*, who was the Ambassador of the United States to England during the Great War, there is an account of a smoking-room chat with the King, which is deeply interesting. " He talked about himself," says Page, " and his position as King." One of the remarks of the King was : " Knowing the difficulties of a limited Monarch, I thank Heaven I am spared being an absolute one." " He went on," Page proceeds, " to enumerate the large number of things he was obliged to do, and the little power that he had, not at all in a tone of complaint, but as a merely impersonal explanation." The reign of King George will be notable for this— that in it a perfect constitutional adjustment of the Monarchy to its contemporary environment, political and social, was effected. And it was effected for all time. The King is sometimes called the crowned President of a Republic. That is no more than a fanciful description of his office. The Government of the country is Monarchical in form, and democratic in practice. What George V really is—as the political events of his time establishes—is a Democratic King. As he was so will his successors be. He has set an example that must be followed and, no doubt, will be, willingly.

*   *   *   *   *   *

King George on his accession became involved in the most serious political crisis since the Reform agitation of the early 'thirties of the nineteenth century, when the same question arose—that of using the Royal Prerogative to overcome the resistance of the House of Lords to a Bill embodying the policy of the Government of the day. As in 1832 William IV was advised by his Whig Ministers to create sufficient new peers to carry the Reform Bill through a hostile House of Lords, so in 1911 King George was advised by his Liberal Ministers to create as many new peers as might be needed to force the Parliament Bill through a House of Lords that was similarly hostile. But there was a vast difference in the number of new peers required on each of these occasions. In 1832, between fifty and sixty would have sufficed; in 1911, no fewer than four or five hundred were contemplated.

This trouble was a heritage from the preceding reign. It originated in the throwing out by the Lords in 1909 of the historic " People's Budget " of Lloyd George imposing for the first time direct taxes on land. The Liberal Government and their supporters thereupon concluded that the veto of the Lords on Bills must be so definitely limited as to establish the House of Commons as the unquestioned organ of the opinion and will of the country. This was to be done by means of the Parliament Bill. It proposed that Money Bills which the Lords failed to pass should receive the Royal Assent at the end of the session in which they were brought in, and that Bills, other than Money Bills, passed by the Commons in three successive sessions should, on the third rejection by the Lords, receive the Royal Assent and become law.

King Edward was informed by Asquith, the Prime Minister, in April, 1910, that if the Parliament Bill were not accepted by the Lords, the Government would either resign or recommend a dissolution of Parliament, but that they would not recommend a dissolution except on conditions which would ensure the judgment of the people, as expressed at the general election, being carried into law in the new Parliament. In other words, before going to the country they would ask the King for guarantees that, if returned again to power, peers would be created in sufficient numbers, if necessary, to carry the Parliament Bill through the House of Lords. The reply of King Edward, as reported in a public speech by Haldane, one of the Ministers, was : " What the country decides that I will accept." King Edward died within a month. This serious situation embittered King Edward's last days with anxiety and irritation—as Sydney Lee discloses in his biography of the King. For the first time in his reign he decided to intervene in party politics with a view to averting the threatened collision between the two Houses of Parliament. The King consulted Asquith, the Prime Minister, and having been advised by him that his interposition would be constitutionally correct, he sent for the Leaders of the Opposition—Lord Lansdowne and Arthur Balfour. His conversations with them were communicated by the King to the Prime Minister in personal audience. Nothing came of them, to the bitter disappointment of the King. The situation had not developed in King Edward's lifetime to the point at which the advice to create peers to provide that the will of the Commons prevailed would have been definitely given to him by his Ministers. But early in the new reign the Parliament Bill, denounced by the Unionists as revolutionary—did it not mean, they argued, the setting-up of Single-Chamber government ?—was thrown out by the Lords. The Government dissolved Parliament in December, 1910, on the issue of " Lords and Commons," and came back with a majority of 120, from the United Kingdom, or, excluding their Irish Nationalist allies, 60 from Great Britain.

Accordingly, King George had to decide whether or no use was to be made of the Royal Prerogative, to an unprecedented degree, by the Government of the day in furtherance of their party programme. The Parliament Bill was brought in again in the session of 1911. It passed through the Commons, and the Lords were determinedly engaged emasculating it, when, on July 20th, Asquith wrote to Arthur Balfour, the Leader of the Opposition in the Commons, telling him that when the Bill returned to the Commons, the Government would be compelled to ask the House to disagree with the Lords' amendments. He added this most momentous statement :

> In the circumstances, should the necessity arise, the Government will advise the King to exercise his Prerogative to secure the passing into law of the Bill in substantially the same form in which it left the House of Commons, and His Majesty has been pleased to signify that he will consider it his duty to accept and act on that advice.

If necessary, the King would create the required new peers ! The excitement was tremendous. The Prime Minister was assailed in the House of Commons by the Unionists with cries of " Traitor " and howled down when he attempted to defend his action. So great was the uproar that the Speaker was compelled to adjourn the House. For the first time in the history of Parliament the Prime Minister was denied a hearing. The Unionist peers were advised by some of their supporters to " give in " ; they were called upon by others to " stand fast " and " damn the consequences." They met in private conference and decided by a large majority to yield. The minority who advocated a fight to a finish numbered fifty. They and their supporters in the Commons were called " Die-Hards." Votes of censure on the Ministry, denouncing the pledge they obtained from the King in regard to the creation of new peers, as " a gross violation of constitutional liberty," were moved in both Houses. In the course of the Commons debate, Asquith disclosed, by leave of the King, the terms of the pledge. Dated November 15th, 1910, the eve of the general election, it stated that His Majesty " after discussing the matter in all its bearings " with the Prime Minister and Lord Crewe, the Leader of the House of Lords, " felt he had no alternative but to assent to the advice of the Cabinet," which came to this— " His Majesty will be ready to exercise his constitutional powers, which may involve the Prerogative of creating peers, if needed, to secure that effect shall be given to the decision of the country." In the Lords debate, on the following day, Lord Crewe, while repeating substantially the account which Asquith gave to the Commons of the interview with the King, made an addition to it of considerable importance, and interest, inasmuch as it indicated His Majesty's feelings in the matter. While it might be inferred from the Prime Minister's statement that the King's independent judgment coincided with the wishes of his Ministers, the fuller version given by Lord Crewe showed some reluctance, or hesitation, on His Majesty's part as to the use of the Prerogative in the creation of peers. " His Majesty," said Lord Crewe, " faced the contingency and entertained the suggestion as a possible one with natural, and, if I may be permitted to use the phrase, in my opinion with legitimate reluctance." *The Times,* next day, stated that this fresh account of the interview was made by the King's request.

The Commons disagreed with the amendments made by the Lords in the Parliament Bill and sent the Bill back to the Lords again in its original form. The question then was—Should the Lords prove obdurate, what will the Government do ? To this a most dramatic reply was given by Lord Morley of Blackburn, on behalf of the Ministry. He read a prepared typewritten statement that if the Bill were defeated that night, " His Majesty would assent to a creation of peers sufficient in number to guard against any possible combination of the different parties in Opposition by which the Parliament Bill might again be exposed a second time to defeat." Lord Morley added that their lordships would deceive themselves if they thought this was " bluff." " Every vote given against the Bill," said he, " is a vote in favour of a large and prompt creation of peers." Lord Lansdowne and Lord Curzon, the Unionist leaders, counselled submission—not to the reason of the situation, but to its force. The Bill was carried by 131 votes against 114—the small majority of seventeen.

The King's feelings, as disclosed by Lord Crewe, call for the utmost sympathy. He was advised by his Ministers to do a tremendous thing—the creation of an unlimited number of peers for the purpose of overcoming the natural, or to be expected, opposition of the Lords to a Bill the effect of which would be to deprive them of all decisive influence in public affairs. Common prudence dictated that His Majesty should safeguard himself against any suspicion of his having taken sides in so grave a situation. He stood outside the party quarrel, strictly neutral, but very anxious. Apart from that, it must be obvious that for King and for Ministers alike there was no alternative to the course each pursued once the Lords had determined to thwart the legislative proposals of the Liberal Government. The King could not constitutionally have acted otherwise, as the responsibility rested upon the Ministers alone, and the Ministers could not politically have acted otherwise, and be true to the pledge they gave to their supporters to make the will of the House of Commons prevail.

*   *   *   *   *   *

So the trouble ended, but only for a little time. It burst forth afresh, in a still more embittered form, over the Home Rule Bill in 1913. The Government were bent on carrying the measure against the Lords by means of the provision in the Parliament Act enabling a Bill passed by the Commons in three successive sessions to go direct to the King for the Royal Assent. Here was His Majesty again in a very awkward quandary, put there by no act of his own, but solely by the political differences of his people. The Liberals undoubtedly occupied the strongest position, taking their stand on the constitutional principle that the King must act on the advice of his responsible Ministers. " What ! " cried Lord Halsbury, a late Lord Chancellor in his eighty-ninth year, putting in a public speech the extreme Unionist view—" Is the King to have no judgment? Is he not to be enabled to say, ' No, this is against the interests of my country, and I must do my duty. I reject the Bill ' ? " " It is said that the King must do what he is bid," continued the old Die-Hard. "If so, it is not much of a King. I say it is for His Majesty alone to decide whether the thing proposed to be done is good or the reverse for his country." The demand of the bulk of the Unionists was in a way more reasonable. It was that the Government should go to the country on the issue of the Home Rule Bill; and that if they declined to do so—which they did, maintaining that they had already got a mandate from the country—the King would be well within his constitutional rights in dissolving Parliament. But this the King was in substance powerless to do. The Sovereign certainly has the discretion to impose on his Prime

Minister a dissolution of Parliament, or to refuse to his Prime Minister a dissolution of Parliament. But, practically, the King could only dissolve Parliament on the advice of his Ministers. Had he determined personally to have Home Rule submitted to the judgment of the electors, his course was well marked out. He would have to dismiss his Liberal Prime Minister and appoint a Unionist Prime Minister to form a Government on whose advice he could decree the election of a new Parliament. There is no constitutional principle more clear than that the King can do no executive act except on the advice and through the agency of responsible Ministers. The dismissal of his Liberal Ministry would, moreover, have been a violation of the principle by which King George had always guided his conduct in public affairs—that of abiding by the advice of the existing Ministers so long as they were supported by a majority of the House of Commons, no matter what might be their political policy.

What the King did do was to endeavour to assuage the violence of the contest by acting as mediator between the parties. In July, 1914, he summoned the leaders to a conference at Buckingham Palace—Asquith, Prime Minister, and Lloyd George, Chancellor of the Exchequer, for the Government; Lord Lansdowne and Bonar Law for the Opposition; John Redmond and Dillon representing the Irish Nationalists, and Sir Edward Carson and James Craig, representing the Irish Unionists, with Lowther, the Speaker of the House of Commons, as chairman. His Majesty opened the proceedings with a brief speech. It is necessary to mention here that very perilous revolutionary stuff was at this time being broadcast in the speeches of leading public men. Carson, speaking in Belfast, had said : " We have the repeated pledges of our great leader, Mr. Bonar Law, that whatever steps we may feel compelled to take in opposition to Home Rule, whether they be constitutional, or whether, in the long run, they be unconstitutional, we will have the whole of the Unionist Party under his leadership behind us." "For months," said the King, "we have watched, with deep misgiving, the course of events in Ireland. The trend has been surely and steadily towards an appeal to force, and to-day the cry of Civil War is on the lips of the most responsible and sober-minded of my people." This passage became the subject of acrimonious speculation. Was it aimed at the Unionists? Was it the King's own voice, or the voice of his Ministers? Asquith explicitly stated in the House of Commons that he as Prime Minister took the whole responsibility for the words. But nothing came out definitely to settle the point whether the King wrote the speech and had it approved by the Prime Minister, or whether the speech was drafted according to custom by the Prime Minister and approved by the King. The probability is that it was due to the King's initiative. It struck an impressive note of warning, and the right to warn, as well as the right to encourage, is the King's when his Ministers consult him. But this can confidently be said that never during the whole of the long controversy did the King make any disclosure of his own personal views regarding Home Rule in his conversations with his Ministers or even with his closest personal friends.

The conference failed. There was no give and take. In truth, the delegates were powerless to agree among themselves to any compromise which they felt would satisfy the mass of their respective followers. Each side wanted to take, but not to give. The prospect seemed, indeed, to be Civil War. Then suddenly and unexpectedly a bolt literally burst from the blue —the World War. And, confronted by this peril to their common country, the divided and distracted parties became one.

*   *   *   *   *   *

The circumstances attending the appointment by George V. of Stanley Baldwin as Prime Minister in place of Bonar Law, who resigned on account of ill-health in May, 1923, were most remarkable and important from a constitutional point of view. In a country so ruled by precedent as Great Britain is, the course taken by His Majesty may be said to have set the final seal to the principle that the people's will, as expressed at the polls, is sovereign, and that the King has no other thought but to ascertain it and carry it out.

For the understanding of the significance of the episode it is necessary to explain the position of the King when a Prime

Minister resigns. As there is no Government then in existence —the other Ministers but formally retain their offices until their successors are appointed—all the powers of the Executive are concentrated in the hands of the King. In this single situation only can the King exercise one of the rights of Prerogative without the advice of his Ministers (there being no Ministers to advise him) and, therefore, solely on his own responsibility. And that particular right is of the highest consequence, being nothing less than the selection of the new Prime Minister, the most powerful man politically in the land.

As a rule the new Prime Minister is clearly defined and known to all, the Sovereign included, and the Sovereign has hardly any choice but to send for this particular individual. If the resignation of the late Prime Minister is due to political causes and involves the fall of his Government—such as defeat in the House of Commons on a question of confidence, or overthrow at a general election—the King sends, as a matter of course, for the recognised leader of the Opposition. In a case of that kind the position of the Sovereign is as Bulwer Lytton once defined it—" seeing the political parties fight and crowning the victor." There may be a slight doubt as to who the victor is, or, rather, as to who is the predominant leader of the party victorious at the polls. But that is an exceedingly rare circumstance. The only modern instance of it arose in 1880 when the Government of Lord Beaconsfield was beaten at the polls. The Liberal chiefs were Lord Hartington, leader of the Opposition in the late Conservative Parliament, and Gladstone who, having retired when defeated at the general election of 1874, had emerged from private life and flamed forth as leader in the successful electoral campaign against the Conservatives. Queen Victoria disliked Gladstone for political reasons. So she tried to shelve him. She invited Hartington to form a Government. He told her that only Gladstone could form a Government, and advised her to send for him. But she was not satisfied. Hartington, at the Queen's suggestion, went to Gladstone to ascertain definitely whether or no he would accept a subordinate post in the new Government, and brought back the assurance from Gladstone that nothing but the Premiership would satisfy him. Then, and only then, did the

Queen send for Gladstone. Describing the interview in his *Diary*, Gladstone says the Queen received him " with perfect courtesy from which she never deviates," but found fault with some expressions in his election speeches. " She said with some good-natured archness, ' But you will have to bear the consequences ' to which I entirely assented." " She seemed to me," Gladstone adds, " if I may say so, ' natural under effort.' All things considered, I was much pleased, and ended by kissing Her Majesty's hand."

In like manner the Sovereign has scarcely any freedom of choice when a Prime Minister in command of an ample party majority in the House of Commons resigns because of ill health or old age, leaving a successor of established title by reason of his party service and distinction in Parliament. There was no question that Queen Victoria was right in sending for Arthur Balfour, First Lord of the Treasury and Leader of the House of Commons, when Lord Salisbury resigned on the ground of failing health in 1902, and that King Edward was right in sending for Asquith, Chancellor of the Exchequer, when Campbell-Bannerman resigned through illness in 1908. In both those instances the Sovereign had no other alternative. The succession of Balfour and Asquith to the Premiership, each in his day, was as certain as the day's dawning.

Indeed, the sole situation in which the Sovereign has the opportunity of personally selecting the Minister who is to form the new Government is the exceptional one of nicely balanced claims between two leaders of the party in power. In such circumstances the choice may be determined by the Sovereign's likes or dislikes, personal or political. The last instance of it arose when Gladstone resigned the Premiership and retired finally into private life in 1894. There were two men in the Liberal Ministry with almost equal claims, in the opinion of the Party generally, to succeed to the office—Lord Rosebery and Sir William Harcourt. Harcourt had the advantage in length and distinction of service, and, was, besides—now that Gladstone was gone—Leader of the House of Commons. In these circumstances, Queen Victoria might well have followed the custom of consulting the outgoing Prime Minister as to whom she should choose to succeed him. Gladstone expected to be consulted, and being opposed to the leadership of Rosebery, and knowing that Harcourt's ill-temper had estranged some of his colleagues in the Cabinet, was disposed to recommend Lord Spencer. But his advice was not asked for. The constitutional practice in such a situation—at least, according to Queen Victoria—was laid down in December, 1852, when the outgoing Lord Derby volunteered the suggestion that the Queen should send for Lord Lansdowne. The Prince Consort, in a memorandum, dated December 18th, 1852, writes :

> I interrupted Lord Derby saying that, constitutionally speaking, it did not rest with him to give advice and become responsible for it, and that nobody, therefore, could properly throw the responsibility of the Queen's choice of a new Minister upon him. The Queen had thought of sending for Lord Lansdowne and Lord Aberdeen together. This, Lord Derby said, would do very well ; he knew that, strictly speaking, the Sovereign acted upon her own responsibility, but it was always said on such occasions, for instance, " Lord John advised the Queen to send for Lord Derby."

Rosebery got the post. It was said at the time that in sending for him, the Queen was influenced by her personal predilection for a Whiggish peer, as opposed to a Commoner of Radical proclivities, rather than by any factor of the political situation. Anyway, Rosebery was accepted by the Liberal Party, with some dissent by the Radical wing, and Harcourt, though deeply sore at the frustration of his ambition, agreed to serve under him.

The next political crisis involving the downfall of the Prime Minister, attended by uncertainty as to who should properly succeed, was in December, 1916, when Asquith, as head of the Coalition Government which he had formed shortly after the outbreak of the Great War, was driven to resign in consequence of his colleagues' dissatisfaction with his conduct of affairs. Bonar Law had been Leader of the Opposition in the time of the preceding Liberal Government. He was Colonial Secretary in the Coalition. Furthermore, he was leader of the largest of the four parties, supporting the Coalition—the Unionist. King George therefore acted with perfect constitutional propriety in first sending for Bonar Law, and then hearing from Bonar Law that the Coalition desired that Lloyd George should succeed, appointing Lloyd George to the Premiership.

*   *   *   *   *   *

In the situation of May, 1923, caused by Bonar Law's resignation of office of Prime Minister—to which he had been appointed as recognised leader of the Unionists so recently as October, 1922, when the Unionist Party decided to end the Coalition—the King acted on the same principle but to an even greater and more striking degree. He had exhaustive enquiries made to find out the man whom the Unionist Party desired to have as Premier. As in the situation which arose out of the retirement of Gladstone in 1894, there were in 1923 when Bonar Law resigned, two men of equally conspicuous position in the Government, and, as in 1894, one was leader in the Lords and the other was leader in the Commons—Lord Curzon, Secretary of State for Foreign Affairs, and Stanley Baldwin, Chancellor of the Exchequer. For whom should the King send? The King was unable to consult the outgoing Prime Minister as, it seems, he desired to do. For Bonar Law, lying ill and voiceless in London, had sent his resignation by letter to the King, who was at Aldershot for military manœuvres. But next day an official announcement of an unprecedented kind appeared in the newspapers. " The King," it said, " is in communication with those whose opinions His Majesty would naturally seek in the exceptional circumstances which precluded him from seeing and consulting the outgoing Premier." Never before did a Sovereign take the public into his confidence as to the line he was taking to decide who was to be Prime Minister.

The King obviously wished it to be known that no personal opinion of his own would in the slightest degree affect his choice. If the King had any prepossession it might be supposed to be in favour of Lord Curzon. For Curzon was an old and valued friend of the Royal Family. He was besides one of that long line of men who have enriched English public life by their gifts and dignified it by their characters. The King, however, allowed no consideration of the kind to influence him.

To obtain the views of the Unionist Party, His Majesty sent his Private Secretary, Lord Stamfordham—this also was announced in the newspapers—to consult with its leaders, including the chairman of the Unionist Party organisation, as well as representative Lords and Commons, and in order to be at the centre of things His Majesty immediately left Aldershot for London. That the new Prime Minister must be in the House of Commons was found to be held widely and strongly in the Party. For one reason, the Labour Party constituted the official Opposition, and Labour had no representatives in the House of Lords. Moreover, political questions and the fate of parties are determined solely by what happens in the House of Commons. Accordingly the King sent for Stanley Baldwin.

One of the most pathetic stories which the history of politics affords is associated with this appointment to the Premiership. It had been Curzon's ambition from his schooldays at Eton to be Viceroy of India and Prime Minister of England—a double honour which so far had fallen to no man. On the evening of the day that the resignation of Bonar Law was announced in the newspapers Curzon, then in the country, got a letter from Lord Stamfordham making an appointment to see him next day in London. " The great moment of his life," says Curzon's biographer, Lord Ronaldshay, " which was to place the crown upon a long and meritorious career of service to the State, was surely at hand." He had been Viceroy of India. He was about to become Prime Minister of England. Curzon came up to London next day, and his pride and exaltation were increased as he read, on the way, in the London papers, that the choice lay only between Baldwin and Curzon and that of the two his claims were vastly superior. A staggering blow awaited him. He received it from Lord Stamfordham's statement of the conclusions to which the King had come. Curzon pleaded for a little delay so that he might submit a memorandum setting out certain considerations which might have escaped the attention of the King in coming to his decision. Too late. He was told by Lord Stamfordham that Baldwin was already Prime Minister. " Such," said Curzon, in some sore reflections which he wrote on the episode, " was the reward I received for nearly forty years of public service in the highest offices ; such was the manner in which it was intimated to me that the cup of honourable ambition had been dashed from my lips." "Oh," he cried, "what a dirty game is politics!" It is not politics that is dirty. Politics is not a game but a mission, as I have observed it for more than forty years—a mission to cure the ills of the State by the application of varying principles, each in its turn. What is dirty is the pettiness, the meanness, of some of those who take part in politics.

Two things were settled by the action of His Majesty, as precedents to be followed by the Sovereign in future political crises of the same kind. One is that the Prime Minister must always be in the House of Commons. The other is that when there is any doubt as to the right and title of two men with equal pretensions to the vacant Premiership, the question is to be settled, not as previously, by the personal inclination of the Sovereign, but by the weight of opinion in the Party to which both men belong.

Have we not in all this the final admission that the Sovereign is not to be expected personally to possess at first hand that knowledge and experience of affairs and sound judgment which alone could enable him to make a right interpretation of the popular will in a political situation ; and consequently that the decision, as well as the responsibility, must be left to the Ministers as the spokesmen of the Party in power ? Do we not see in all this the British Monarchy bending its head for all time in willing submission to the opinion of the majority, no matter what the principles or the aims of the majority may be ? Some may say that this is but following the line of least resistance. Even so, it surely is the right line for a constitutional Sovereign to follow. The King has his sense of the tangle of things, but it is not for him to attempt to set them right ; he recognises that his position requires him to leave it to his Ministers to do that—if they can. This course surely is the one most favourable to the continuance of happy relations between King and people, and to the strength and stability of the Monarchy.

* * * * * *

On two occasions King George took action to repel aspersions upon his honour as a man, and his political neutrality as a Sovereign. On his accession to the Throne a story was circulated that he had been married before his marriage to Queen Mary, and that his first wife was alive, but unacknowledged, as the marriage, being morganatic, was constitutionally illegal. It was but a manifestation of that unhappy trait of human nature which gives the ignoble and the malicious joy in defaming the noble. The story was denied and refuted, after the most searching inquiry, by the Archbishop of Canterbury and W. T. Stead, a distinguished journalist. But it got into print in an insignificant paper called *The Liberator*, an Indian revolutionary organ, published in Paris and circulated in London. The statement was definitely made that the King in 1890—he was then Prince George and serving in the Navy—married at Malta a daughter of Admiral Sir Michael Culme-Seymour, and it was contended, consequently, that the subsequent marriage to Princess Mary in 1893 was bigamous and shameful.

The writer, Edward Mylius, was arrested and tried for criminal libel before the Lord Chief Justice and a special jury. Evidence was given that the King was not at Malta between 1888 and 1901. The Maltese registers were produced, and shown to contain no record of any such marriage. Admiral Culme-Seymour absolutely disproved the whole story. He said he had no daughter whom the King could have married in 1890. One of his two daughters died unmarried in 1895 and had never known the King ; and the other, who was married, had not met the King between 1879 and 1898. The prisoner was convicted and sentenced to two years' imprisonment. The Attorney-General then read a statement written by the King in which he said he had never been married to anyone but the Queen, and that he would have attended in person to give evidence had not the Law Officers of the Crown insisted that it would be unconstitutional for him to do so. The King had no skeleton in his cupboard.

The other occasion, which arose in July 1921, was wholly political, relating solely to His Majesty's conduct as King. Lord Northcliffe, the owner and controller of *The Times* and *Daily Mail*, then on a world tour, was reported in the London newspapers to have said to an American Press interviewer that the King was very angry with his Ministers over the unhappy condition of Ireland in the Sinn Fein rebellion, and the measures being taken by the Black and Tans to suppress it; that he angrily burst out at his Ministers, exclaiming, "I cannot have my Irish people killed in this manner," that he went to Belfast to open the Northern Parliament in June 1921, putting aside a speech of blood and iron against Sinn Fein which his Ministers had prepared for him, and making instead his own conciliatory speech, appealing to all classes in Ireland to forgive and forget for the sake of their common country, and that he brought about the conference between the British Government and the representatives of Sinn Fein which led to the establishment of the Free State. Lord Northcliffe denied that he had made the statements.

The King took an unprecedented step to contradict them. He sent a categorical denial to the House of Commons, which was read by Lloyd George, the Prime Minister, in the House of Commons, July 29th, 1921. "The statements contained in the report are a complete fabrication," said the King. "No such conversations as those which are alleged took place, nor were any such remarks as those which are alleged made by His Majesty." The King added—"His Majesty also desires it to be made quite clear, as the contrary is suggested in the interview, that, in his speech to the Parliament of Northern Ireland, he followed the invariable constitutional practice relating to speeches from the Throne in Parliament." It is probable, however, that there was more in this episode than was allowed to come out at the time, for State reasons. The King may have, for once, come between his Ministers and his people, with happy results. It is significant that when, soon afterwards, the Irish Free State was founded, His Majesty publicly expressed "his great happiness to have contributed, in a small way, by his speech at the opening of the Northern Ireland Parliament, to this great achievement."

*   *   *   *   *   *

And what are the Royal Family paid for their services to the State and community? Under the Civil List Act of 1910—passed after the accession of George V "to make provision for the honour and dignity of the Royal Family"—the King gets £470,000 a year of which £110,000 is for his Privy Purse or personal use. He has also the revenues of the Duchy of Lancaster, which amounts to about £50,000 a year. Queen Mary continues to receive the annuity of £10,000 which was voted to her "for her sole and separate use," when she became Princess of Wales. There is also a provision that in the event of the Queen surviving the King there shall be paid to her an annuity of £70,000—the sum which was paid to Queen Alexandra as a widow. The income of the Prince of Wales is derived from the revenues of the Duchy of Cornwall, made up of royalties and leasehold property in the West of England and in South London, and amounting to about £80,000 a year. In the event of his marriage the Princess of Wales is to receive an annuity of £10,000 to be increased to £30,000 should she survive her husband. The Civil List Act of 1910 further provides that the younger sons of the King are each to receive, on reaching the age of 21, an annuity of £10,000, which is to be raised to £25,000 when he marries. A daughter gets £6,000 a year on coming of age or marrying—the annuity that is being paid to Princess Mary, Viscountess Lascelles.

At the accession of Edward VII it was officially stated that His Majesty received much less than the majority of foreign monarchs, the income of the Czar of Russia being £2,050,000, the Emperor of Austria-Hungary, £780,000, the King of Prussia, £770,000, the King of Italy, £614,000, and the King of Spain, £280,000. It is not too much to say that Royalty would be well worth the cost of its maintenance—about threepence per head of the population of the Kingdom, or a farthing apiece taking in the whole Empire—if it were only for the examples it sets of devotion to duty and of gracious manners in an age in which so many are disposed to be rather lax and rude ? Admiration, gratitude and affection—those are the feelings which the Royal Family evoke in all classes of society. The good derived by the community through being moved by such uplifting and refining sentiments cannot be measured in money. And that apart from the advantage of the Nation having an hereditary Head, in the freedom it gives from the distraction and animosity associated with the election in a Republic of the President.

END OF BOOK VI

BOOK VII

IN THE ROYAL CIRCLE

CHAPTER I

THEIR MAJESTIES' COURT

LORD MORLEY, in his *Reminiscences*, mentions that while he was staying with King Edward at Balmoral as Minister-in-Attendance in the Autumn of 1907, His Majesty took him for a drive through the district's splendid forest scenery. "I did not much wonder," he says, "when the King told me that if he could have chosen his life he would have liked to be a landscape gardener." One can understand why the King's confession caused Morley no surprise. A republican at heart, Morley himself would no doubt prefer to be a landscape gardener rather than a King. Indeed, who—not of the Blood Royal—would not? But it was not the case with Edward that being a Sovereign, and unable to adopt a lowlier lot in life, he had to subdue himself, or reconcile himself, to his uncongenial but unavoidable Kingship. He showed no other feeling—in public certainly—than one of pride and glory at being King of England.

King Edward had a passion for Royal pageantry. His frank delight in acting the principal part in Court ceremonies was plain to be seen. He spared no expense or personal care to secure that they were perfect in ritual and splendid in representation. He was hospitable as well as kingly. The cloud which fell on the Court at the death of the Prince Consort, and lasted throughout Victoria's reign, was dispelled by him. The Court became the most brilliant in Europe, and London that was rather a dull city, on its Royal side at least, was transformed into one of the gayest capitals of the world.

The most splendid and interesting of the Court ceremonies is the presentation to the King and Queen—that high festival of womanhood. Queen Victoria discontinued the Courts, after the death of the Prince Consort, and held Drawing Rooms instead. The Drawing Rooms, being held at 3 o'clock in the afternoon, were but spectral and wan imitations of the Courts. The ladies to be presented had to leave home in their carriages for Buckingham Palace not later than one o'clock. They were not allowed to be escorted by their male relatives. There was no music and no refreshments. King Edward revived the Courts, and holding them at night, imparted to them the glow of electric lights and joyousness of wine suppers. As the King associated his Consort, Queen Alexandra, with these functions, they came to be officially known as " Their Majesties' Courts." They were on a larger and more magnificent scale than ever before. They were not so exclusive. The Drawing Rooms of Queen Victoria, as well as her earlier Courts, were most select. The favoured few admitted to them belonged to what Disraeli used to call " the highest nobility." King Edward and Queen Alexandra sent their commands, or invitations, to a far wider circle. They transferred the scene from the Throne Room, where Queen Victoria held her assemblies, to the more spacious and lofty Ball-room. The King and Queen stood in front of two Chairs of State set in the centre of the room—Edward in the scarlet and gold of a Field-Marshal, Alexandra, in full dress and the beauty and stateliness of the First Lady of the Land. As the King looked upon his fair subjects he was, in appearance and manner, regal, proud and imposing. There was in him no suggestion of the Monarch who wished in his heart to be a gardener.

*   *   *   *   *   *

Their Majesties' Court derives its glory from the splendour of woman—contrasting the freshness and daintiness of the maid with the matron's mellowness and strength of character. The girls in their white frocks and laces may be compared to Spring's lily of the valley. The matrons in their brocaded silks and satins look like the autumnal aster. It is a sight which few can see—few males certainly, and not at all unless they belong to one of four very limited categories : diplomats, or officials in foreign Embassies, and Legations to the Court of St. James ; Ministers of the Crown, heads of departments of the Civil Service, or Officers of the Royal Household. Men of the first three categories possess what is called at Court the " Entree " ; those of the fourth are present by right of service. Otherwise only women are admitted, for the ceremony marks an important stage in the social life of womanhood, as well as deriving from womanhood its ineffable grace and charm.

The main purpose of a Court is the presentation of ladies of birth, wealth and distinction to the King and Queen. For men there is the Levee, which is held by the King (unaccompanied by the Queen) in St. James's Palace at midday. To be presented at Court, to pay Their Majesties homage or reverence with a curtsey, to get a bow and a smile from them in return, gives a lady—or is supposed to give her—a recognised position in the social scale that cannot be obtained in any other way. To put it more relevantly to the actual state of things, a lady presented at Their Majesties' Court obtains a higher standing in her own particular set, and, should she visit a Kingdom abroad, a title to be received at its Court.

Even as recently as the later days of Queen Victoria, the honour of presentation at Drawing Room or Levee was undreamed of except by those who were already included in what was called fashionable society. It was confined chiefly to the families of the aristocracy and country gentry, and the higher ranks of the Church, the Navy, and Army. Distinguished members of the medical and legal professions were also regarded as entitled to the privilege. To Literature and the Stage, and more so to trade the Court showed a face of reserve. Those engaged in manufacture and commerce on a large scale were not debarred, but the line was strictly drawn at trade, known as retail trade, however extensive its operations. But the daughters, so far as I have been able to gather, of wealthy commercial men were not excluded from Drawing Rooms in the later Victorian period, if their education, social associations and moral character were above suspicion. At this time of day the advance of democratic ideas has almost obliterated fine differences of social rank, or made them less rigid or definite, converting the " Upper Ten " into the Twenty Thousand, and therefore many a class who hitherto thought their appearance in the Royal Presence a glory beyond their dreams of social distinction may now hope to bask in it.

But the Court serves a sweeter and more romantic purpose than that of giving a mark of social status.

> " Maiden with the meek brown eyes,
>   In whose orbs a shadow lies.

Standing with reluctant feet,
Where the stream and river meet,
Girlhood and womanhood sweet."

For the girl "coming out" it is the decisive step from the
obscurity and limitations of the family circle, into the spacious-
ness and entrancing light of Society. She puts away her girlish
things for ever, discards plaits for short hair, and gets into
skimpier frocks, for the whirl of the world of youth—a succession of dinners, balls, garden parties, at homes, concerts, plays.
The transformation is wrought by the command to meet her
King and Queen which comes right Royally on a card of gold
lettering and gilt-edged. Court day is, next to her wedding day,
the most important of her career, perhaps. Ah, the excitement
and delicious palpitation as she goes in her white dress and
plumes to Buckingham Palace. The King and Queen smile
upon her as she passes on, with a curtsey—a vision of virginal
loveliness, to meet Life and all that it has in store for her, of
weal and woe, as sweetheart, wife and mother.

And how is a girl, in her coming-out season, to get that
magical card of invitation? A mother may present her
daughter, or daughter-in-law, if she herself has already been
presented. The privilege of presentations is restricted to married ladies. No spinster can make a presentation. Should a girl
have no near relative who is entitled to present her she must
seek the favour of a lady friend who has that privilege and who
is willing to stand sponsor for her moral and social fitness.
Two cards must next be applied for at the Lord Chamberlain's
Office, St. James's Palace, and having been filled up with the
name and address of the girl to be presented, the names and
rank of her father and mother, and the name of the lady who is
to present her, they should be returned to the Lord Chamberlain. The names are submitted to Their Majesties, or are supposed to be, and, if approved of, cards of invitation, or rather,
of command, to attend the Court, are sent three weeks or so
beforehand. There are several hundred presentations at each
Court. The debutante must be accompanied to Court by the
lady who is to present her. A lady who has been presented may
attend any subsequent Court. A lady presented before her

marriage would have to be presented again after her marriage ; and the ceremony would have to be repeated after the conferring on her husband of any new title or rank, or on her second marriage. Ladies who have been presented and desire to be commanded to a Court have to make written application to the Lord Chamberlain, and the card is sent subject to the rule that a lady must not attend a Court more than once in every three years. This regulation, introduced by King Edward, has enhanced the prestige of presentation and at the same time has made the Court circle wider still and more representative, by enabling a larger number of presentations to be made at each Court. Another rule of King Edward permits each lady making a presentation, to bring—on giving due notice—her husband with her to the Court, and, if the lady to be presented is married, her husband also. No other male relative or friend is allowed to accompany the ladies. But even husbands cannot attend their ladies unless they have been presented at a Levee.

*　　*　　*　　*　　*　　*

In times past, the King, holding a Court, used to give his right hand to each lady to assist her to rise from the low curtsey she dropped to him; then, drawing her close to him, His Majesty implanted a kiss on her cheek. The salute was known as the "Kiss of Fealty." No doubt it tasted as sweet by that as by any other name. King William IV was the last King to avail of this privilege. His sons by Mrs. Jordan, the actress, who were given the name of "Fitz Clarence," were always about the Court, and as young men were noted for their familiar and boisterous manners, following in that respect, at least, their father's footsteps. It was their habit to wait at the exit door of the Presence Chamber, and as the young ladies bashfully came out, to greet them with the rude inquiry, "Well, how did you like being 'bussed' by Dad?" "Dad" himself enjoyed the "bussing." So much so indeed, that anything which interfered with the unction of it greatly irritated him. The curled plumes worn by the girls in their hair were so long that they drooped over the face, and the old King—good natured but irascible—was often heard swearing to himself when his lips encountered feathers instead of the roses and

cream of a girl's cheek. But that was not his only vexation.
The paint on the faces of the matrons made him swear audibly.
" It makes my lips stick together so," he used to complain.

When a lady attending a Drawing Room of Queen
Victoria entered the Throne Room and her name was called
out by the Lord Chamberlain, she found herself in the presence
of a little stout lady in a plain black gown, that was relieved
by the blue of the Garter Ribbon worn across her breast.
There were groups of brilliant figures in the room—members
of the Royal Family, Ambassadors and Ministers and their
ladies and the ladies and gentlemen of the Household. But
this little old lady in black stood out prominently and alone,
with the Throne as a background—a burnished structure of
elaborate carving, with hangings of rich crimson velvet
showing the Royal Arms wrought in gold. She extended her
right hand, and the debutante, placing the back of her own
ungloved hand underneath, kissed the Royal hand as she
curtseyed. Now and then there was a change in this procedure.
The Queen, instead of giving her hand to certain ladies to be
kissed, kissed them herself on the forehead or cheek. The
ladies thus singled out were the daughters of earls, marquises
and dukes, who were being presented for the first time. The
daughters of the two lowest ranks of the peerage, barons and
viscounts, were not kissed.

At one Drawing Room the wife of a knight was announced,
and Queen Victoria, in a moment of mishearing or inattention,
was about to salute her as a daughter of a peer, when a Gentle-
man-in-Waiting, shocked out of his good manners by the
impending breach of Royal etiquette, called out, loud enough
to be heard by all present, " Don't kiss her, Your Majesty;
she's not a real lady." The Queen drew back in time, and, instead of kissing the lady, gave her hand to be kissed. There was
much awed speculation in Court circles afterwards as to what
would have happened had the Royal kiss been given. In Spain,
such slips in Royal etiquette would have consequences, serious
or ludicrous, as one pleases to regard them. The King of
Spain told a muleteer, whom he stopped to talk with on a
country road under a broiling sun, to put on his hat. His
Majesty forgot that by commanding a subject to cover himself

in the Royal presence he created him a Grandee. But the situation was saved by one of the King's suite hastily knocking the muleteer's hat out of his hand, and setting his foot upon it as it lay upon the ground. Another King of Spain unthinkingly addressed a groom of his horses in the second person singular instead of in the more formal third person. Fortunately the man was an Englishman, for, as a chamberlain afterwards represented to His Majesty, a Spaniard spoken to with this familiarity would have claimed that his King had dubbed him cousin—that is, had ennobled him. Therefore the question is sometimes frivolously asked in Court circles : had the knight's wife been kissed by Queen Victoria would she have become the daughter of an earl, marquis or duke.

Queen Victoria, who was a bit of a prude—being, perhaps, over-sensitively modest and reserved—was nevertheless unable to confine her kissing to ladies. As all Sovereigns look upon themselves as brothers and sisters they greet one another with a kiss. Queen Victoria kissed Napoleon III, and he returned the salute, on his visit to England as Emperor for the first time in 1855 ; and when she made him a Knight of the Garter at Windsor, she again kissed him on both cheeks. It was done with grand ceremony in presence of the assembled Court and the Knights of the Garter. Nevertheless there were irreverent giggles among the young Maids of Honour.

King Edward did not revive the Kiss of Fealty at his Courts. His Majesty was content to smile and bow his head as each lady, on presentation, curtseyed to him. Kissing, in fact, has fallen out of fashion at Royal functions. When George IV parted with the Duke of Wellington and Sir Robert Peel, on their quitting office as Ministers of the Crown, he kissed them both. King Edward, one may be sure, did not kiss Arthur James Balfour when he resigned the Premiership ; nor did King George thus salute Asquith on parting with him during the Great War ; or Lloyd George on parting with him after the Great War. But those who were admitted to Paddington Railway station one day in the Autumn of 1907, as I was, when the German Emperor, on a State visit to Windsor, came up to London for a luncheon given in his honour at the Guildhall by the City Corporation, saw the kiss of greeting exchanged by King Edward and the Kaiser. Their Majesties put their two hands on one another's shoulders, and twice laid their cheeks together, left and right.

*　　*　　*　　*　　*　　*

As the debutantes, accompanied by the ladies who are to present them to Their Majesties, mount the grand staircase from the main entrance to Buckingham Palace, they encounter on the top landing another stream of persons in which there are gentlemen as well as ladies on their way also to the Court, and the two streams are diverted into different corridors by stalwart troopers of the Household Cavalry. In that other stream may be recognised some of the ministers of the Crown, and the permanent chiefs of the Government departments in Court dress, but it is in the main composed of Ambassadors, Ministers and officials from the various foreign Embassies and Legations in London, in a striking variety of uniforms. These are the classes, Cabinet Ministers, leading Civil Servants and diplomats, who have what is called the privilege of the " Entree " to the Presence. They are accompanied by their wives. Having the " Entree," these gentlemen and ladies enter the Palace by a side door as it were—or, as it is officially called, the Pimlico entrance on the south side of the Palace. Intimate friends of the Royal Family also attend the Court in the same way. These classes are particularly numerous at every first Court of the Season. They are the first to be presented.

The diplomatic circle was noticeably large in the first Courts held by King George and Queen Mary after the Great War. This was due to the rearrangement of the map of Europe out of which several new States had been evolved. The ladies of the diplomatic circles are attired like the other ladies attending the Court—all plumes and trains. The gentlemen—Ambassadors, Ministers, and the principal members of their staffs—are brilliantly dressed. Crimson and gold are the predominant colours. Before the World War the German Ambassador wore, perhaps, the most striking uniform in the circle. After the War, as the representative of a Republic, he joined the Ambassador of the United States as the wearer of evening dress and knee breeches. The French Ambassador wears Court costume to which distinction, or individuality, is given by the broad red sash of the Legion of Honour. It was not until about the middle of the nineteenth century that the representatives of the United States discontinued the wearing of the recognised official dress of the Courts to which they were accredited. In 1853 the Government of the United States sent an order to its Ministers abroad that they must appear at Courts " in the simple dress of an American citizen." The American Minister at the Court of St. James at the time was a man who afterwards became President of the Republic—James Buchanan. He adopted the American evening dress of the period. " I appeared at the levee on Wednesday last," he wrote in February, 1854, "in just such a dress as I have worn at the President's a hundred times—a black coat, white waistcoat, and cravat, and black pantaloons and dress boots, with the addition of a very plain black-handled and black-hilted sword—this to gratify those who have yielded so much and to distinguish me from the upper Court servants." He says he knew he would be received at Court by Queen Victoria in any dress he might wear, but did not anticipate that he would be received in so kind and distinguished a manner as happened when he made his first appearance in evening dress. " As I approached the Queen," he goes on, " an arch but benevolent smile lit up her countenance, as much as to say, ' You are the first man who ever appeared before me at Court in such a dress.' I confess that I never felt more proud of being an American than when I stood in that brilliant circle ' in the simple dress of an American citizen.' " As late at King Edward's reign the American Ambassador and his suite at a Court wore trousers. They wear knee breeches now. Republics of South America have not followed the example in that respect of their elder big brother of the North. Their representatives wear gorgeous uniforms. And Ambassadors of ancient countries and first-class Powers are less insistent than they on the recognition of their diplomatic privileges. In the enjoyment of these privileges they include their servants. It was the representative of a South American republic who wrote to the Home Secretary in high indignation: "I have this day got a severe blow from a policeman's baton on the head of my valet."

* * * * * *

But the Guards' band in the Presence Chamber is playing the National Anthem as an announcement of the entrance of King George and Queen Mary, accompanied by members of the Royal Family. They are preceded by a large company of the officers of the Household, headed by the Lord Chamberlain and the Lord Steward. These are variously dressed. Those who are Army officers wear their uniforms. Others are in the dress of their offices—the difference being in the amount of gold embroidery and the number of gilt buttons on their single-breasted coats, but all these have breeches of white kerseymere, white silk hose, black patent leather shoes, and swords in black scabbards with gilt mountings. Most of them carry long white wands. And all are walking backwards at a slow pace facing Their Majesties. The King wears the uniform of an Admiral of the Fleet, or that of Colonel-in-Chief of one of the Life Guards or Foot Guards. The Queen is always richly and beautifully dressed. At one Court her gown was of gold cloth woven in varying tints which gave it a sunset glow.

We talk of Kings as Crowned Heads. But the King of England is not to be seen, even at Court, with this golden symbol—and burden—on his head. The Queen, however, does wear a light golden and jewelled Crown over her hair. Both display across their breasts the broad blue riband of the most illustrious of the English Orders of Knighthood, and the first in the world—the Garter, of which the King is the Sovereign and the Queen the Lady. No other decoration could be more appropriate for this high festival of womanhood. For it is emblematic of the chivalric ideal of woman's purity and honour. We know the story, or tradition, of the origin of the Order of the Garter about the middle of the fourteenth century. The Queen of Edward III dropped her garter at Court. There was a titter among the ladies and gentlemen as the King picked up the garter and rallied the Queen upon what would be thought of her. " Honi soit qui mal y pense ! "

she cried. (" May he be dishonoured who thinks ill of it.")
And the King, to emphasise the rebuke, placed the garter
below his left knee as a proud decoration.

But the King and the Queen have now taken up their
positions before the dais upon which the Throne is set. About
them are grouped the members of the Royal Family and the
Ladies-in-waiting. The Ambassadors and Ministers and their
ladies also remain in the Presence Chamber. The Throne
Guard—consisting of twelve members of the Honourable
Corps of Gentlemen-at-Arms (distinguished Army officers)
in scarlet coatees with epaulettes of gold bullion and gold-
chased helmets, with plumes of swan's feathers—are drawn up
in a line close at hand. At the doors are posted parties of
the other Bodyguard of the King, the Yeomen of the Guard—
old non-commissioned officers with fine bearded faces that
become their ruffs and scarlet skirted coats and puffed sleeves
of Tudor times. All is ready for the debutantes and the ladies
who are to present them. The young novices come in, one
at a time, the name of each being announced by the Lord
Chamberlain. Many types of beauty are to be found among
them, but they all have one charm in common—the freshness
and bloom of budding womanhood.

Before the debutante enters the Presence Chamber her long
train, which she is carrying over her arm, is let down by a
Gentleman Usher, or a Gentleman-at-Arms, and deftly spread
in its full length along the floor. She moves forward over the
crimson carpet—a fairy-like being, bright and spotless, in
white, or pearl grey, with three plumes mounted in her hair
and a bouquet or feather fan in her right hand. She is all
alone, and the great moment has come. She has only a dim
perception of the splendour of the chamber in white and
gold, and the flood of light from the cut-glass electroliers.
But she sees the King and Queen clearly enough. Down she
sinks with a graceful sweep in her first curtsey before the
King. She does not kiss hands. But regaining her footing,
makes two paces sideways to the right, and sinks down a
second time in salutation of the Queen. As she leaves the
Presence, her train is lifted up, folded, and placed over her
arm again by a Gentleman Usher or a Gentleman-at-Arms.

She has passed through the gateway of Life. The school girl has become a woman of Society. The ladies join their male escorts in the outer rooms and partake of the supper which Their Majesties have provided for their guests.

The spectacle has a certain solemnity calculated to inspire awe. Rarely has anything happened to mar it. At the worst a debutante may, in her excusable agitation, walk past Their Majesties without stopping to curtsey. The wonder is that so cool and collected are the girls that most of them go through the ceremony with all the ease of experienced dowagers. Once, however, a most unexpected thing occurred. It was in June, 1914. The militant suffragettes were agitating for the parliamentary vote, and several of them were in prison refusing to take food—on " hunger strike," as it was called—as a protest against their incarceration. So a debutante went down on her knees before King George, and in a loud voice exclaimed, " Your Majesty, for God's sake, stop torturing women." The sensation was immense. Yet there was no interruption of the proceedings. The girl was lifted from her knees by a Gentleman-at-Arms and gently carried out of the Presence. The band went on playing soft music. The debutantes continued coming in, and as they curtseyed they were smiled upon by the King and Queen.

*   *   *   *   *   *

As lovely woman is seen set in the beauty of raiment, so brave man shines forth solicitous to dazzle in the brilliancy of uniform, spangled with decorations and orders, at the Levee. The general public have a better opportunity of seeing what men look like than what women look like when they come to pay their respects to the Sovereign. Levees are held in the afternoons of the early months of the year. A stroll in the Mall on a Levee day is well worth while for the sight afforded of the men coming out of St. James's Palace, after their presentation, in scarlet tunics and plumed hats ; lace cravats, knee breeches, and silver-buckled shoes, with the fresh greenery of St. James's Park as a background. The peacock in the park in all the glory of his erect and spreading tail has but little more to boast of in the way of splendour and pride than man in the gay and varied bravery of his Levee dress.

No command is issued by the King for attendance at his Levees. His Majesty simply makes public announcement that it will be his pleasure on an appointed day to receive gentlemen wishing to be presented. Levees, in fact, are the modern equivalents of the public receptions held by earlier Sovereigns when every subject had the right—at least in theory if not in actual practice—to enter the Presence in order to testify to his allegiance and loyalty or to petition for a favour. Admissions to Levees are necessarily subject to certain regulations. A civilian applicant for a card must supply the Lord Chamberlain with particulars of his profession or calling, and also give the name of a sponsor who guarantees his respectability and who himself has been presented. Diplomatists, members of His Majesty's Government, Permanent Secretaries of Civil Service departments, and others, have the " Entree." Navy and Army officers obtain their cards from the Admiralty and War Office. Indian civil servants from the India Office, Dominion civil servants and officers of the Forces from the Dominion Office, mayors, sheriffs, and magistrates from the Home Office, Judges and King's Counsel from the Lord Chancellor's Office.

The assembly in the saloon adjoining the Presence Chamber before presentation is large, numbering several hundreds, and is singular in its variety of uniform and dress and its richness in colouring. There are King's Counsel in silk gowns and full-bottomed wigs ; soldiers in scarlet and sailors in dark blue and gold epaulettes, outshining airmen in the severe simplicity of their light blue ; and different groups of civilians— civil servants, medical doctors, authors, musicians, artists, commercial men—in Court velvet coats and shorts or frock-dress with trousers. Other contributions to the colour scheme of the company are the lovely tints of Indian turbans; the lawn and scarlet of ecclesiastics ; mayoral furred robes and gold chains of office ; the gold lace of lord lieutenants of counties ; the gold embroidered dark blue of diplomats ; the red and black and grey of Judges of the High Court; the

273

medals and ribbons of Army and Navy officers; the decorations and orders of foreign attachés.

Court officials marshal the company into the single file which is to pass before the King in the Presence Chamber. Each name of those in the gay and glittering line is called out as he passes the King with a bow. Formerly the King shook hands with everyone who was presented. The custom at Levees held by Queen Victoria was for the person presented to drop on one knee and kiss the Sovereign's hand. More often the Levees were delegated by the Queen to the Prince of Wales, and presentation to him was equivalent to presentation to Her Majesty. King Edward introduced the present habit of the Sovereign smiling and bowing as his subjects pass by.

As I have said, it was an ancient right of the subject in England to enter the presence of the Sovereign. As late as the Stuart Kings the Palace of Whitehall was an open house. All and sundry made their way into the Palace. Macaulay, in his *History of England,* contrasts the easy and familiar ways of Charles II and James II with the dourness of their successor, William III :

> One of the chief functions of our Sovereigns had long been to preside over the Society of the capital. That function Charles the Second had performed with immense success. His easy bow, his good stories, his style of dancing and playing tennis, the sound of his cordial laugh, were familiar to all London. One day he was seen among the elms of St. James's Park chatting with Dryden about poetry. Another day his arm was on Tom Durfey's shoulder, and His Majesty was taking a second while his companion sang " Phillida, Phillida," or, " To horse, brave boys, to Newmarket to horse."

King James, with much less vivacity and good nature was, Macaulay says, accessible, and, to people who did not cross him, civil. But of this sociableness King William was entirely destitute.

> He seldom came forth from his closet (Macaulay writes) and when he appeared in the public rooms he stood among the crowd of courtiers and ladies, stern and abstracted,

making no jest and smiling at none. His freezing look, his silence, his dry and concise answers which he uttered when he could keep silence no longer disgusted noblemen and gentlemen who had been accustomed to be slapped on the back by their Royal masters, called " Jack " or " Harry," congratulated about race cups or rallied about actresses.

The Hanoverian Kings went further in separating Court life from national life. It was Queen Victoria who restored something of the old intimate personal relations between the Sovereign and his subjects by the giving of garden parties at Buckingham Palace. This custom was not only carried on but developed by King Edward and King George, so that garden parties have become by far the best known and most popular of State functions. Commands are sent to many thousands of men and women well known in their walks of life and representative of all classes. The King and Queen walk about among their guests in the extensive and beautiful grounds of the Palace. Tea and music are provided. But presentations made at garden parties are not equivalent to presentations at Court or Levee.

CHAPTER II

AT HOME

THE management of the State functions of the Court, and of the daily routine of the King's Household, is an elaborate business. For the ensurance of due order and regularity it is divided between several departments. These are conducted by officials who have invariably been carefully selected for their ability and experience in organisation, as well as for their social position, good appearance, and engaging manners.

The Officers of the King's Household and the Court are of two classes. There is the political class, who are appointed by the Prime Minister, and, being members of the Administration, go out of office when there is a change of Government. Their duties are principally ceremonial. Then there is the permanent and more important class for the conduct of the domestic business of the Household. These appointments are made by the King, and are held during His Majesty's pleasure, independently of the Government. Formerly the Lord Chamberlain was at the head of the political Ministers of the Royal Household. In November, 1924, on the return of a Conservative Government, following the defeat of the first Labour Government, the Lord Chamberlain, the Lord Steward, and the Master of the Horse were given a non-political character and accordingly do not now change with the Government. The Lord Chamberlain's chief function is the regulation of Drawing Rooms and Levees. He is also responsible, curiously enough, for the licensing of dramatic entertainments. His salary is £2,000 a year. He has two offices—one in Buckingham Palace and the other in St. James's Palace. The Master of the Horse looks after the horses, and the carriages, the coachmen and footmen. The domestic economy of the Royal Household is the concern of the Lord Steward. In the service of a dinner to the Sovereign formerly the Lord Chamberlain found the table linen and crockery, the Lord Steward the food and wines, and the Master of the Horse the footmen to attend at table. The Master of the Horse has also a privilege which no other Minister of the Household enjoys—the private use of a royal carriage and pair with royal footmen in attendance. He arranges royal processions, such as the procession from Buckingham Palace to Westminster, when the King and Queen go in State to open Parliament. Lord Albemarle, a Master of the Horse in Queen Victoria's early years, claimed the right to accompany Her Majesty in the State coach to Westminster. The Queen objected, and the matter was referred to the Duke of Wellington. " My good fellow," said Wellington to Albemarle, " the Queen can, as she pleases, make you go inside the coach, or outside the coach, or run behind the coach like a tinker's dog." Still, the Master of the Horse is a great officer. In State processions his place is next after the Sovereign.

There remain only three important appointments of a political character. They are offices subordinate to the Lord Chamberlain and the Lord Steward. The Vice-Chamberlain of the King's Household acts as assistant to the Lord Chamberlain, and as his deputy in his absence. The Treasurer of the King's Household is next below the Lord Steward, and his deputy in his absence; and the Comptroller of the King's Household ranks next after the Treasurer in the Lord Steward's department. These posts carry salaries of £700 a year. The Court duties of these political officers of the Household have become nominal in a large degree. It is the Government that commands most of their services. Whether they be Lords or Commons, they act as deputies to absent Ministers, or as assistant Whips in their respective Houses. The original purpose of changing these and the other political officers with each change of Government was to prevent party intrigues with the Sovereign. All that has been past and done with long since.

* * * * * *

" Oh, the rapture of a dull evening at home." One can imagine the King indulging in this cry of the heart as, escaped from the ceremonial restraints of the Court, he sinks into an arm-chair in his " den," with a cigarette and a book in all the abandon of slippered and jacketed ease.

The King labours under social, as well as political, disabilities. That he can never wholly disappear for awhile must be one of the most irritating—never even shake himself free of his official self to the extent of becoming just an ordinary man, meeting ordinary men and women on the footing of a common humanity, giving free expression in talk with them to the thoughts that arise in his mind. There is no man in the world to-day in regard to whom public curiosity is so unrelaxing, on whom the glare of the limelight is so unremitting, as the King of England. All his movements are daily chronicled in the *Court Circular*, which is compiled by the Court Newsman, and distributed every night to the daily newspapers of the Kingdom. If he goes for a week-end to a country house the visit is written about in the papers. There is not a day of his existence that the public do not know where he is and what he is doing.

Only in the home circle, as distinct from the Royal Household, is the light that beats upon the Throne really turned off. Only at home do the King and Queen enjoy some measure of the privacy which is the common possession, almost the Divine right, of their people. The home life of Their Majesties is wholly isolated from the pomp and circumstance of the Court. It is quietly spent in the seclusion of the innermost private apartments of the Royal Family, whether in Buckingham Palace or in Windsor Castle—a little oasis of cosy domesticity set in a wilderness of spacious salons, wide floors, high ceilings, approached by stately and cold marble staircases. Their Majesties are very homely folk. Society does not greatly appeal to them, nor company either. The King does not dine out as his father used frequently to do both as Prince of Wales and King, with men only—small parties, as a rule of no more than half a dozen, but remarkable for the evidence afforded of Edward's disregard of racial and social prejudices in the selection of his intimate acquaintances. It is impossible, perhaps, for the Sovereign to surround himself with a circle, close in personal relationship, unembarrassed and disinterested. The main attraction of friendship with Royalty is the gratification of vanity, or the hope of advancement. The sense of equality is particularly absent. By all accounts King George's intimate friends are few in number. He has not that gregariousness or sociable instinct, which enabled his father, in whom it was strongly developed, to make " familiars," remarkable in their numbers and variety of character and of position.

At Home

The home is the centre of King George's happiness. Queen Mary is the most domesticated of women—a true housewife. The houses which the Queen graces with her presence as guest are very restricted in number. And it is no hyperbole to say that the suburban villa—the home of the great middle class—may see in the Palace a replica of itself, on a higher plane, and in more luxurious surroundings, no doubt, but in things essential presenting the same kind of domesticity. Perhaps the only really striking difference between the one home life and the other is in regard to card-playing. Bridge is a popular pastime around Hampstead and Streatham. Neither the King nor the Queen cares for cards. In this respect they differ widely from King Edward, with whom card-playing was a passion. King George and Queen Mary have that love of music which has always been a characteristic of the Royal Family. King George's favourite masters are Mendelssohn and Gounod. He also greatly enjoys an old ballad sung to her own accompaniment by Queen Mary.

But the truest picture of the Royal home life is one which presents the King at rest after a hard and trying day, reading the latest book of travel or biography to the Queen, while the Queen is engaged with busy fingers on crochet work for charitable gifts. There is nothing in the couple, as they thus sit together of an evening after dinner, to suggest those awe-inspiring personages, anointed and crowned, whom we have hitherto been considering. They are "Mary" and "George" to one another. In former times the King or Queen was allowed hardly a moment of privacy. Sleeping or waking, dressing or undressing, eating or drinking, walking or sitting, in doors or out of doors, there was always some Court functionary, male or female, in close attendance, from whom there was no escape. At home, King George and Queen Mary see to it that they are untroubled by the attentions of Gold Stick in Waiting, or Silver Stick in Waiting, or even Silver Stick Adjutant in Waiting. Whatever attendance they require is supplied by their own domestic servants. In a word, the King and Queen are their simple, natural selves in the narrow inner home circle of the Court.

Nevertheless, it is at home that the King feels most the

pressure of the cares and responsibilities of his position. For it is at home that he has to deal with most of the work—vast in extent and varied in character—which his part in the administration of Government entails. He is an early riser. Before breakfast he reads two or three of the London daily newspapers. Practically all the leading newspapers, London and provincial, are taken in at the Palace, and carefully gone through by members of the Private Secretary's department. News and announcements of special interest to the King are marked with a blue pencil, and his attention is called to them by the Private Secretary. After breakfast His Majesty goes to his office, a large room on the first floor with an outlook on the gardens, lake, and woodlands of Buckingham Palace. There are two roll-top desks in the room—one for the King and the other for his Private Secretary. Here His Majesty sits for hours reading State documents, official letters, and despatches from abroad, as well as his own private correspondence. The room is like the office of a banker, or head of a commercial firm, so furnished is it with labour-saving appliances—card indexes, telephones, speaking tubes. On a table within easy reach of the King's hand is a row of despatch boxes, among which he distributes letters and papers with his annotations. There is a constant daily flow of these red boxes to and from the Government departments in Whitehall. Only by the most methodical system is it possible to cope with the vast mass of documents which have to be read or signed. As it is, the King is fully occupied until luncheon time. And besides dealing with his correspondence, he has to see Ministers of the Crown and Ambassadors for whom " audiences " have been appointed, or other people whom he has arranged to "receive." There may not be any very substantial power or authority attached to those duties, but their prompt discharge is necessary to the constant movement of the mighty machinery of Government and administration. Ministers may decide things, but it is the King who sets them in motion. Were he to cease to perform his duties the whole machinery of the State would be paralysed.

*   *   *   *   *   *

Queen Victoria made a labour of State business, but it was labour she rejoiced in. So high was her sense of the importance of the work, and her personal responsibility, that she insisted upon reading all correspondence on State and political affairs, and writing most, if not all, the replies in her own hand. During the greater part of her reign there were no labour-saving appliances, such as the telephone, shorthand, and the typewriter. Even if there had been, she would probably not have availed herself of them. She declined to use them when they were introduced in her later years. To have done so would, she thought, be derogatory to her office, and also lacking in respect for her correspondents, whether Ministers of the Crown, foreign Royalties, members of the Royal Family, or private friends. She was conservative in every-thing and old fashioned. Besides that, two of her favourite maxims were: "If you want a thing done well, do it yourself," and, "If you want a thing kept secret, keep it to yourself."

All her statesmen from Melbourne to Balfour also laboriously wrote their State correspondence with their own hand. That was the fashion of their age. Had they departed from it, the Queen would certainly have called them to account. As she wrote all her letters herself, she insisted that her Ministers should write all their letters to her themselves. She discarded even the one aid to the saving of labour that existed in her time—the copying clerk who wrote a good round plain hand. Never in her old age, any more than in her youth, did she fall victim to the temptation to do things with as little effort as possible. She was never perfunctory. To the end she followed the plan which Prince Albert laid down for her, never to sign anything until she had read it, and, as a further precaution, always to make and retain a note of its purport.

All this kept her very busy every day of her life, and some-times even till late at night. She was enabled to keep it up without overtaxing herself, mentally or physically, because of her sound constitution and her clear, strong mind. But as a precaution, her Physician in Ordinary, Sir James Reid, saw her twice daily, morning and evening, and there was also a weekly consultation with Sir William Jenner. Seventeen times a week her pulse was felt, she was sounded, and she put out her tongue for a physician to look at ! And yet she was not a bit hypochondriacal ! She liked writing, and she wrote with ease, giving expression to her thoughts in an artless and unstudied way that is most pleasing. She began to keep a Journal on her thirteenth birthday, May 24th, 1832, at her mother's request, and continued it until her death, describing the places she visited and the people she met. The last entry is dictated and dated January 12th, 1901. She died on January 22nd, 1901. There are over one hundred volumes of the *Journal* in the archives at Windsor, and with them are over 1,200 large folio volumes of her correspondence. What a remarkable monument of her industry and conscientiousness ! And, in addition, she had to sign her name to at least 50,000 official documents every year—an average of about 160 for each working day.

* * * * * *

The postal letters and telegrams of the King are looked after by a special department consisting of the Court Postmaster, an assistant overseer, and two or three telegraphists. This department accompanies Their Majesties as the Court is removed to Windsor, Sandringham, or Balmoral. The miscellaneous postal correspondence includes some extraordinary letters ; but they are by no means so numerous as might be imagined. It would seem that people out of their minds have sense enough left not to bother the King unduly, or else the feeling of loyalty is so powerful that it survives even in lunatics. What is also remarkable is that the great middle class rarely if ever trouble His Majesty with communications of any kind. And is not loyalty more predominant in this section of the community than in any other ? All letters are read by the Private Secretary or members of his staff. None are ignored. Even the trivial and absurd are acknowledged. Those of a reasonable character are submitted to the King personally, and replies are sent of a kind to afford gratification to the writers. Begging letters are very numerous. Assistance is given out of the Privy Purse, or the appeal is sent on to some charity organisation which deals with cases of the kind.

The private benefactions of the King amount to a large sum yearly.

The presents the Queen receives by post form a curious collection. Royalty never accept gifts from persons with whom they are not acquainted. All such presents are returned with a polite note explaining this rule. Poets send her poems ; tradesmen, specimens of their wares ; ladies, mittens, stockings, and other articles of attire worked by themselves. At Christmas the Queen is the recipient of some hundreds of Christmas cards, many of them of the most expensive nature.

The Private Secretary has much more to do besides dealing with the correspondence of the King. His duties require close observation of current events and also a talent for intelligent anticipation. Expressions of the Royal pleasure and sympathy must be well-timed. " Slips " are occasionally made, though they are very few considering the variety and extent of the communications. Queen Victoria had down to Windsor, for the entertainment of the little Princes and Princesses staying with her, a troupe of performing geese then appearing in a London music-hall. The custom of sending a polite message of inquiry as to the safe return of the company after a " command performance " was followed, in this case, without any change in the usual phraseology. " I am commanded by Her Majesty," Sir Henry Ponsonby, then Private Secretary, wrote to the manager of the troupe of geese, " to express the hope that the ladies and gentlemen of your company have safely returned to town." A mistake of a more serious kind almost led to foreign complications. Among the countless messages of condolence received by King Edward on the death of Queen Victoria was one from the Legislature of Kansas, United States. In the acknowledgment that was sent in the King's name, His Majesty was made to express his gratitude for " the loyalty and sympathy of the people of Kansas." The word " loyalty " aroused such resentment in Kansas that the message was ordered to be expunged from the State records. A few weeks later, Choate, the American Ambassador in London, sent to the Legislature the regret of King Edward for the unfortunate wording of the message. He explained that a form of message used in letters of acknowledgment to countries and towns in the British Empire had, through an oversight, been sent to Kansas. He added : " I have learned that the King was much pained when he heard of this blunder." Some member of the Royal secretariat had imagined that Kansas was a Crown colony.

The utmost precautions are taken to ensure the secrecy of the King's postbag. There is no duplicate of the gold key with which His Majesty opens his private writing-desk. There are two keys of the despatch-boxes in which all State papers are kept until they are dealt with by the King. His Majesty has one of the keys and the Private Secretary the other. The final depository of State documents are safes in the secretariat department, the keys of which never leave the possession of the Private Secretary. When the King leaves his office or room where he deals with his correspondence, no servant is allowed to enter until an assistant secretary has destroyed the contents of the waste-paper basket and the blotting pads.

* * * * * *

Above all, it must be ever present to the mind of the King and his secretaries in dealing with State documents that anything His Majesty may officially do wrongly will entail an immense amount of trouble in the undoing. It has been held, even by great jurists, that if the Keeper of the Great Seal—the highest symbol of Kingly authority—should affix it, without taking the Royal pleasure, to a patent of peerage or to a pardon, the instrument, to quote Macaulay, " cannot be questioned in any court of law, and can be annulled only by an Act of Parliament," though the Keeper may be held guilty of a high offence.

* * * * * *

The German formalism and stiffness introduced into the Royal Household by the Prince Consort, and continued more or less by Queen Victoria in her widowhood, has long since entirely disappeared. Domestic servants addressing the young Princes and Princesses had always to say " Your Royal Highness." King Edward, when Prince of Wales, adopted the style (which was followed by King George) of having the children called by the servants, " Prince Eddie " or " Princess Louise." On the other hand, Queen Victoria disliked being addressed as " Your Majesty." She always insisted on the use of the old-fashioned and homely " Ma'am." It was extremely disagreeable to her, particularly in her old age, to be stared at by the domestic servants. Those who had occasion to enter her presence had strict orders not to look at her on any account. Any infringement of this rule met with a severe reprimand. There is one little rule introduced by the Prince Consort which still holds good. An officer of the Household who encounters the King as he is walking through any of the rooms or corridors, bows to His Majesty ; and a domestic servant, in like circumstances, turns his face to His Majesty and stands at " attention."

Another rule introduced by the Prince Consort was that Queen Victoria should allow no man to sit in her presence —except at dinner. Queen Victoria, on the other hand, forbade her Maids of Honour from addressing any remark to the Prince Consort or sitting in his presence. Indeed, she required her Maids of Honour to stand, when in attendance upon her, and rarely invited them to sit down. This rule applied even to ladies who were guests at Royal dinners or receptions. Lady John Russell with her husband, then Prime Minister, dined at Buckingham Palace shortly after her confinement. When Queen Victoria and the other ladies retired to the drawing-room after dinner, Her Majesty invited Lady John Russell to sit down, remarking that she must feel weak after her maternal ordeal. But the Queen arranged that when the Prince Consort and the other gentlemen joined them, Lady So and So, who happened to be of a stout habit, should stand in front of the Prime Minister's wife, so as to hide her from the sight of the Prince, who would be annoyed if he saw her sitting.

Prime Ministers had also to stand—as well as their wives— in the Presence. Disraeli, in a letter written in 1874, describing a visit, as Prime Minister, to Queen Victoria at Osborne, says the Queen was most pleased with the way he had conducted the parliamentary session. " To think of you having the gout all the time ! How you must have suffered ! " She added : " And you ought not to stand now. You shall have a chair." Disraeli was highly delighted. Lord Derby, his predecessor as Conservative Prime Minister, once told him, as proof of the Queen's favour, that when he had an audience after his recovery from a severe illness, she remarked to him, " How sorry she was she could not ask him to be seated. The etiquette was so severe." " I remembered all this as she spoke," Disraeli continues. " So I humbly declined the privilege, saying I was quite well, but would avail myself of her gracious kindness if I ever had another attack." Gladstone relates that in his later years as Prime Minister Queen Victoria always asked him to sit down.

There was a story once current that Queen Victoria was invited to sit down in Buckingham Palace by one of her subjects, and as the subject happened to be Carlyle, the story was thought not improbable. Carlyle was asked to the Palace. As the Queen stood—so the story went—Carlyle could not sit. He said : " If your Majesty would be seated we could carry on this discussion with greater ease," and the Queen, taking the hint, sat down and he with her. In Carlyle's own account of the interview, given in a letter to his sister, Mrs. Aitken, he says that after some conversation with the Queen, who was seated on a sofa, he asked, " as an old infirmish man," Her Majesty's permission to sit, which, he states, was " graciously conceded."

Etiquette, in the opinion of the Prince Consort, apparently, was a code of rules by which great people kept lesser people at a proper and respectful distance. King Edward introduced simpler and more rational manners, and they have been improved upon by King George. People visiting Buckingham Palace to be received by the King are treated with every courtesy as, of course, they deserve to be, calling as they do by His Majesty's command. Gentle or simple, King George always invites his visitors to be seated.

*　　*　　*　　*　　*　　*

The Palace of the King anciently formed a separate criminal and civil jurisdiction. It was subject to the Court of the Lord Steward, held in his absence by the Treasurer or Comptroller of the Household or the Steward of the Marshalsea. In 1541—the thirty-third year of Henry VIII—an Act of

Parliament was passed for the punishment of murder and bloodshed within the King's Court, or within any house in which His Majesty was abiding. Trials for the crime were to be conducted by the Lord Steward. The penalty for murder was death and forfeiture of property. For striking, the offending right hand was to be cut off. It was provided that the Chief Surgeon was to be present " to sear the stump with a hot iron when the hand is stricken off," and that the Sergeant of the Cellar was to be ready to give a pot of red wine to the offender after the stump had been seared. The Act was not to apply to noblemen, or other persons who might strike his or their servants within the Palace, or the house where the King was abiding, " with his or their hands or fists or with any small staff or stick," for correction and punishment of offences committed ; nor to any of the King's officers and servants " that shall strike any persons within the said Palace or house." This criminal jurisdiction fell into disuse in the eighteenth century. The civil jurisdiction remained until 1849 when, by Act of Parliament, it was transferred to the Court of Common Pleas or the County Court. But one office created by the statute of Henry VIII still survives. This is the Coroner of the Royal Household for the holding of inquests in respect of sudden deaths occurring in any of the Palaces, including the Palace of Westminster in which Parliament sits. The jury is always formed from Officers of the Household.

CHAPTER III

IN SOCIETY

THERE is one sphere in which the pre-eminence of the King is universally recognised. This is Society. His Majesty is the leader of Society and sets its habits and fashions. To entertain the King is an honour that is much coveted by the exalted and wealthy in Society. But it is not open even to the greatest noble of the land to ask His Majesty to be so gracious as to spend a week-end at his country mansion. A King is not to be invited by a subject. As King he has the freedom of the country, and the doors of all its big houses are open unto him to enter as he pleases. He " commands " his hosts as well as his guests. That is the etiquette of the matter. But His Majesty knows full well, that whatever hospitality he may desire in a country house, whether for a night or two, in the course of a ceremonious visit to the district to lay a foundation stone or open some institution, or for a week's game shooting, can be given without undue strain on the host's purse, and will be given with a heart and a half. The would-be host may, of course, intimate to the Private Secretary that it would give him the greatest pleasure to entertain the King, should it meet with His Majesty's gracious wishes. But the date of the visit and its duration—however it may be arranged, whether directly or indirectly—are fixed by the King. Before the invitations for the house-party to meet the King are sent out, the host submits the list of proposed guests to His Majesty. A name may occasionally be added to the list—that of a particular friend—but seldom, if ever, is one deleted. An invitation to meet the King at a country house amounts to a declaration of the King's desire for the pleasure of one's company, and therefore it is regarded as imperative as the King's personal command to a Royal function at Buckingham Palace or Windsor.

When the King is accompanied by the Queen to a country house, the visit is more ceremonious. The visits of the King alone for a week-end, or for a week's shooting, are somewhat informal. The suites of apartments in which Royalty is lodged must be out of the way of the rooms of the other guests, and, if possible, have a separate and private entrance from outside. Rooms have also to be provided for the King's gentlemen and the Queen's ladies, and for their personal servants—valets, footmen, and maids. In addition, motor-car drivers, and, if the King is down for shooting, a loader of his guns, have to be accommodated. Telegraphic instruments are usually installed in a country house where the King is staying, especially if the visit be prolonged, and the house is connected by a special wire with the nearest telegraph office. There must be facilities for instant communication between the King and Downing Street and Buckingham Palace, so that His Majesty may quickly attend to urgent State business and be informed of important events without delay. The King's private telegraphist has charge of the special wire.

No Sovereign is so safe among his people as the King of England. Nevertheless, no risks are taken. The King is guarded with the utmost vigilance. For there is no accounting for lunatics with grievances, real or imaginary, and notoriety-hunters of unbalanced minds. There are small and specially organised bodies of detectives for the protection of the King and the Prince of Wales. Each is under the control of an inspector—a well-dressed man, with a keenly-watchful eye and a strong sense of suspicion, who attends the King or the Prince at public functions, but unconspicuously, being never in the way and yet never out of the way. In like manner there is no parade of the detectives on duty when the King is staying at a country house.

*   *   *   *   *   *

The King is regarded as head of the house during his visit. The Royal Standard floats over the house. But the visit is regarded as private or formal to the extent that while it lasts the issue of the *Court Circular* is suspended. The plans for each day are submitted for the King's approval. Dinner is usually the only meal at which His Majesty joins the house party. He always breakfasts in his room. Not even a brief visit to a country house frees the King of the responsibilities and cares of his office. Besides the communications that are constantly coming by telegraph, messengers are ever on the road to and from London with despatch-boxes containing papers which require immediate attention. His Majesty devotes the morning to them. Should he be down for game shooting, a different course is followed. As he likes to be out at the coverts early, State business is postponed until the return to the house for afternoon tea.

The guests assemble in the drawing-room to await the King's appearance for dinner. Should His Majesty be accompanied by the Queen, the order of going to the dining-room is quite a stately rite. The gentlemen line up on one side and the ladies on the other, and as the King taking in the hostess and the Queen following with the host pass down this alleyway, the ladies curtsey and the gentlemen bow, and then fall in according to rank. At dinner the King and Queen are waited upon by their own footmen in livery, the rest of the company being attended to by the servants of the house. Dinner does not last long. The heavy meals of Victorian days, with their numerous dishes, were abolished by King Edward, who set the fashion of five or six courses quickly served. Formerly, after the ladies retired, a good deal of drinking was indulged in by the gentlemen. King Edward stopped this also by having cigars and cigarettes immediately handed round at his own table, and when he had smoked one cigar himself, he proposed an adjournment to the drawing-room. There was usually some little conversation and music in King Edward's time, but soon the company in the drawing-room settled down to bridge until bed-time.

Card-playing was the favourite indoor pastime of King Edward. Gladstone mentions in his *Diary* that when he was the guest of the Prince of Wales he was invited by the Prince, after dinner, to play whist. " I said, ' For love, sir ? ' He said, ' Well, shillings and half-a-crown on the rubber,' to which I submitted." Gladstone adds : " The Prince has apparently an immense whist memory, and plays well, accordingly." King Edward's stakes at bridge were half-a-crown points. Etiquette then required that all money passed to the King should be new and unused ; and, in order that the house party might be enabled to comply with it, the host took care to obtain beforehand a supply of new coins and fresh notes, for which his guests exchanged their own money.

In 1891 there was a grave Society scandal arising out of card-playing at Tranby Croft which was brought into a court of law. King Edward, as Prince of Wales, was of the house party, and was examined as a witness at the hearing of the case. The Prince was censured in the Press—particularly in the Evangelical and Radical section of it—more censured than he had ever been in his career as Prince. He was very annoyed. He wrote a letter to Dr. Benson, Archbishop of Canterbury, the most outspoken and emotional he had ever penned. It shows that he was smarting keenly under a sense of injustice.

The letter was in reply to one of sympathy from the Archbishop. " A recent trial which no one deplores more than I do, and which I was powerless to prevent," he wrote, " gave occasion for the Press to make a most bitter and unjust attack upon me, knowing that I was defenceless, and I am not sure that politics were not mixed up in it." He referred again to " the torrent of abuse " which was poured upon him, not only by the Press, but by " the Low Church and especially by the Nonconformists." He went on to say : " they have a perfect right, I am well aware, in a free country like our own, to express their opinions, but I do not think they have a just right to jump at conclusions regarding myself without knowing the facts." He declared that he had a horror of gambling, regarding it, like intemperance, as one of the greatest curses which a country can be afflicted with. " Horse-racing," he said, " may produce gambling, and it may not, but I have always looked upon it as a manly sport which is popular with Englishmen of all classes, and there is no reason why it should be looked upon as a gambling transaction." This outburst caused general surprise. Royalty usually treats malignant stories and criticisms with a proud and silent disdain. The Prince, by all accounts, was a stickler for the proprieties. He made allowances, but any flagrant violation of good manners met with his unmitigated censure. A word of condemnation from him, as Society's mentor, meant for the offender that all was lost.

As leader of fashion, women of Society copied the Princess of Wales more than men copied the Prince. Once after a serious illness the Princess was noticed to walk with a slight limp. Immediately women who desired to be regarded as fashionable assumed what came to be known as the " Alexandra limp." Some of the early portraits of the Princess, after her marriage, show that it was her custom to wear two long locks of her hair, on each side, over her shoulder and down her breast, which was admirably suited to her graceful neck and slender form. The fashion was universally copied. By ladies of Society it was called " love locks." Among girls of the people it was known as " follow-me-lads." When the Princess became Queen it was her custom to drive in Hyde Park with one of her grandchildren seated on her knee. This had a very charming result. The dogs which Society ladies used to carry on their laps when out driving were replaced by children.

*　　*　　*　　*　　*　　*

King George contributes his share to the common stock of a house-party's entertainment by his easy and playful sociability. It is a breach of etiquette to speak to the King unless spoken to. His Majesty must make the approach and start the conversation. Nevertheless, hosts and other guests talk and laugh and amuse themselves ; and the King enters heartily into everything in his simple, unaffected way. He puts people at their ease by putting himself at ease with them. From cards he derives but little enjoyment. In fact, it is not too much to say that he dislikes them. He prefers a game of billiards. But he would rather give the time to talk. He likes to meet any notable exponent of the art of conversation, which the vogue of card-playing, with its absorbing silences, has almost destroyed. He has a relish for matters of concern, be they social, scientific, literary, historical, sport, manners and customs—anything but political, in the party sense—and enjoys the clash of opinion that arises when a subject is regarded from as many different views as there are different temperaments present. His own part in the discussion is distinguished by the depth of thought and the breadth of outlook of a grave and sympathetic mind. He also loves a good story well told, and shows his enjoyment of it in a very hearty laugh.

His Majesty is not much of a smoker. He likes a cigarette better than a cigar or pipe.

For any of the company, lady or gentleman, to withdraw before the King gives the signal for the break up of the party by himself retiring would also be a breach of etiquette. That rule applies not only to house parties but to such gatherings as balls, wedding receptions and garden parties at which Royalty is present. Gladstone, in 1883, when he was Prime Minister, wrote this humble letter of apology to the Prince of Wales : " I am very much shocked at an omission which I made last night in failing to ask your Royal Highness' leave to be the first to quit Lord Alchester's agreeable party in order that I might attend to my duties in the House of Commons. When I was a young man, not only did the company remain united if a member of the Royal Family were present, but I well recollect the application of the same rule in the case of the Archbishop of Canterbury." The host always attends the King to his rooms when he retires for the night.

The servants of a country house are as delighted and flattered by the visit of the King as are their master and mistress. They are also handsomely remunerated for the extra trouble to which the household is put. The King's douceurs—to call them " tips " might be regarded as unbecoming—are, again to use language appropriate to the subject, wholly consonant with his august rank. The average guest, peer or commoner, staying at a country house for a week's shooting gets off with £20 or so. The King leaves as much as £100 to be divided up among his host's servants. Even the stable boys, or the boys of the garage, get " paper " in the distribution. In addition, the King and also the Prince of Wales, before leaving the house, usually sends for the cook and thanks him or her personally for seeing to his comfort. The host and hostess are not forgotten, of course. They receive a handsome souvenir—a pin, or brooch or cigarette-case, with the Royal initials in diamonds. The King is very careful, as well as generous, in the selection of gifts. He chooses them himself, with an eye to their fitness, and presents them himself, knowing how the personal touch is esteemed in all such matters.

*   *   *   *   *   *

The English King

King Edward and Queen Alexandra made the English Court famous throughout Europe for splendid hospitality. Sovereigns, Presidents, Princes, and other potentates, succeeded each other as the guests of Their Majesties at Buckingham Palace or in Windsor Castle, and the entertaining was magnificent. Over it all was the dazzling glory of St. George's Hall on a night that supper was served there after a ball or theatrical entertainment in the Waterloo Gallery. The famous gold plate displayed on the buffets blazed under a thousand electric lights. These festivals, incidental to the exchange of courtesies between Crowned Heads are now, as a consequence of the Great War, exceedingly rare. As the sovereignty has become more democratic so has its hospitality. In it all classes of subjects participate. It has varied forms. There are State dinners at Buckingham Palace at which thirty or forty guests may be entertained—Ministers of the Crown, leading members of both Houses of Parliament, distinguished Churchmen, Judges, and officers of the Navy and Army. When the Court is at Windsor there are week-end visits to the Castle. This hospitality is attended with considerable state. At the railway station a Royal carriage awaits the guest, and he is received at the Castle by an officer of the Household. Two footmen are stationed outside his rooms to render whatever services he may require. He meets Their Majesties in the drawing-room with his fellow-guests before dinner. Breakfast is served in his rooms. And he leaves, as he came, in a Royal carriage. The Garden Party in the beautiful and extensive grounds of Buckingham Palace, at the end of the Season, is now the most popular form of Royal entertainment. Commands to attend it are widely distributed—to representatives of all the professions, and all industrial, political, social and religious movements, as well as to the aristocracy. And an exceedingly pleasant open-air function it is on a fine afternoon, with its thousands of guests, its tea and its music, and the presence of the King and Queen. It is a typically English scene—a full-dress out-of-door five o'clock tea marked by the minimum of formality and the maximum of sociability. Lastly, there are the house-parties for deer stalking at Balmoral, and game shooting at Sandringham. These, of course, are intimate social gatherings of the King's particular friends. But not always. Henry Broadhurst, one of the first Labour representatives, who worked as a stone mason until he was elected to Parliament, spent a week-end at Sandringham as the guest of the Prince of Wales. " On my arrival," Broadhurst writes, " His Royal Highness personally conducted me to my rooms, made a careful inspection to see that all was right, and stoked the fires ! " As he did not possess a dress-suit, dinner was served in his room. " I spent three days with the Prince and Princess," Broadhurst adds, " and I can honestly say that I was never entertained more to my liking, and never felt more at home."

For full State banquets at Buckingham Palace, the famous Crown dinner service of solid gold—each plate is said to be worth £400—is brought from the strong-rooms in Windsor Castle. The laying of the Royal table is, on such occasions, a ceremony in itself. First come the " upholsterers," whose duty it is to see that the table is well and truly placed in the room, and is in fit condition to bear its precious and heavy appointments. Next come the " table deckers," who lay the snowy napery, worked with the Royal Arms, the knives and forks and spoons and the drinking glasses. The napkins are never twisted into fanciful shapes, being always plainly folded. The Yeomen of the Gold and Silver Pantries then arrange the gold and silver appointments ; and, finally, other " deckers " adorn the table with flowers and trailing greenery.

The custom of providing finger-bowls, containing scented water for dipping the fingers in before taking fruit at dessert has become almost a thing of the past ; but even when their use was the vogue they were never seen at the Royal table. They were banished early in the reign of the House of Hanover, for the reason that when the toast of " The King " was given the Jacobites were enabled really to drink to the Pretender by the device of first passing their glasses over the finger-bowls, which meant—" the King over the water." It may not be generally known that it is permissible to drink to the King with water. King Edward, who was appealed to on the point, declared that he would appreciate his health being drunk with water just as much as with wine. He also put an end to the custom of standing up when the toast of " The Prince of

Wales " was proposed. At a public dinner which he attended, when Prince of Wales, he waved the company to sit down, saying : " I am only a subject of the Queen."

*   *   *   *   *   *

The sojourn of the King and Queen at Balmoral, and subsequently at Sandringham, after the close of the London Season, is perhaps the nearest approach to the homeliness of private life which they are enabled to enjoy. Etiquette, though never entirely banished, becomes less rigid through being tempered by a certain informality. It is at Sandringham that the hearts of King George and Queen Mary are set and their first fond hopes remain. It is their country seat, as it was the country seat of King Edward and Queen Alexandra. This estate of over 7,000 acres in Norfolk was purchased in 1861 for the young Prince of Wales for £220,000, out of moneys saved by the Prince Consort from the revenues of the Duchy of Cornwall during the minority of the Heir Apparent. The mansion, of red brick and Elizabethan in style, standing in a park of 200 acres was built in the early 'seventies. There is another house known as York Cottage, also in the park. It was occupied by King George and Queen Mary when they were Prince and Princess of Wales. Thus the home associations of the Royal Family cluster round Sandringham.

A very pleasant country it is, with its fir plantations and its stretches of bracken and heather on dry sandy soil, and the grassy swards flanking its roads abloom with wild flowers in their season. There are four villages on the estate, Wolferton, Babingley, West Newton and Appleton, and part of Dersingham—all with a charming air of rural simplicity. They are also rather secluded. The nearest town, King's Lynn, is seven miles away and the nearest railway station, Wolferton, is three or four miles from the house. Besides the primary schools in the villages there are two central technical schools for boys and girls, the boys being taught carpentry and cabinet-making and the girls, cooking and dress-making. The place is without a public-house. But at West Newton, the most central of the villages, there is a club-house for the men and boys of the estate in the midst of a flower garden, where books and papers may be read, chess and bagatelle played, and each member may drink a pint of beer a day but no spirits. There is a church in most of the villages. Sandringham Church is in the park, near the house. Its clock, like the clock of the mansion, is always half an hour fast. For punctuality in all things is one of the attributes of Royalty. In the churchyard may be seen the grave of an infant Prince, Alexander by name, who died in 1871—one day old. A window in the church commemorates him—" Christ blessing little children."

Sandringham is one of the best sporting estates in the country. About 10,000 pheasants are reared there annually. There is an entire absence of warnings, so familiar elsewhere, as to prosecutions for trespass and pains and penalties. But the King's preserves are never poached. This is to be attributed more to the loyalty of poachers than to the vigilance of keepers.

The King's favourite sport was game-shooting. As a shot he had very few equals. It is doubtful whether any adept at the gun could do much more than hold his own with the King at driven birds. From his earliest years he also delighted to tramp through reed beds, mud and water, in search of snipe, wild fowl or outlying game. At York Cottage, there is a glass-case containing two woodcock. They fell to right and left shots from the King—an exceptionally fine thing in shooting. Rarely do two woodcock rise together, and more rarely still are they brought down by the one gun. Many stories are told of King George's fine shooting. One relates to grouse at Balmoral. The King, with his two guns, was in a butt towards which eleven driven grouse came flying, but on reaching the butt the birds turned and crossed the line. Nevertheless, His Majesty brought down four of the birds in front of the butt, and four behind—a feat in shooting with two guns which for rapidity and precision it would be difficult to beat. In pheasant shooting at Sandringham, His Majesty's average successes used to be over eighty per cent. of the cartridges fired.

To be so good an all-round shot as King George was requires uncommon steadiness of nerve, quickness and accuracy of vision. These qualities can only be secured by simple and plain living and regular exercise throughout the year. His Majesty is probably the most temperate and abstemious King

297

that ever sat on the English Throne. Walking was the form of exercise he preferred. He liked it better even than riding. At Balmoral, in the autumn, there is not only grouse shooting, but deer stalking also. A very trying and tiring sport physically is the stalking of a stag in the forests and on the moors of Balmoral. But the fitness of the King was equal to it, despite his advancing years. And in illustration of His Majesty's skill with the rifle, it is told that once two stags came within range which to an ordinary shot would mean that one of the deer would escape, but the King got them both.

At Sandringham the King farms a thousand acres. He breeds horses and cattle. He competes for prizes at local and national agricultural shows. He enjoyed the role of country squire, in perfect freedom and lightness of heart. He used to be seen about the fields and roads taking his favourite exercise on foot with his steward—clad in a tweed knickerbocker suit and soft hat, a stout stick in his hand and a couple of dogs at his heels. This was always an engaging glimpse to have caught of the man, apart from his office.

*   *   *   *   *   *

King Edward enjoyed the telling of stories, but there was one subject on which he would not allow the irreverant to trespass. Sir Felix Semon, the Court physician, relates in his *Diary* that, meeting the King in Society one day and being asked what was " the latest," he ventured to tell His Majesty about a Scottish doctor, who was also a professor at Edinburgh University, who put upon the door of his lecture room in the University the announcement, " The Queen has been graciously pleased to appoint Professor —— her Physician in Ordinary." Whereupon the students wrote under it, " God save the Queen." The King, Semon says, did not even smile. On the contrary his face stiffened and he turned away. The King or Queen must not be made the subject even of such harmless little jokes.

Splendid as may be the people's idea of the dignity of the Kingship, it paled before Edward's conception of it, that is, according to another story told of him when he was Prince of Wales. London was visited in 1881 by a coloured potentate, Kalakana of the Sandwich Islands, who was popularly known

as the " King of the Cannibal Islands." It happened that the
Crown Prince of Prussia (afterwards Frederick, German Emperor) and his wife, the daughter of Queen Victoria and Princess Royal of England, were in London at the same time.
When the parties met at Royal functions, as they did on two
or three occasions, the Prince of Wales decided that Kalakana
should have precedence of the Crown Prince. He was a black
man and only half civilised. But he was a King, aye, though his
palace might be a mud hovel, his throne, a derelict barrel
picked up on the seashore, his crown, a battered silk hat, or
else a biscuit-box, his robe, the cast-off shawl of a Lancashire
mill girl, his sceptre, the shinbone of a rival chief slain in
battle, and though only a couple of tens of thousands of savage
natives recognised him as master and ruler.

Accordingly, King Kalakana led out the Princess of Wales
for the opening dance at a party given at Marlborough House,
and at a reception in the South Kensington Museum he walked
at the head of the procession between the Prince and Princess
of Wales, and preceding the German Crown Prince and the
Princess Royal. The German Embassy afterwards sent an
indignant remonstrance to the Prince of Wales, to which the
Prince is said to have given the reply—" Either the brute is a
King, or he is an ordinary black nigger, and if he is not a King,
why is he here at all ? "

CHAPTER IV

WITH THE PEOPLE

SOCIAL service has become a tradition of the Royal Family. It was started by the Prince Consort, whose consuming sense of duty to the Nation wore him out at a comparatively early age. The Royal Family are always in ready sympathy with the joys and the griefs, the aspirations and ideals, the customs, sports and amusements of the people. And in return the people associate themselves whole-heartedly both in the joys and the sorrows of the Royal Family. This intimate association of the Royal Family and the Nation was emphasised by the Prince Consort, speaking at a public dinner in 1853, to the toast of the Royal Family. He truly said that one of the blessings attaching to the British Monarchy was that the domestic relations and domestic happiness of the Sovereign were inseparable from the domestic relations and the domestic happiness of the people at large. " In the progress of the Royal Family through life," he said, " is reflected, as it were, the progress of the generation to which they belong, and out of the common sympathy felt for them arises an additional bond of union amongst the people themselves." Undoubtedly, this feeling in regard to the Royal Family helps to transfuse the whole community with the spirit of one common family life. The domestic events of the Royal House are the domestic events of the nation.

The members of the Royal House to-day have the most sensitive conception of the obligations to the people which their exalted position imposes upon them. For them a round of duties, social, charitable, and national is ordained. Their desire is that the discharge of these duties should be attended with as little as possible of the formality of reception. The Duke of York, one of the busiest of them all in social work, must have expressed the genuine feeling of each when he remarked, " I am a very ordinary person when I am allowed to be." Swelled head is by no means an attribute of the Royal Family. In public company they are simple and natural. There is an utter absence of condescension on their part. If anything, they are a little diffident and shy. In all that they do there is manifest a desire not to hold themselves aloof but to meet people on their own ground, to enter into the closest fellowship with all classes in the corporate life of the community. They do seem really to love to come out of their Palaces and mix with the warm, palpitating masses engrossed in labour, in buying and selling—carrying on the business of the country from day to day; to show their interest in the happiness and contentment of the community; to give what help they can to advance its moral and economic progress. In their desire for service the members of the Royal Family are disposed to say " Yes " to every possible request; and " No " only when it is absolutely unavoidable. This has not been always so. We need not go very far back in the nineteenth century to get to a time when such condescension by a King or Queen would have been considered very lowering to their dignity.

Punctuality is another characteristic of the Royal Family. They are never a second late in keeping public appointments. A good memory also seems to be a Royal attribute—a good memory for persons, faces, incidents. At public functions members of the Royal Family may be noticed intently looking round the company so as to be certain to recognise and give a nod and a smile to those whom they had met before. A story of King Edward, when Prince of Wales, affords a happy illustration of Royalty's readiness of memory. The Prince met Mark Twain, the American humorist, at Homburg, and they walked and talked together. As they were parting, the Prince said, " Well, good-bye. I am glad to have met you again." Twain was smote to the heart. As they had never met before, the Prince, he thought, had mistaken him for someone else. " Why," said the Prince laughing, " don't you remember when you met me in the Strand, London ? " The reference was to a humorous account which Twain had written some years before of an imaginary meeting with the heir to the British Throne. " The Prince was at the head of a procession in the Strand," Twain wrote, " and I was on a 'bus."

I have read that Society ladies find Queen Mary reserved and not easy to get to know. That is not so in the case of humbler folk whom Her Majesty visits in their homes and workshops, and in hospitals and other institutions. They get to know the

Queen as a womanly woman, interested in the daily round and common tasks of their lives, and adept at talk of a kind which they understand, and can take part in. I recall, for instance, a visit which Her Majesty made to a home for crippled boys at Blackheath. In the schoolroom, where the boys received her by singing " God Save the King," a photograph on the wall, taken some years previously, showing her carrying Prince George pick-a-back, caught her eye. " Ah, there is my little George," she exclaimed. On entering the kitchen she found there the cook and the housemaid at work. " What a nice airy room ! " she said to the cook, " and that stove looks useful too." The daughter of the superintendent of the Home, who attended Her Majesty on her round of the institution reminded her that the King, when he opened the home several years ago, warmed his hands at the kitchen fire. " Really," said the Queen, " Was it as cold as that ? " A black kitten was curled up on a chair in the kitchen. " What a dear little thing," re-marked the Queen as she played with the kitten with the end of her fur boa. In the workshops where shoemaking and tailor-ing were taught Her Majesty saw some of the boys repairing footballs for a large private school. She took up one of the balls, and having examined it, complimented the matron on the workmanship. She talked to several of the boys, and praised one bright lad of 15—who lost both his legs in a street acci-dent—on the way he had turned an old coat which he was wearing. " It really looks as good as new," she said. We can well understand what pleasure the Queen and her talk gave to the inmates and staff of the home. A very striking demon-stration of the intimate feeling of personal affection for Her Majesty took place during a visit to the Black Country in which she accompanied the King. At one of the great iron foundries the workmen, numbering several hundreds, sang a song, popu-lar at the time, " My Mary," and beat time to the refrain, with ringing effect, with the clanging of their hammers :

> " Kind, kind and loving is she,
>   Sweet is my Mary,
>   The apple-blossom on the tree
>   Is not so fair as Mary."

The workmen were very shy about it beforehand. They asked the manager to inquire whether Their Majesties would like it, and of course Their Majesties were cordial and unembarrassed. The performance particularly pleased the Queen. Homely talk and kindly incidents mark the naturalness of the relations between King and Queen and people when Their Majesties go avisiting.

I can remember also being present at a visit of the King and Queen to working-class houses built by the London County Council at Wandsworth. When their Majesties passed into the little garden plots at the backs of the dwellings the interest of the King was immediately attracted by rows of small earthenware pots placed on sticks, with their mouths downwards, along the flower borders. He enquired what they were for and was amused to learn that they were traps for those unpleasant garden pests, earwigs. The earwigs come out at night and nibble at flowers to get at the nectar, and in response to their habit to seek shelter in crevices before dawn, they cluster into the cosy grass-lined pots, only to be immolated by the gardeners in the morning. Whether the surprise of the King was real or simulated it certainly gave the greatest pleasure to the inhabitants of the county council houses. It was the subject of lively reminiscences and discussions in the settlement for many a long day afterwards.

Royalty, no doubt, is more accustomed to another kind of earwig—the one that whispers flattery in the ear. We do not know, to what extent, if any, King George has come into contact with this kind of earwig. His Majesty seems to be of a sort, straightforward and simple, to whom flattery would be distasteful. It would, at least, leave him unspoiled. His immense influence is derived in a large measure, no doubt, from his long descent, as a wearer of the Royal purple and wielder of the Sceptre ; but in this democratic age it is derived to a still greater extent from qualities that are pleasing in men of all stations, but are particularly graceful and winning in a Monarch —simple dignity and courtesy, frankness, good nature, plain common-sense, and, with these, whole-hearted devotion to the interests of his people and solicitude for their well-being.

Anyone who is present at a public function which the King

attends in State, such, for instance, as the opening of a dock or
a municipal building, or the laying of the foundation stone of a
great institution, cannot fail to notice that when the time comes
for His Majesty to speak, the Home Secretary, who is usually
the Minister in attendance on these occasions, gives to the King
a typewritten document which His Majesty proceeds to read.
This is an indication that what the King says—though he himself probably has written the speech—is said on the advice of
his Ministers, just as what he says in his speech from the
Throne to the assembled Lords and Commons is said on his
Ministers' advice. Such an incident was witnessed, for example,
at the opening of the County Hall, Westminster Bridge, July,
1922.

But at the more numerous public functions of a different
kind which the King attends in London and the country, His
Majesty speaks what he feels and from his heart. These
speeches denote an intensely sensitive and sympathetic nature.
The King sorrows over the trials and sufferings of his people ;
he glories at everything that tends to their progress and happiness. No wonder that he is so esteemed and loved. Has ever a
Sovereign of England had so wonderful and unique a popular
reception as that which greeted King George at Wembley
Stadium on that memorable Saturday afternoon in April, 1923,
when the final tie was played for the Football Association Cup.
The Stadium was designed to hold 125,000 spectators. Over
200,000 entered it. Tens of thousands of them made their way
in by force. Barriers were stormed ; the playing-field was
invaded. All was confusion. The swaying and crushing of
the multitude were alarming to see and their cries painful
to hear. The ambulance corps were busy carrying away hundreds of injured women and men on stretchers. Then suddenly
the band played the National Anthem announcing the arrival
of His Majesty. At the sight of King George standing in the
Royal Box silence fell on the crowd, all stood to attention and
bared their heads. " God Save the King " was sung by myriad
voices, followed by three great echoing cheers that assailed
the skies.

Then there was the long and critical illness of King George
in the winter of 1928-29. For several weeks a cloud lay over

the Kingdom. Nothing like the tension of the public mind had ever been known before. With what eager concern were the physicians' bulletins awaited, read and discussed! The unifying effect of this crisis in the King's life was most remarkable. It brought out fellowship of one's kind—the obliteration of class distinctions, the mingling of social degrees, the sinking of differences and prejudices. It fused the diverse elements of the land into a national solidarity. It made the whole civilised world sympathetic sharers in the trouble of the British Empire. His Majesty during his illness was continuously and prominently in the world's news. It was a wonderful manifestation of the spell which the English Throne has cast upon the world. More than that—abroad, as well as at home, the King's character was rightly gauged and worthily esteemed. His Majesty had justified to the world his people's faith in the British form of democratic sovereignty, and there was a universal prayer that his wise reign might be long prolonged.

INDEX

INDEX

Index

Index

Index

315